How Long's the Course?

'The secret is silver, it's to shine and never simply survive.'

Roddy Frame of Aztec Camera

'You surely are a truly gifted kid, but you're only as good as the last great thing you did.'

Paddy McAloon of Prefab Sprout

How Long's the Course?

My Autobiography

Roger Black

with Mike Rowbottom

ANDRE DEUTSCH

Mike Rowbottom is
athletics correspondent for the *Independent*.

First published in 1998 by
André Deutsch Ltd
This edition published in 1999 by
André Deutsch Ltd
76 Dean Street
London WIV 5HA
www.vci.co.uk

1 3 5 7 9 10 8 6 4 2

Typeset by Derek Doyle & Associates
Mold, Flintshire
Printed and bound in the UK

A catalogue record for this book is available from the British Library

ISBN 0 233 99644 3

Cover designed by Design/Section
Cover photographs: Action Plus, Allsport

Plate Section designed by Design 23

Picture Acknowledgements
Page numbers refer to plate section only.
Allsport 5 bottom, 13 both; Allsport/Reebok 15 bottom;
Empics/Tony Marshall 10 middle;
Robin Jones 2; McConnell's 9;
Mark Sherman 3, 4 middle and bottom,
5 top, 10 bottom, 11, 12.

All other photographs come from Roger Black's personal collection.

CONTENTS

PREFACE

I was at Heathrow Airport with the British team when I spotted him. 'There's Van Morrison,' I said to my coach, Mike Whittingham.

Mike was a big Van Morrison fan – he'd seen him in concert at least ten times – and as luck would have it he was carrying one of the great man's tapes. So the two of us walked over and Mike said: 'Van Morrison, I'm a huge fan of yours. Would you mind signing this for me?'

'Sure,' drawled Van Morrison. 'So what are you guys doing?'

'Well, this is Roger Black, the athlete, and we are with the British team which is going to the European Cup final in Frankfurt. There's Linford Christie . . . and that's Sally Gunnell.'

'Right,' said Van Morrison, looking blank. 'Athletics. Is that like, er, running and . . . jumping?'

Mike and I looked at each other for a long moment. He seemed to be asking the question in all sincerity.

'Yes,' we said.

'Right,' said Van Morrison cautiously. But he still seemed troubled by another detail. 'So . . . how long's the course?'

1

THE PERFECT RACE

Peace is not something you would expect in a stadium filled with 85,000 people. But as I crossed the line at the end of the 1996 Olympic 400 metres final in Atlanta, peace was what I found. After a career which had switchbacked between triumph and disaster for ten dizzying years, I had an Olympic medal. It was silver. It felt like gold – because it testified to a race which I had run to perfection, something I had been striving for since first setting foot on a track.

I didn't whoop. I didn't holler. Despite the urging of the British supporters, I didn't join the winner, Michael Johnson, on a lap of honour, because that was his moment. Slowly, very slowly, I looked around the Olympic stadium, taking the whole thing in, reflecting on the path I had travelled to arrive at this high vantage point. I was surrounded by noise, knowing millions worldwide were watching on television. I absorbed all the energy, all the emotion of the occasion. This was my moment, and I told myself to seize it, to be grateful for it, because I knew the good times didn't last for ever. But I had come far enough to know that neither did the bad times.

For most of my career I had feared I might never perform to my satisfaction at the supreme sporting occasion. Eight years earlier I had been forced to miss the 1988 Games with a foot injury which prevented me running for eighteen months. 'Olympics' equals frustration. Four years later I made it to the

Barcelona Olympics, but again I was carrying an injury, and subsequently suffered a bout of glandular fever so severe that my whole career was in jeopardy. 'Olympics' equals disappointment. Now, at the age of thirty, I could associate the word 'Olympics' with success.

When I crossed that line, I could have given you a huge list of people who had helped me in the course of my career. But the basic satisfaction was that I had finally taken control of my own destiny. I am a championship performer, thank goodness. I'm not particularly good at turning up to one-off meetings in Zurich or wherever and running a fast race, but I have always been able to beat people who are faster than me on paper when it comes to the big occasion. My greatest strength is my ability to focus, to be cool under pressure. And that's what four races in four days is all about. It's about being able to go out, run the first round and then as soon as you have crossed the line, saying, 'That's over. Forget it. Move on.'

I had gone into the semi-final with the prime concern of trying to win it to earn a good lane draw for the final, but it produced a bonus for me when Butch Reynolds, who had set the world record of 43.29sec in 1988 and was most people's bet for second place behind Johnson, dropped out after running the first 100 metres. I knew that was going to happen, because Butch had turned up beforehand with his leg heavily bandaged and he did not do any kind of warming up, whereas before the previous rounds he had prepared for almost an hour and a half.

Butch was behind me in lane one. When it happened, I heard the crowd go 'Ooh' and I thought, 'There he goes.' That meant I could win the semi-final virtually unchallenged, which I did. It felt so easy – I was in such great shape.

On the way back to the athletes' village afterwards I was on a bus with the world and Olympic 400m champion Marie-Jose Perec, whom I knew through my girlfriend, Elsa. Marie-Jose said to me, 'So you're going to get your silver medal.'

'Yeah. And you're going to get your gold medal,' I replied.

'Yeah.' We were both right.

You try to deal with the Olympic final in the same way as the previous rounds, but with the best will in the world, you can't regard it as just another race. If you think that, you shouldn't be there. The Olympic final is unlike any other race. It's like playing backgammon with a doubling cube for the first time – the stakes are so much higher and the game takes on a whole new dimension. Despite that, I had established a routine by then which I tried to keep up. On the morning of the final, the first thing I did when I woke up in the Olympic village was to go for a little jog, do some stretching and some drills. I was delighted to see that it was cloudy, with a hint of rain. For the whole of the previous year we had been told it was going to be impossibly humid and hot in Atlanta. But every time I ran it was fine.

I was rooming with my old friend Jon Ridgeon, who had made an astonishing comeback from injury to compete in his first Olympics since 1988. On the day of the race, he reminded me that most of those I would be racing against had no idea what it was like to have recovered their career from some of the setbacks I had overcome. As I did my drills on a grass field opposite our apartment block, I was aware that I was tired – but I knew everyone else would be too.

Later I had lunch in the athletes' restaurant – my normal chicken and rice – with Jon and another long-standing training partner, Sven Nylander. There is an underlying tension at such times, but different people express it in different ways . . . You keep looking at your watch, but you can't speed time up. So you just kill it. I try to have a bit of a laugh or I read.

People come up to you saying, 'Good luck, good luck.' I recall Keith Connor, the former British triple jump record holder who now coaches, saying to me, 'You're going to get your silver medal. And the reason is that you've got ten years over most of those other guys. There are guys out there who will just not be able to hack it.'

It was very strange being so close to the biggest race of my life. The temptation was to think about what it would mean to me if I got an Olympic medal, but I tried not to dwell on the subject. After lunch I sat in the room with the other guys who were in my apartment. Jonathan Edwards had left by then, so it was Jon, Steve Smith, and the 800 metres runner Curtis Robb, with whom I whiled away a little time by playing lightning chess. Steve was recovering from having a drop too much the previous night – he'd just got his bronze in the high jump. Looking at his medal, I found myself thinking, 'I could have one of those by tomorrow.'

When I got to the stadium I went to see Mark Zambada, my massage therapist. Before my previous three rounds he had spent at least half an hour working on me. This time he did a brief check and then just looked at me. 'Nothing to do, is there?' I asked.

'I'm not going to touch you. You're ready.'

I try to relax at such times by listening to music on my Walkman. I make a compilation tape every year of music that means something to me. The intention is to create a positive state of mind. In the early part of my career it was mostly upbeat material, but I came to realize that that didn't work. By the time of the Atlanta Games I had evolved as a runner, and so had my musical tastes. That year I was trying to create a state of mind of relaxation and enjoyment, and the music had to reflect that. I had Aztec Camera, 'Just like the USA', and Tears for Fears, 'Break It Down Again', at the start, which was ideal for a short period of jogging. Then I had a thirty-minute section for when I was doing stretching exercises featuring Sting, Van Morrison's 'Crazy Love' and Paul Weller's 'Broken Stones'. Then came Oasis, 'Champagne Supernova' – music to get up and go with. Your body clock knows what time you've got to leave.

I didn't want anyone around me at this point in my day – I like to go into my own little corner away from everybody. 'You know it's the Olympic final,' I was thinking. 'But don't think about the Olympic final. Just think about running the perfect race. Think about enjoying it.'

Four years earlier I had entered the Barcelona Olympics

knowing I was only 80 per cent fit because my hip was troubling me. In that situation your mind is on your hip, and not on your zip. When you're not injured, you're not worrying about whether this hurts or that hurts. You're only thinking about executing your running. That's why an athlete who is not injured is so powerful. I've had just two years in my career without being troubled either by illness or injury – 1986, when I won the European and Commonwealth titles, and 1996. I don't care who you are – if you're carrying an injury, if your body hurts, then anaesthetic injections or not, you know about it. I can remember saying in 1986 that I never got injured. What did I know? I was twenty years old. My views had changed even by the time I reached twenty-two.

After doing the warm-up, your spikes and numbers are checked before you board the bus that takes you round to your holding position in the stadium. And as the door closes, it comes home to you what you are about to do. There are just eight of you – reality checkpoint. This time our concentration was interrupted by the cheery greeting of the official accompanying us – the same man who had been there for earlier rounds. 'Well hi, fellas!' he said with a grin. 'Here we go again then!' For us it was the prelude to the most important race of our lives; for him, we were just another busload of runners.

I always sit near the back on these occasions and concentrate on breathing and relaxing, trying not to think of anything at all. You don't say, 'Hi, Michael, how're you doing?' or 'All right Davis, have a good one.' By and large, each athlete is in a world of their own, and although you are not supposed to be listening to music at this time, I was. You can tell which competitors are uptight because they're the ones who are looking around. I remember thinking to myself, 'You should be like Michael Johnson, or like me – don't show anything.' I didn't say anything, not even to my fellow Briton, Iwan Thomas, who was quiet but tense. He knew the score as well as anyone.

People and cameras were waiting for us as we got off the bus. Television monitors showing the action in the stadium seemed to be everywhere. You try not to look at them, but you can't help it. It is all very distracting – but when you've been doing it for eleven years, you get used to it. We walked into a little holding room where our spikes and numbers were re-checked. It was possible then to do a few strides on an indoor strip of track. Other races were going on ahead of us, people were coming off the track and filing past us, some of them elated, some destroyed.

You're in the holding room for about twenty minutes. But you can go in and out, which is what I do. Then you get called through to the tunnel, and you have to sit on a bench, lined up in your lane order, and they check your numbers once again. That's when you start to see the crowd, a little bit of the crowd through the tunnel. And you start to hear the noise. If you're going to crack, *that's* where it will happen. I was just internalizing it, as ever. I was switching to automatic pilot now, switching to, 'This is my territory. There's no reason to be scared here.' I wasn't thinking, 'Right, race plan, RACE PLAN' – that was all done. I knew what I was doing.

The others were right next to me. Michael was on my right, because he was drawn in lane four, one lane outside me. Davis Kamoga, the Ugandan runner, was on my left. There is so little space that we were jammed up against each other, touching legs. Still, no one talked. I'd run against Michael many times, and had a beer with him. But this was the Olympic final.

I don't wear socks when I compete, so before races I put talcum powder on my feet to prevent them getting sweaty and slippery. As I was doing so on this occasion, I slipped, and spilt some powder on Michael and his kit bag. I was mortified. The thought went through my mind that this might have appeared like a crude effort at gamesmanship, but as I turned to say something, I checked myself. This was not the time or the place. And Michael never uttered a word.

The people who consistently perform where it matters, the champions, have the ability to perform under pressure. When you walk into the Olympic stadium and there are 85,000 people in it – 80,000 of whom are chanting for Michael Johnson – and there are a million people back home staying up until three o'clock in the morning, all wishing you well, when the hopes of the nation are fully fixed on your shoulders, and there are a billion other people around the world watching on television – that is pressure. In such circumstances, you resent even the smallest alteration in your routine.

In the first three rounds the organization had been very slick. It had been a case of, walk to your marks, get your tracksuit off and away you went. But it proved too much to hope for that that routine would be maintained for the final. No sooner had we got to our blocks than we heard, 'Hang on, guys. Ten minutes for some TV commercials.'

Ten minutes! Before an Olympic final! We just sat on the track and I tried to collect my thoughts and relax as best I could. They were the longest ten minutes of my life. Finally we heard what we were waiting for, 'Right. Tracksuits off, gentlemen.' Then it was that minute when you're standing behind the blocks and being introduced in various languages. Two important things happened next.

Since the start of my career I have had a nervous habit of putting my hand on my heart to check my pulse before starting a race. In those early days my heart would be thumping really quickly because I was so nervous, but it gets harder to create those nerves when you get older. I went through a phase between 1990 and 1995 when I was thinking, 'Why am I not nervous? That's not good.' I had said that to myself as I had lined up for the final in the previous year's World Championship in Gothenburg. This was the Olympic final. And when I put my hand on my heart, my pulse felt slow and steady. This time I was thinking, 'You're ready.' I had this over-all sensation of calm. Some people have to be uptight for such an occasion, but not me. Over the years I had come to learn that I needed to be cool, calm and collected. I was nervous. But my heart was not pounding madly.

As I went down to my marks, something else happened.

'This is for you, Jenks,' I said. I don't know why. I hadn't been consciously thinking of it. And there are certainly people in the sport who wouldn't have liked to hear me mentioning David Jenkins because he is, after all, a man who has served time as a drug smuggler and has admitted to taking drugs while competing for Britain in the 1970s and 1980s over 400 metres. But *I* knew how much his advice had helped me prepare for my highest moment of achievement. That is what I felt; and that is what I said.

When you get called to your marks it's the same routine, whether you are running in the Olympic final or the British League. You've done it hundreds of times before. Friends and family tell me that as spectators they go through anguish at these moments. It is ten times worse for them than for me for one simple reason – *they* have no control over what happens. None at all. For me it's not that bad, because this is my work environment.

The key to running fast is relaxation. I know that may sound a paradox to most people, especially when you are talking about 400 metres. When you see schoolchildren running, the strain on their faces shows they're trying as hard as they can, working to the 'No pain, no gain' theory. But at the highest level you learn that that is not the case, because it has been proven that the human body and the muscles work far more efficiently in a relaxed state than a tense one. If you are tense when you are running, then obviously your body is going to run into fatigue quicker than it would if it was relaxed. The secret of any good runner is to be able to run quickly and relaxed. Steve Cram, Ed Moses, more recently Wilson Kipketer – these are great athletes who were able to combine the two things beautifully. Kipketer is probably the greatest example of this that there has ever been. He's a man who is running incredibly quickly, but it doesn't seem so because he is so relaxed.

When you're relaxed you are handing over ultimate responsibility to your body. By pushing it you feel as if you are really working, you feel as if you are moving faster, but when you run in a relaxed state you allow your body to work for you – in many ways it feels easier. It takes a lot of confidence and understanding to believe that you are running faster by relaxing than by pushing. There's no doubt it works. Linford Christie has broken down the elements of 100 metres running and put them back together again. And his focus is relaxation. It looks as if he is just a powerhouse, but he's not. He is power driven by relaxation. In the 400 metres, relaxation is the difference between swimming in lactic acid, or coming through the line comfortably and feeling strong.

So I was standing there trying to be relaxed. What I do is go through an anchoring routine, as the scientists would call it. I stand behind the line in a specific pose, with my left foot forward and my right foot slightly back. Athletes talk about being in 'the zone', this state of optimum performance when you have a sense of confidence, of being in control, of being able to block out everything else around you. There are degrees of this control. When you have 85,000 people in a stadium, it's very hard to block them out totally.

Visualization is a very powerful tool to get yourself into 'the zone', and people can use it in lots of ways. One way is to see your own lane in a certain colour, different from every other lane. You can see your lane in blue, while you perceive all the other ones as red. What I do is something which is called phasing left – I don't look outwards, to the right of me. I look to the inside lane. I focus left to internalize, rather than externalize my thoughts. I can't see anyone, because the competitors inside me are all further back down the track.

As I stood there in Atlanta, I needed to keep my focus away from my competitors because I had worked on the concept of running *my* perfect race. I believed in that concept. I tried to internalize my thoughts. 'It is just me here and I am going to get the maximum I can out of *this* body at *this* moment in time.' I accepted fully that my competitors would affect me, just by being there, but that was the extent to which I was prepared to let them affect me. I did not want to get to the point where I simply reacted to what they did. I was in lane three, Michael Johnson was in lane four. If I was to focus out, the first person I was going to see was Michael Johnson.

My whole season, my whole career, had been leading to this moment. I had run the perfect race physically two or three times prior to this final. I had run it mentally hundreds of times using visualization. By lying in a deeply relaxed state I would often 'see' myself running the perfect race from different perspectives – sometimes as if I was in the crowd looking in, sometimes as if I was inside my body looking out. I could see my lane, rehearse every movement from being focused in the starting blocks to coming around the final bend and running for the finishing line where the fatigue would be setting in but 'teaching' my brain to send the right messages to my body … relax, relax, relax. I could feel, see, hear and even taste the sensation of running the perfect 400 metres, and I had prepared both my mind and body to switch to autopilot once the starter's gun was fired. When athletes talk about their greatest races they often say, 'It just happened. I don't remember it.' It is at that point you have achieved the ultimate, you are running on the subconscious, not the conscious level. That is where you want to be. I had run it mentally about 500 times. Research has shown that the nervous system cannot tell the difference between a real experience and a vividly imagined one.

Waiting for the gun I was conscious that there was no logical reason for me to make a mistake because I had run so well in the earlier rounds. When the gun went, I went into autopilot. I was aware that there were other great athletes around me, but I was not aware of the crowd. I kept talking to myself throughout the race. The things going through my mind were to get out well, and then from 100 to 300 metres to relax. The one word that went round in my head was 'Relax, relax, relax'. I was focusing on keeping a high hip position, because the first thing that happens when you hit fatigue is that your hip level drops and then you lose your form. The beauty of this kind of mental exercise is that it keeps you thinking about what you can control, your physical position, rather than using up energy on what's going on around you. If you can focus inwards, you'll still have something left with 50 metres to go.

I remember being aware of Johnson, but I was not thinking, 'At what point is he going to go, what's he going to do?' I was not questioning. I had already rehearsed his race in my mind – any idiot could work out what he was going to do. He would run to 200 metres at about the same pace as the rest of us, 21.3, 21.4 seconds, and then between 200 metres and 300 metres he would take five metres out of the rest of the field. He is the only man in the world who is capable of doing that and then hanging on for the last 100. For him, it is a painful jog to go through in 21.5. He starts his running at 200 metres.

We got to 200 metres pretty much together. Johnson was probably a fraction ahead, and when he started to kick, I did not respond. That was the defining moment for me. In earlier years I would have gone with him, and blown myself out of the race. As we reached the 300 metre mark, he was five or six metres ahead, but I was in second place, and I knew that, if I maintained my composure and ran my own race, no one was going to come past me. I was unaware that Kamoga had been coming up like a train behind me, but fortunately he didn't catch me.

Johnson won in 43.49sec, I was second in 44.41, and Kamoga got the bronze in 44.53 with Iwan Thomas finishing fifth. If Johnson had pulled up lame I would have been aware of it, but I would have just flipped back into my mode, maintained my run. I didn't even hope he would. The whole principle for those four days of Olympic competition was that anything which I could not control was not in my mindset.

I'm sure athletes' senses are refined. Their instincts, for instance to know they've crossed the line first when it takes the technology of a photograph to confirm it, are finely tuned. Sprinters, even in a blanket finish, can usually tell the order in which they have finished.

But as I crossed the line I was not aware of Kamoga. I

glanced over, as I always did, to look for Brendan Foster, who was there for the BBC. I just needed the nod that I had got the second place. I got the thumbs up. Then there's that instant, 'I've done it.'

My initial feeling was almost trance-like. My automatic reaction was, as it always has been, to go and shake hands with the others. I congratulated Michael. We shook hands, but I don't think he said anything. He had just become Olympic champion, so his mind was off in the clouds.

I turned to find Iwan, and he congratulated me. I then noticed Kamoga lying flat out and I tried to pick him up, which seemed to annoy him because I think he just wanted to lie on the floor for twenty minutes.

There is no doubt that what Michael Johnson did in Atlanta was superhuman. What he did in the 400 metres was phenomenal. If you watch it, it's a massacre. He won by 10 metres. (It's ironic, isn't it? You can get beaten by 10 metres and people still know that yours is a great achievement.) It is particularly amazing considering what he did two days later – demolishing the world 200 metres record. It's not just the times he ran, it's that he ran them back to back. The physical demands on the body of doing that are immense, which makes the results all the more astonishing. If other athletes have called those performances into question, I choose to give Michael the benefit of the doubt. It was a staggering feat.

Anybody who watches me in that Olympic final – it's clear if you see it in slow motion – will notice that I have a pained expression when I cross the line. I remember watching a replay on television, and there's this wonderful shot of Johnson and myself coming down to the line. Johnson's face is absolutely relaxed and expressionless, and there's me, absolutely writhing in agony, scrunching my face up. So there is an area I do have to work on. Obviously I'm not getting it exactly right if there's still tension anywhere, even in the face!

There is a routine after a big championship race, just as there is a routine leading up to it. Once you walk off the track, everybody wants to interview you, and the television people get the first shot. As I approached the media scrum around the tunnel, I felt unable to let out the overwhelming emotion of the occasion, the sheer joy at what I had done. I suppose that because I had spent the previous six months of my life internalizing the race, my way of enjoying the moment was an internal one. I looked for my girlfriend Elsa, of course, and spotted her in the stand. It was so frustrating for her because she wanted to hug me but she couldn't get down from where she was sitting, close to the TV cameras. But there was this huge smile on her face, perhaps because she was thinking, 'Good, now we can afford to move house!' Which, in fact, we did, soon after I returned . . .

As I was walking off the track, I saw John Smith, who coaches some of the most talented sprinters in the world including Maurice Greene, Ato Boldon and Marie-Jose Perec. He was one of the first to congratulate me:

'You deserve that. There may be guys who are faster than you, but you did it.' That was a great feeling.

Jon Drummond, another of John Smith's athletes, was there, devastated after having a very disappointing Games. And John said to him, pointing at me, 'Look, hang on in there. If you need an example of why it is worth carrying on trying, there it is.'

That was ironic, as I had tried without success to join John Smith's group the previous year. As things turned out, that would have been a bad move for me for all sorts of reasons. But I didn't know that at the time.

You do the BBC interview first, with Brendan. It was my first one of the Olympics, because I don't believe in giving interviews between the rounds. As soon as I cross the line in the rounds, it's over. I want to move forward, and I don't want to reflect on it. After the BBC you go to whoever gets you, and in my case on that day it was three French channels, for whom I demonstrated my far from perfect command of the language which I have picked up through having a French girlfriend. I do remember saying hello to all my friends and family on the island of Martinique, which is Elsa's birthplace, and I subsequently discovered it had made a huge impact. When I next went to Martinique, I was invited on their TV channel and asked to explain fully why an Englishman who had just won an Olympic silver medal would think to mention a little island in the middle of the Caribbean. Of course, this Englishman knows that he is going to spend a lot of his future life on that island. So I suppose you could call it British diplomacy! Next stop was the British athletics writers, who were all there. And it was nice for me to be able to share the experience with the likes of Colin Hart (of the *Sun*), Neil Wilson (of the *Daily Mail*) and Mike Rowbottom (of the *Independent*) who had been on the journey with me almost from when I started.

After that, you get marshalled in to speak to the world's press, and that was how I found myself with Michael Johnson for a couple of minutes, waiting for the bronze medallist to arrive before we went into the conference room. Michael was repeating, 'I can't believe it, I can't believe it.'

'You're joking, aren't you? It's probably the easiest race you've had all year, isn't it?' I asked.

'Yeah, but it's never easy. And I'm Olympic champion.'

It was really good to see that it meant so much to him. After what had happened at the 1992 Olympics in Barcelona – he failed to reach the 200 metres final because of food poisoning – he had clearly not been taking anything for granted. He's always given me respect, partly because, after his Barcelona experience, he knows what it's like to be down in a trough and pull yourself back up, and also because I'd been around for ten years, and most runners don't manage that.

Facing the world's press, I was sitting up on this big stage with Michael Johnson and Davis Kamoga. And after about ten minutes I thought, 'What the hell are Davis Kamoga and me doing here?'

It is at that point that the reality of 'They're only interested in the champion' hits you hard between the eyeballs. I had been asked a token question, I think, but the focus of the world's press, quite rightly, was on Michael Johnson. Immediately after the race he had been asked by a television crew how long he would need to prepare himself for his next event, and he had replied: 'Give me another twenty minutes.' Two days later he achieved the seemingly impossible – he lowered the world 200 metres mark to 19.32 seconds.

Next stop for us was the drug-testing room, where you're asked to give the routine urine samples which are required from the first three in each event. Now that was an interesting environment, because anyone who made it there had won an Olympic medal – quite an exclusive gathering, when you think about it.

Two things always go through your mind when you are being drug tested – and they were particularly vivid then as it was the aftermath of the greatest occasion for any athlete. The first thing is, 'I hope they do this properly. I don't want any complications for me personally.' And then you look around at all the others waiting to produce samples and you can't help but wonder if any of them are about to be caught out. Not at the Olympics, if they have got any sense. But then Ben Johnson didn't seem to have any sense at the 1988 Olympics, so it *is* possible.

You get people who are fed up with having to wait because they can't pee; invariably there will be a couple of athletes sitting in the corner who have been there for two or three hours, desperately drinking. And you get people who are really uptight and want to make sure that everything is done correctly. There is a very strict procedure that has to be followed – and rightly so. You give the samples in curtained cubicles and a doctor always has to be in attendance. Your life is in their hands. I had a clear conscience. But every innocent athlete still has that fear at the back of their mind that a mistake in the testing procedure, or a failure to store their sample properly, could lead to a positive finding and subsequent ban from the sport.

When that procedure was over, it was a case of waiting to receive my medal. And it was then that I chose to be alone. I was jogging down a tunnel outside the stadium, in what I can only describe as a wash of satisfaction. How can you express how you feel when you have achieved your goal? It really is an incredible state to be in, and I wanted to be on my own to take it all in. I think this was a sort of transition stage I needed. I needed to really look forward to going out and getting the medal, and to think about all those times that I'd dreamt of being on the Olympic rostrum. Carl Lewis, who had just won the long jump to huge acclaim, and Michael Johnson were also running around nearby, surrounded by a mass of people. It felt funny to be a part of all this, even though I was no Lewis or Johnson.

So there I was, jogging around in the area beside the main stadium, when I was approached by a man heading a camera crew, who introduced himself as Bud Greenspan, the American documentary maker who has made films at the Olympics over the course of thirty years. 'Roger,' he said, 'could we have a few words? Because we see you are on your own and you are about to go out for an Olympic medal, and that seems very strange when you see that Carl and Michael are surrounded by people.'

So I told him that this was something I often liked to do, and I did a little piece to camera which I believe they included in the film of the 1996 Games. That was quite an honour for me, because Bud's reputation as a film-maker is huge.

Before the presentation, you sit in a little holding room. I waited there with Davis Kamoga and the gorgeous American models who were carrying the medals out. Michael was waiting separately, surrounded by people, and joined us as we were called forward. It was obvious that Davis still had not come to terms with what he had just done. He couldn't believe it, because he had taken nearly a second and a half off his personal best in the course of the Games. It was for him the beginning of what I believe will be a great career – he went one better in the World Championships in Athens the following year by filling the silver medal position behind Michael Johnson.

I noticed that Alberto Juantorena, the great Cuban who had

won the 400 and 800 metres at the 1976 Olympics, was in the presentation party. I was delighted about that.

As we walked out into the Olympic stadium, all I could see was Union Jacks. All over the place. Two hours earlier I hadn't been aware of a single one as I had walked out for the final, which was an indication of how attuned I had been to the task ahead. I had felt like a pressure cooker immediately after the race, bubbling away and maintaining myself, knowing full well that at some point it was all going to explode. And of course the moment it happened was when I walked out to get my medal. This huge smile came on to my face, and I think it stayed on my face the whole time. I was saying to myself, 'This. Is. Great.'

I remember standing behind the rostrum and just beaming happiness, and sharing the odd aside with Michael – you feel in a privileged position when you are sharing something like that. And then, purely by chance, I caught sight of a huge, madly waving figure right in the middle of the VIP section – an old friend of mine from California, Joe Donohue. He was just standing there screaming 'Yeahhhh!!' I have no idea how he got there. Then I saw Mike Whittingham, my manager and friend, making his way down to Joe, and he had his Roger Black T-shirt on from when I had started a fan club after the 1991 World Championships.

The British flag went up alongside the American one, and when the 'Stars and Stripes' began to play, in my head I was singing 'God Save the Queen.' All the time I was just saying to myself, 'Savour this moment, savour this moment.'

As I walked off I waved to the British fans who had been so loyal to me over the years, and I went to find Mike and Elsa to show them the medal. Then it was a case of 'What now?' You always have this sense of 'What now?' after moments of high achievement, and the answer is usually something mundane. In this case it was to get on a bus and go back to the Olympic village, which is what Elsa and I did. All the seats were full with other athletes. So we sat on the floor.

2

HEART OF THE MATTER

My athletic career was almost over before it began. Every year of my life since I was eleven I have had to have a check-up by a cardiac specialist following the discovery of a potentially serious heart problem. The condition – caused by a congenitally defective valve – has remained a secret over the years to all but a close circle of relatives and friends.

When the heart murmur was discovered, during my first senior school medical, I was referred by my doctor to the heart specialist at Southampton General Hospital, Dr Neville Conway. The heart has four valves, and one of mine leaks. With a healthy valve system in the heart the blood always goes one way and it doesn't come back. Because of my defect – in medical terms, an aortic incompetent valve – the blood goes out, and some of it leaks back. I have kept Dr Conway's letter to my GP, which warned of the possibly dire consequences if I overtaxed my body. On 3 October 1977 he wrote:

On examination I think he has aortic regurgitation. His pulse is collapsing in quality . . . he has an aortic ejection click, followed by a short ejection systolic murmur . . . What has happened has been presumably that the bicuspid valve . . . has begun to leak, perhaps because of growth or perhaps because of the development of floppiness in its connective tissues.

My view is that for the next six months in the first

instance at least, he should not undertake any special training ... my reason for saying this is that if aortic regurgitation has appeared relatively suddenly, this might prove too much of a load. If in six months time things have not changed at all and this situation continues over the succeeding years I think we will be able to allow him to do a little more.

One other factor has to be taken into account for all of this, and that is growth. As I have already suggested, it is not uncommon for the bicuspid valve to start to leak as it increases in size and this is another factor that must be watched carefully.

When the family heard the diagnosis, I remember they were pretty shattered, because I was to all intents and purposes a very fit and healthy boy. I didn't fully understand the implications of this news, mainly because I didn't actually feel unwell. Nobody fussed – that was not the way of things in our household.

When I look back on my childhood, the word drama was just not in our vocabulary. But I was aware that my parents were greatly concerned for me, particularly as my father, who was a practising GP himself until he retired in 1991, also had a heart problem. In fact, there was no link between the two conditions, but I felt my father was worried about what might happen to me in later life. As a doctor, he knew that my condition might eventually require open heart surgery – he had diagnosed cases himself where surgery had been needed to rectify the problem. At that time such an operation would have meant replacing my defective valve with an artificial one, which would almost certainly have put a stop to any sporting career, and would almost certainly have prevented me becoming a world-class 400 metres runner.

My father recalls me being deeply disappointed at the time, but it was not a case of running crying to my room or anything like that. The biggest cause of distress as far as I was concerned was that I was not allowed to represent the school in any sport. When it came to rugby matches, the most I could do was be touch judge because it was considered too dangerous for me to play. I was also banned from doing cross country.

The situation was not without its fringe benefits, however. Not having to do cross country was a cause for celebration as far as I was concerned – I have never been a long-distance runner. It was something that greatly annoyed my friends as they were forced to labour round in the mud. More than one was seen clutching at his chest and asking to be excused – but it never seemed to work for them . . .

It also brought me closer to my father – I'm the only one of his four children who has a heart problem. But what it meant on a more serious level was that I was under surveillance for the rest of my life.

The time leading up to my annual check-up back at Southampton General Hospital is always deeply worrying for me. I have lived with the fear of knowing that I could walk out of the hospital doors having been told I could never do sport again. That is a reality I have had to face to the present day. I have always known that if I was advised to stop I would have no choice. And who knows what might happen later in life?

As I started to achieve in the athletics world, the significance of this check-up became greater and greater, because it was something that could take away the essence of my being. Even during the height of my fame, every time I went into that waiting room I still felt like the scared eleven-year-old boy who had first been there in 1977. As a child, I had found the whole experience very scary and intimidating. I would sit in the waiting room in the cardiothoracic department with people who had severe heart problems. It was very obvious in some cases, because they looked as though they had had the life sucked out of them.

Although Dr Conway has retired now, I still see the same nurse who took me in on the first occasion more than twenty years ago. The basic procedure is always the same: I am attached to an echo-cardiogram and then I have an ultrasound scan, an X-ray and a physical check up. Medical science has developed over the years and the machines have become more efficient and easier to use, but when I first went there I had to have suckers put all over my body, and the nurses would use a gooey white cream to get them to stay on. Sometimes they had to use tape as well. The whole thing would take more than an hour, and I felt like Frankenstein when everything was in place. A few years ago it all changed. There was no more goo, it was simply a matter of clipping things on and then throwing them away after one use. The ultrasound machines have also improved. You can now see very clear images of your heart on screen. When they found out during my sixthform days that I was planning to go to medical school, they used to talk me through the pictures as if I knew what it was all about. And, of course, I would just nod my head at the appropriate moments – even though I hadn't a clue what they were talking about.

In March 1985, soon after I had started training with Southampton Athletics Club, Dr Conway wrote my father a letter in which he expressed continuing concern about my well-being:

> I naturally want Roger to excel, since he has such tremen-dous talent. I think you will understand my position, however, if I express some reservations about the severity of the training he will have to undergo and its possible effect upon his myocardium. I have to do this for reasons you will appreciate ... In short, I cannot give you carte blanche.

Clearly my father was concerned about the possible effects of my taking up athletics seriously. In the early days, especially after I had started training with Mike Smith, he always asked me the same question: 'Are you more out of breath than anybody else?'

I used to reply that I didn't think I was any more out of

breath than the others. I do have a naturally low heart rate – my resting pulse is about 44 beats per minute, well below the average rate of around 72 and pretty low compared to most 400 metres runners. In training, I have always tended to recover very quickly. In those early years, however, there was a continuing worry that I was putting myself through things that the human body shouldn't be subjected to – certainly a body with a defective heart valve, which is understandable when you consider that athletes' heart rates can approach 200 beats per minute during arduous sessions such as hill work.

I know that Dr Conway, who used to run marathons, was very aware of that. Looking at his face, I knew he was thinking, 'I don't know how this guy manages. This doesn't make sense.' And he always said to me, 'If you are aware of feeling excessively tired you must, must contact me immediately.'

As my heart grew, the leak neither improved nor got any worse. After a few years, Dr Conway started to wonder whether, ironically, I might have gained as an athlete because my heart had overcompensated to cope with its congenital defect. In January 1987, the year after I had won both the European and Commonwealth 400 metres titles, he wrote again to my father:

Delighted to see Roger in the clinic and to see how well he is. I see no reason why he should not go on to the very top and look forward to following his career.

As I said to him, I wonder if the aortic incompetence, by causing the small increase chronically in his stroke volume, has in fact helped him rather than hindered him. Too much, I am sure, would be bad, but perhaps it has stretched his myocardium and enlarged his left ventricular capacity a little. Having said that, I do not think I would recommend it for all athletes!

Have I, because of my athletic prowess and natural fitness, helped myself and actually combated a potentially serious defect? The question fascinates the doctors, because what I have been able to do in the circumstances is illogical – particularly as the strain you put on your heart in the 400 metres is phenomenal. Of course, we don't know for sure, but I like to think it has, because I have learned throughout my life that out of apparent adversity can come great benefit. People often ask why I have been able to bounce back from so many setbacks in my athletic career. Maybe it was because at the age of eleven I had a potentially huge setback and moved on with it. I have always had the attitude of trying not to complain, of just getting on with things, because the reality is it could all end tomorrow. I am always fully aware of that.

Throughout my career there have been times when I have suffered chest pain. Certainly when I had glandular fever in 1993 it happened a lot. The alarm bells go off, and I mention it to the doctors, but it is probably just a muscular thing. Having said that, I carry the worry with me always.

My heart condition also makes me prone to a potentially dangerous infection – bacterial endocarditis – so any time I have dental treatment, or any kind of operation, I have to have full antibiotic cover. That is a lesson I learned to my cost just as I was preparing to return to action in 1989 after two long, painful years out with injury.

Early in October, I started to get sweats and feel pretty rotten. Then I began to *really* sweat, and feel *really* rotten. Being the son of a doctor, I grew up in a household where the phone was always ringing with people saying, 'Oh, I've got a sore throat. Can you come and see me?' And my father would get so upset at having to go out in the middle of the night, or in the middle of supper, when he'd rather be with his family, for someone who had a cold. So it needed something very serious for me to phone up the surgery and I spent three or four days feeling pretty ill before I called my GP. He came round and told me I needed to go straight to hospital because I had a potentially serious heart problem.

So it was that on Thursday 19 October, I wrote the following in my diary:

This is good. This is very good. I'm sitting in Ward E3 of the cardiothoracic wing of Southampton General Hospital. Why am I here? Well, the last nine days I've had flu – hot and cold sweats, feeling lethargic, etcetera. So I saw my GP today because Pa said there may be a chance I'd got infected during dental treatment because I didn't have antibiotic cover. The GP agreed, and spoke to my specialist, Neville Conway. This is why I'm here.

The situation is this. If I have got bacterial infection on the heart valve that is faulty I've got a big problem. They need to do a lot of tests on me here to make sure I haven't got infected. It will take four to six days to get the results required so I'll be here for quite a while. If the result is positive, then I'm in hospital for six to eight weeks on intravascular drips and antibiotics. Not much fun. The bacteria will then die. If they don't die then I'll have to have a heart operation to get a new valve. We are talking open heart surgery here. Which would put me out a little after everything I've been through.

I've just got bad flu – I hope. It's easy to be jolly now but this will really test me. No matter what the outcome, I should have known better and I should have had antibiotic cover. Saying all that, I hadn't realized how severe the consequences of infection might be.

It is quite a shock to find yourself in a heart ward for four or five days undergoing tests. I was lying in bed thinking, 'This is unreal. This isn't really happening.'

Friday, 20 October: Last night I lay in bed and the reality and possible consequences of this situation began to sink in. I know it's so unlikely, but if I had to stay in hospital for eight weeks I would have to reassess my whole situation. Obviously the 1990 Commonwealth Games would be out. So would training in California for a while. I don't know how much effect the treatment would have on my body, so possibly the whole of 1990 is out as well. I can handle it. I have to. But it would be so hard. It's as if I got over the foot problem only to have a more serious one thrown at me now. I know it's unlikely, but you do think the worst at times.

Saturday 21 October: It looks less and less likely that I do have bacterial endocarditis. The illness I have suffered is viral pneumonia. The X-ray of my chest has shown this and the symptoms are usual. I have to stay here for five days until I've had twelve blood cultures which show up negative. Then I can go on antibiotics for the pneumonia. I feel a lot better but my throat is very sore and I'm sweating a little. It was quite a scare, though. I was pretty worried the other day.

Monday 23 October: I should have been sent home today but I have to wait until tomorrow which is quite a pain in the arse. Tests are negative and I am on antibiotics.

Friday 27 October: Been back to hospital. Blood tests have given a definite diagnosis. I have caught a virus called psittacosis, which is in my system. Apparently it's caught off parrots or budgerigars or pigeons. I don't know how I've caught it, but at least they know what it is. Thank God it's not bacterial endocarditis. All this has been very worrying, very frustrating, but c'est la vie. How I got it I don't know. I had birds in my roof, I remember that. Maybe it was that.

The bottom line is that because I have a leaking heart valve, if I got a bacterial infection in a valve it would have very severe consequences – the valve would get infected and would have to be replaced. I must be sure that when I have dental treatment or any operation I also have anti-bacterial cover. I always have to remember to tell the doctors. And I must carry a special card around with me for reference, in the event of an emergency.

That incident in 1989 was the only time that my heart problem has really scared me. As an athlete, your instinct is to put the whole thing to the back of your mind, because you have to think of yourself as invincible. But at that time I was unable to – it reminded me of my human frailty.

Over the years, obviously, a lot of people have noticed me sitting in the waiting room of a consultant cardiologist. But the reason nothing has ever leaked out – if I may use that phrase – is twofold. Firstly, the secrecy to which the medical profession is bound. And secondly, the fact that for a professional athlete medical checks are not unusual – well, athletes get checked up all the time, don't they? So I could always have said, 'Oh, I'm just having a routine check-up to see if I'm in good nick.'

Although I have always tried to prevent it becoming public knowledge because I didn't want that kind of attention, I do find it amazing that my condition never did come out. I think what I did well was to play the whole thing down, which stopped family and friends from seeing it as a problem. Only my father, my doctor, myself and my coaches fully understood its real seriousness.

I know Dr Conway has sometimes pointed me out to some of his younger patients as an example of what can be done despite a heart condition. I have seen a lot of children in hospital since 1977, and I have also seen the worry on the faces of their parents. I don't know what their problems were – but it would be nice to think I could have given one or two of them a degree of hope. I hasten to add that many others who had to attend that clinic were much worse off than me. I did need help – but my problems were relatively minor.

There has been just one year since 1977 when I haven't been for my annual check-up. And that was the Olympic year of 1996. The check-up always comes at around the same time, in

January or February – but I was conveniently unable to make my appointment on that occasion. I did not want to go because I knew it was irrelevant. Whatever I was told, I knew that that year of all years, I would not have stopped running for anything.

3

IN THE BEGINNING

I was born in 1966, on 31 March – coincidentally the day on which Harold Wilson's Labour Government was re-elected. I wasn't quite an April Fool, but I wasn't far away from it. Forty minutes later, my twin sister Julia arrived.

This population explosion – as my father wryly referred to it – meant we had to move to somewhere larger. My parents bought a 1930s five-bedroomed detached house half a mile inland from the beach at Gosport. There were six of us initially: Julia and myself, our two elder brothers, Alastair and Nigel, my mother, Thelma and my father, David.

I didn't really know my brothers that well as they went away to school when I was still young. Nigel, who is nearly six years older than me, was a musical scholar at Kings, Canterbury, and has gone on to be a successful musician. He is now the principal horn player with the Philharmonia Orchestra in London. Alastair was the oldest – he is nearly eight years older than me – and he went to Marlborough College before joining the Royal Navy and then working as a business consultant.

So Julia and I were left to get on with each other. We were inseparable and very rarely argued about anything. I remember being happy in my childhood. I was apparently a really easy child, very laid back. Julia was the bossy one, I was always bossed around. I was slow, she was very quick, always a step ahead of me, much to my frustration. While neither of my brothers was particularly athletic, she was good at sport from an early age. She was particularly good at sprinting, but unfortunately developed a form of junior arthritis when she was sixteen which prevented her from doing as much sport as she would have liked.

As we got older I was the one who had more success at studying. My sister didn't get into the girls' high school and went to the local comprehensive instead while I went to a good school, an academic school. In those days it made a huge difference being at a grammar, so we were in effect set on very different paths for the first time in our lives. We led different lives at different schools with different friends and interests. I think my parents, my mother in particular, felt guilty about that. I excelled at sport and did well academically – Julia didn't. I felt we seemed to drift apart for several years.

Although Julia didn't pass many of her exams, it didn't seem to do her any harm. She's been working for the past ten years for Esso as a sales manager, and she's done very well. And last summer she had a baby girl, Caitlin. Recently I have recognized that my relationship with my sister is a lot more important to me than I think I ever realized for the first twenty-five years of my life.

In the early days of my success, I carried an enormous amount of guilt around with me. I felt guilty because I seemed to have everything. That is something you probably experience more acutely if you are a twin. But to Julia's great credit, there was never sibling rivalry between us, although she did find it hard to adjust to the changes which occurred when I suddenly became well known after winning at the Commonwealth Games and European Championships in 1986.

Julia had been on holiday in Australia when all this was happening, and when she came back she suddenly found herself being referred to not as Julia Black, but as Roger Black's sister. That really upset her and things became difficult for her. Our relationship hit an all-time low. As I hadn't had a serious argument with Julia until I was twenty-three, when it happened, during Christmas 1989, it caused me real gut-wrenching pain. The row erupted in the family kitchen when we were all helping to wash up after Christmas lunch. My sister felt that a troubled relationship I was having with a girlfriend was causing me to take my family and close friends for granted. It was not a prolonged argument, more of an explosion. But it shocked everyone. I acknowledged I had been at fault, and we made up. From that day onwards our relationship has been fantastic. That was the moment I realized how important my sister is to me. She hates watching me run and is, from all accounts, a nervous wreck at those times. She looks forward to the day when I finally retire so that she too can escape from the pressures that I put myself under and therefore indirectly she also feels as my twin sister.

As a youngster, life was very simple for me. Life was football. When I was in junior school I played the game all the time. When I came home, I would go out to play football with the other kids on the beach. I was centre-forward for the Alverstoke Junior School team. I had a hugely powerful kick, so very often the ball would be passed to me from kick-off and I'd have a go from long range. Every now and then it would come off as the opposing keeper hadn't yet got his concentration. I nearly managed the feat to spectacular effect in the Gosport Schools Cup final against our big rivals Elson School. We eventually lost 2-1, but things might have been different if my mighty effort from the halfway line had gone in, rather than cannoning off the bar.

We lived in Gosport, which is next door to Portsmouth, and all my friends supported Portsmouth. But for some reason my father took me to Southampton's ground, The Dell. So, although I started out being a Liverpool fan, I was soon hooked on Southampton Football Club. Football was a bit violent in those days, but I used to love watching the likes of Peter Osgood, Mick Channon, Steve Moran and Kevin Keegan.

When Keegan returned from Hamburg and joined

Southampton it was a massive event for me. People often ask me who was my hero when I was young, assuming I am going to mention some Olympic athlete. But I only had one hero, and that was Kevin Keegan. You could buy kits to make plaster cast footballers then, and I remember buying Keegan and painting in all the details, even down to his perm. He is the personification of everything I respect in a sports person. He wasn't outstandingly naturally gifted, although he had greater ability than he was sometimes given credit for. He just worked and worked and gave everything.

I actually got to meet Kevin Keegan in 1995. We had been invited to dinner by a mutual friend, Len Hatton. For the first few minutes after we had been introduced I was like a little kid. It was such a strange experience because you never forget that feeling of hero worship but then you realize that your hero actually knows who you are, and wants to talk to you too.

We got on really well, and it soon became clear that we had very similar views on many things. I am very interested in what makes one person fulfil their potential and another one not, and I discovered that Kevin has read the same books and assimilated the same principles on achievement that I have. We talked about the same psychological theories. His passion for sport is the same as mine. But he's still my hero.

At the time I first met him he was manager of Newcastle United, and he invited me up to one of the games. I took a fellow athlete, John Regis, with me because they were playing Liverpool that day and John supports them. We were given the whole tour by Kevin and met the players. And I was thinking to myself in the course of the visit, 'What is it that makes this man great?' I think it was because he could mix with everybody and yet always be himself – whether he was talking to the players, the chairman or the cleaning staff, he was always himself.

Of course the big day for me as a Southampton supporter was when they beat Manchester United to win the 1976 FA Cup. That is one of the greatest memories of my life. I watched the match on television – wearing my full Southampton kit –

but I kept running out of the room every few seconds because I was so nervous. Then Bobby Stokes scored the only goal in the eighty-second minute. Channon to Jim McCalliog to Stokes. 1-0 to the Saints. It was unbelievable. I ran out to the park and re-created that goal a hundred times.

Becoming an athlete gave me the opportunity to meet many of the players who were such heroes of mine. I met Bobby Stokes at a charity function in Southampton a couple of years before he died, and I said to him, 'I want to thank you, because you created one of the happiest days of my life.' I was glad I was able to tell him that. He was a man whose life ended when he stopped playing football. I think he was running a chip shop in Portsmouth Harbour. Two years later he died. From all accounts life was never the same for him after becoming a Cup final hero. All sportsmen and women who have experienced a moment of supreme achievement need to remind themselves as they stand on top of their mountain and take in the winner's view that it doesn't get any better than this. What, for example, can compare to winning Wimbledon or the Ashes, standing on the medallists' rostrum or, in Bobby Stokes' case, scoring the winning goal in the FA Cup final? To return to a normal life after such experiences takes enormous adjustment and I guess Bobby Stokes found the transition harder than most. What happened to him was so sad.

As a kid, when I wasn't playing football I was singing. I became head choirboy at St Mary's Church in Alverstoke, which was about a mile from our home. It was not that my parents were ultra-religious – I just happened to be a good singer. When my voice broke I became a server along with my best friend at that time, a boy called Michael Marks. Our task was to help the vicar with the service, and our duties included tidying the church, taking round the collection boxes, helping with the bread and wine and of course snuffing out the candles at the appropriate moment with our snuffers, which were like long witches' hats on sticks.

I have to confess that we spent an awful lot of time mucking about. We used to sabotage candles by getting them to burn down the middle so that when an unsuspecting server attempted to put them out the flame was too far below his snuffer to be extinguished. The victim would be left stranded at the altar as he either resorted to performing a hasty operation with his forefinger and thumb, or was forced to take the candle from its holder and blow it out. The greater the embarrassment, the greater our enjoyment.

But I tired of this, and at some point I started to question what I was doing. For as long as I could remember I had spent three days a week going to church and I never once prayed. I never once went for the right reasons. I went just to sing, or to make a bit of money by performing at wedding ceremonies, or because my best friend was going. I could recite all the prayers, all the psalms, everything, without looking, but I never gave one thought to what they were about. I'm not saying you should, not at that age. But I decided I was not there for the right reasons, so I left. And I've always been uncomfortable going back to church since.

Then my parents put me in for the entrance exam to Portsmouth Grammar School, and I didn't want to take it because they only played rugby there. I wanted to go to St John's College in Southsea because they played football. But my parents insisted I went to Portsmouth Grammar School, and I was devastated.

The vast majority of the pupils at my new school had been to the Portsmouth Grammar lower school for the previous four years. I was one of the very few there who had come up through the state system. So they all knew each other – and they were all a good two years ahead of people like me in academic terms – while most of my friends had gone to the local comprehensive, Bay House, where my sister was.

I was not naturally academic. I will never forget my first day at senior school. I was sitting in the front row with a piece of paper in front of me and I had a fountain pen, which I had never learned to use. I stuck my hand up and asked the teacher, 'Do we write inside or outside of the blue line?' I'd never seen a margin in my life before. I was just a local state school boy who played football. Everyone laughed. Fellow pupils still remember that. From then onwards it was tough. I felt like an outsider and it took me a long time to get accepted at the school. I remember crying in the morning and not wanting to go.

My journey to school was long. As I lived in Gosport, it meant getting a bus to the local ferry, which took half an hour, crossing over to Portsmouth, and then walking from the ferry to school. I spent the years between eleven and eighteen doing that trip in my school uniform. Having to wear the uniform – we were forbidden even to remove our caps – made me an easy target for ambushes by the local boys as soon as I got off the ferry. It was a long walk home, and on some days it seemed interminable as I suffered the taunts and abuse of the kids from the local school. I did what I could to hide my uniform – I removed my cap despite the school rules, and took to wearing an army jacket. But I was always recognized. Luckily, one of my old footballing friends was usually on hand to make sure I didn't suffer from anything more severe than a verbal hammering.

At the end of my first term, I was chosen to sing the solo in the school carol service – 'Once in Royal David's City' – and my grandparents and parents came to watch me. There is a top note in the solo at the point where it goes 'Mary was that mother mild' and I was desperately worried that I was going to miss it. Anybody who has been in the same position will fully understand my anxiety. There I was, this new kid, singing unaccompanied in front of the whole of Portsmouth Grammar School – and my family. It was my first experience of having to deliver under pressure and I failed miserably. When the moment came, my voice wobbled, my legs turned to jelly and I missed the note. Several of the boys who subsequently became good friends of mine at school remember killing themselves laughing. The embarrassment and pain of that moment was huge.

I was the butt of many a joke. But I had one saving grace – I was the fastest runner in the school by miles. That ability came in very useful at the start of my school days. The school playing fields at Hilsea were about eight miles away, and on games afternoons the boys would arrive there – either by bike or bus – some while before the teachers did. As first years, we were known as 'turds', and we were soon introduced to the great PGS tradition of turd-bashing, which involved the older boys chasing us all round the pitch before whipping us mercilessly with rolled-up towels. But they could never catch me. Not once was I brought to ground by the pack of baying second years. And as a baying second year myself, I bashed with the best of them.

The warning I had received over my health might have put some people off doing sport. But I was eager to do as much as I was allowed, and although my heart condition never disappeared, the restrictions placed on me were cautiously relaxed over the period of a year or so as my heart condition remained stable. My sporting prowess meant that I was able to establish my place in the school through sports days, cricket and rugby.

It was the latter sports which aroused my enthusiasm in my early school years. Despite my natural speed, I didn't choose to do athletics in the summer term games lessons because I didn't like individual sport. And the thought of training for athletics – I could think of nothing more boring. Instead, I played cricket, even though I wasn't particularly good at it. I always function better as part of a team because I like the supporting role. People might turn round and say, 'Rubbish' but I never strove to be a star.

If you talk to John Regis about why he loves athletics, he'll say that when he played football, even if he had a great game, someone else could make a mistake and his team would lose. He wants to be in control of things himself, and his attitude is typical of most top athletes. I would always be the opposite. I didn't relish the pressure of athletics, and I liked the fact that if we blew it the whole thing didn't come down to me. The team was more important, and the most important thing was being on the team bus and having fun and being with my friends. I was a competitive person, I liked to win. But it never was the be-all and end-all.

For all that, I found myself earning increasing attention through my athletic achievements. I was obliged to run in the annual sports day, and in 1980, at the age of fourteen, the times I recorded were sufficient to get me into the Hampshire Schools meeting, where I won again. That meant an invitation to take part in the English Schools' Athletics Championships for the first time. I was quite happy to run the odd race, and three outings a year on the track suited me well enough. But I resisted all efforts to get me to train properly. On more than one occasion, representatives from local athletics clubs came to my door to try to persuade me to join them, but I resisted the idea. Over the years, I have grown to love the sport – but at that time, it was just another thing that I did.

In my selection letter from Hampshire Schools, I was given the details of where to catch the bus up to the championships – being held at Kirkby in Liverpool that year – and I was told that I had to wear school uniform for the trip. So the Portsmouth Grammar School boy got on the bus in full school uniform. And all the other athletes were in tracksuits, jeans and T-shirts. Spot the wally. I thought, 'Oh no.' I walked to the back of the bus and sat down while everyone thoroughly enjoyed the spectacle.

A year later, boarding the bus for my second English Schools' Championships, in Birmingham, I had learned from my experience and wore casual clothing. But I was still an outsider on the scene. I knew no one as I moved down the bus and ended up sitting on my own. It was then that I met someone who was to play a major part in turning me towards a career in athletics – Fayyaz Ahmed. Or Fuzz, as he is known. He came and sat next to me and we struck up a conversation. And from that day onwards we've been close friends.

At those first Schools' Championships, all I had was my Green Flash trainers, a beat-up pair of spikes, a really old tracksuit and a blue, V-neck sweater which I used to like to wear. Everybody else seemed to have all the proper gear, and I thought, 'What the hell am I doing here?' I never warmed up – I didn't know what stretching was.

One year I won the 200 metres by a large distance at the Hampshire Schools' Championships. My father overheard one of my beaten rivals being reassured by his own father, who was telling him that he should understand that he had been beaten by a competitor who was highly trained and carefully coached. My father didn't have the heart to tell him the truth. I managed to come fourth or fifth the three times I went to the English Schools' Championships, but I always felt out of place. I look back now and it seems so ironic that I'm an Olympic silver medallist. And so many of those other athletes, who were all stars in their own right at the time, have not come through to the top level. Perhaps one of the advantages I had over them was that I wasn't set on athletics from an early age, so by the time I did decide to concentrate on it at the age of eighteen, I was not burnt out as so many other promising talents are.

By 1981 I was also playing rugby for Hampshire and the South of England, and I even got an England under-16 trial the following year. But I was just a reserve winger so I only played for about five minutes, and I never actually made the team. Rugby for me was just about being on the wing. My team-mates would chuck me the ball and I'd run with it. I loved playing, and in the sixth form I became part of a very success-ful team, captained by Mike Wedderburn, who went on to play rugby for Harlequins and present *Rugby Special* on television with John Inverdale. We won the Hampshire Schools Cup in 1983 in conditions that the local paper described as 'cloying, ankle deep in mud, torrential rain and a fierce, cold wind'. Enough to make a serious athlete shudder.

Two of my former team-mates, Edward Richards – who recently became Controller of Corporate Strategy at the BBC – and Guy Knight – who read law at Oxford before becoming a solicitor – often remind me of those glory days on the rugby pitch. Our deftness of touch, awesome power and shimmying skills are grossly exaggerated as we reminisce over the classic matches we once played in. Messrs Underwood, Bracken and Leonard should all think themselves lucky that we chose different fields in which to display our talents!

When we played weekend matches, all the fathers would be on the touchline, including mine, who was always shouting out in a booming voice that could be heard above all the others, 'Go, PGS, go!' It was a complete embarrassment at the time and I would think to myself, 'For God's sake, shut up!' But now I look back I think it was wonderful that they were always there.

I loved rugby. But as I came towards the end of my school days, I was beginning to realize that I was cut out for a different sport. I was running to maintain my fitness and began to think that this other sporting path held richer potential for me. On one occasion in my final year, my father vividly recalls me arriving home with an injured ankle after playing in a seven-a-side rugby tournament. I told him I would never play rugby again – and I never did. It was an early signal that I was taking my running increasingly seriously.

The sensation of running was one I had always enjoyed, and I used to run round a crescent at the back of our house which must have been about 600 metres long. Not too far off my natural distance! One Christmas after I had been to church with my parents, they were about to get into the car when I said to them, 'I'll beat you home.' I ran and I ran. I can remember racing along that road, and passing cyclists at one point. And I just managed to get there first. But the day I actually realized that I was special came when I was in the lower sixth form and I took part in a 100 metres race against the two other fastest runners in the school, both of whom were in the upper sixth. One was called Justin Allen, the other was Mike Wedderburn. The whole school was betting on the outcome of the race, and a lot of money changed hands. Although I had never been beaten I was a year younger than Justin and two years younger than Mike.

The race was held in Portsmouth at the Burnaby Road stadium, which was absolutely packed. It was the only time I think there had ever been real anticipation for a school race. I was running something that wasn't my strongest event, and I remember going to the stadium feeling very unsure and uptight. It was then that I discovered I had the reserves within me to perform under pressure. Up until then athletics was just something I had done and it wasn't a big deal, but this mattered, because it was the school and everyone was speculating. And I destroyed the opposition. Thus by 1983, as a seventeen-year-old sixth former, I had lowered the school records for the 100 and 200 metres to 10.7sec and 21.65sec and I had my picture and profile in one of the local papers.

I've spoken to Mike Wedderburn about that race since, and he said it was a very significant day for him. I think everyone sort of stood back and realized, 'This guy is a bit special.' Looking back, I think if I saw a kid of eighteen running the 400 metres at the school sports in around 48 seconds, as I did, I would have thought, 'That's astounding, that's astonishing.' But at the school sports they said, 'Ooh, well done, school record' – that was it.

In my lower sixth year, I was selected once again for the English Schools – but I didn't go. Gilbert and Sullivan came first. Together with three friends I had formed a punk rock group – 'The Psychopathic Vegetables'. In order to practise or jam we chose music as a minority subject. I was on bass guitar. And we were rubbish. There were two hangers-on as well. They had to do a minority, and it was better than doing minority French or something even worse.

One day the music teacher, Mr Bluff, came up to us and said, 'Right lads, you've got minority music this year, and that means you are going to be Gentlemen of Japan in the school production of Gilbert and Sullivan's *The Mikado*.

'What? You are joking, right?' we said in horror. We really didn't want to do it.

'We need some Gentlemen of Japan, and you lot are going to do it.'

It would be fair to say that we went along to the first rehearsal reluctantly, but it turned out to be enlightening, because much to our delight, the girls from the local high school had also been press-ganged into being Ladies in Waiting so there was a constant incentive to attend rehearsals and they were some of the happiest days of my life. But then the problem of the English Schools' Championships came up. They coincided with the weekend of *The Mikado* performance.

I had spent two months rehearsing for *The Mikado*. Although it was something I had never wanted to do in the first place, the bottom line was, now my heart was there rather than on the athletics track. I was summoned to see the headmaster and he said, 'Look, it is a great honour for the school and the county for you to be asked to go to the English Schools' Championships, but I hear you are not sure you want to go.' I told him I wanted to do *The Mikado* instead. I think the head thought I had put loyalty to my friends above the individual glory I might have gained from running. We performed *The Mikado* twice, on Friday and Saturday, and what fun we had. I never had any regrets about the decision.

In retrospect I think that decision was one of the reasons why I was asked to be head boy. It always seemed a curious choice to me. Traditionally, the head boy was an academic and was in the combined cadets force. I was neither. I hated the cadets, and came very close to getting a 'dishonourable discharge' because I never went to summer camp. I had no affinity with guns and aeroplanes, or going to boot camp. I didn't need that to toughen me up. Sport gave me all that. There were three other prefects in the running for the post, and they had all been head boys of the lower school. But I got summoned to the headmaster's office and he said that he would like me to be head boy.

I said, 'You are joking. I'm not the right person.' All I was worried about was how unfair it was on the others – they'd done everything right. All three of them were trying to go to either Cambridge or Oxford, and I was never going there. But his reply was, 'You should take it, because you are the right person for it. And don't worry about how the others feel.' Despite that, it took me about two days to come to my decision. When one of the masters suggested that it would look good on my CV, that tipped the balance.

I'm not saying I was a lad at school, but I wasn't the conventional perfect schoolboy. I wore my Doc Martens, and my closest friends were not the academics. Nor were their minds on the gold and silver buttons which denoted senior prefects. We would do all the usual things – we were into smoking, The Stranglers and chasing the local high school girls. But, because of my sport, I knew a broad range of boys at the school, and that perhaps was why I was offered the post. Of course this was the perfect opportunity for my friends to indulge in a little healthy blackmail. Unlike my less careful friends, I was never caught in my wrongdoings. But once I was head boy they constantly reminded me of the dirt they had on me and shamelessly exploited their position to negotiate the use of my office – which was in a ranch house some way from the main school block – for illicit or immoral purposes.

I wore the gold buttons of rank but never felt totally at ease with the situation, despite its obvious perks, probably because I never strove for or expected to achieve such an elevated position. Although I felt a degree of guilt at being made head boy, I have come to realize that feeling guilty for being successful is a limiting belief and that everyone's definition of success and rules for success vary. Success is just the by-product of the decisions that we choose to make everyday and not necessarily something that can be actively pursued.

I realize I could be resented by a lot of people. 'Roger Black seems to have everything.' But the guilt I have often felt is illogical. I couldn't control the genes I was given. And I didn't just become the Olympic silver medallist – I went through four operations and a serious illness first. I've made hard decisions in my career and I've had the courage to do things that a lot of people wouldn't have done to make the best of the talent I've been given.

I didn't just pass my exams, either – I worked extremely hard for them. I have to admit the academic side of school was always a chore for me. I never excelled at and didn't appreciate any subject. I know I ended up getting ten O-levels and three A-levels, but that was because I knew how to work so I could pass exams. My O-level year, that was just hell. But it made me realize that if you put in a couple of months' hard effort you reap the reward later on. I think that was something I got from my father. He never instilled it in me, it was just natural. It was just common sense really – two months of pain could give me great reward. With my A-levels, it was more a case of six months of pain. I worked so hard. We had an old air raid shelter at the bottom of our garden where Nigel used to practise his music. I would spend hours there on my own revising. I covered every exam paper you could ever have seen, I did projects and everything. The pressure I felt at that time was so great that I have nightmares about it to this day. For some curious reason I am sitting an exam in Geography – a subject I didn't take at A-level – without having done any preparation for it. Let the psychologists speculate on that one. I hated it all but it was worth it in the end because it was going to give me options in my life.

Throughout the sixth form I had been wondering, 'What am I going to do after school?' And never once did I think, 'I'm going to become an Olympic athlete.' The honest truth is I chose to do maths, chemistry and biology because I didn't like any subject, but I preferred sciences to arts. I still had to decide what I wanted to do with my life. I wanted to go to university, but I didn't want to do any of those subjects, so I was left with being a doctor, being a dentist, or being a vet. Well, I didn't want to work with animals and I didn't want to spend my life looking at people's rotten teeth. My father's a doctor, so I thought, 'Well, I might as well have a challenge, I'll try and get into medical school.' I knew it would make my father very proud if I did follow him, though he never said to me, 'Son, you're going to be a doctor.' And I had the vague notion that studying medicine would offer me a good quality of life – a statement of obvious naivety as any overworked houseman would be happy to testify.

Originally my teachers weren't sure it was worth trying for medical school, because they thought the academic standards would probably be hard for me to attain. But I did all the interviews, and I got offered a place at St Bartholomew's Hospital, which is where my father had been, on the basis of getting at least three Bs in my A-levels. Nowadays I would probably have needed three As. So there was the goal. Get three Bs at A-level, and go off and become a doctor. And for a year of my A-levels I worked my socks off, I put in the hours, I did all the stuff that a keeno swot would do. I just knew that if I got the A-levels, it would give me opportunities for the future.

I even did the optional A-level biology project – something only usually done by members of the Biology Club. Well, I did it in a manner of speaking. I actually copied most of it straight out of a book, and it ended up costing me one or two minutes of sheer panic. You were advised to do a project because if you did a good one you could push your grade up a level. My friend Nigel Jones was in the same boat as me – he wanted to become a doctor, but he knew he needed every bit of help he could get. One day he said, 'Look, we have just got to do a project.'

'Oh no, I don't want to sit out in the marshes for the whole of my summer doing some biology project,' I replied.

We didn't want to spend too long deciding what project we wanted to do and decided the smart thing to do would be something that wasn't going to take up too much of our time but would produce the right return. Not actually doing a project would save an awful lot of time. So I went to the local library, and looked up the oldest, most unreadable biology book of experiments. In it I found an incredibly boring experiment involving fruit flies and larvae and I thought, 'Great!' I didn't copy it word for word, but I took all the principles and the graphs and pretended I had done the whole thing. I sent off to an obscure laboratory in Cambridge for all the larvae and fruit fly samples, and made out I was coming in regularly to conduct all these experiments in the laboratory, drawing pictures and what have you. But all I was doing was meaningless, because I already knew what the results were going to be. Even that operation took a lot of effort, though. I had to write it up, type it – my sister typed it for me, actually – and add illustrations. It did occur to me on occasions that it might have been quicker to have done the whole thing properly.

Finally the day came when Nigel – who had done the same kind of thing himself – and I faced our one-to-one viva with the examiner. And we were suddenly scared stiff because he'd obviously been through the whole thing very carefully. At the end of the project you had to put down your bibliography, so I wrote down a long list of books I'd used – with one important exception, of course. I had this premonition of walking in and hearing the examiner say, 'Ah, Mr Black. It's not on your list, but do you recognize this book?' It didn't happen like that, thankfully, but I hit an awkward moment when we were looking at the larvae, and he said, 'How do you differentiate between the sexes?' At which point I had a mild panic because sexual differentiation between fruit flies in the larvae stage is not as obvious as it sounds. But I managed to drag up the information from some recess of my brain – as I recall, something protruded, and something else didn't.

Nigel was next in, and I waited outside for him to come out. 'How did it go?' He was devastated. He just sat down with his head in his hands and said, 'I've been rumbled.'

His experiment involved three temperature settings, one of which was minus 20 degrees C, and the question was, 'How did you create it?' He sat there, and he thought, 'God, God, how did I create minus 20°C, I have no idea.' And in the end he said, 'I just chucked them in ice.'

So the examiner looked at him as if to say, 'Look son, I know you haven't done this project.' But in the end he had mercy on him. He didn't disqualify him. I like to think the examiner had the foresight to look beyond the issue at hand and recognized that Nigel and I had done something you are not taught at school – we had used our initiative. We both got grade As for our biology – and Nigel did go on to become a doctor.

I went back to the school the other day and saw my old biology teacher. He's a lovely man, and I said to him, 'I got an A in biology, it was one of the subjects I really did enjoy.' And he said, 'I always remember you did that marvellous experiment on fruit flies.' I was very close to telling him the truth, but just couldn't do it. I wanted to tell him, but I just couldn't. So if and when you read this book, Mr Knight, I am *so* sorry. One of my A-level maths papers brought about what I regarded then as the worst day of my life. I was proficient at maths, I'd done a lot of past papers, and I was faced with one of those questions where you were given the answer and you had to show how you'd got the answer. I knew what to do, and remember thinking, 'Great.' But I just couldn't get it – I was miles out.

I went back and started again. I couldn't work it out. I was missing something. I went over it for the third time, and I was starting to panic. And I panicked more that day than I have ever panicked in my life. More than at any Olympic final. Nothing has ever come close to that moment. Even now I can see the room, I can smell it. I sweated everything. I spent forty-five minutes on that question, and I couldn't get the answer out. When I left the exam room I had only finished about 50 or 60 per cent of the paper. I had wasted forty-five minutes on that one question, and I knew I wouldn't get a grade B. Which meant Barts wouldn't accept me. It was the turning point in my life, and I was devastated. I remember standing on top of the Gosport ferry on my way home and looking down into the sea thinking, 'I've blown it. I've blown it. All that effort for nothing.'

To this day it frightens me when I think that if I had got that question right, and got a B in my maths A-level at the first attempt, I would without a doubt have gone straight to medical school and never been a serious athlete. I am not religious, but I like to think that as I was sitting that exam, someone somewhere was looking down on me and some kind of divine intervention was taking place.

4

TO B OR NOT TO BE

I was supposed to be a doctor. I was going to be a doctor. But I didn't become a doctor. I became an athlete instead. One moment of total panic in an examination had created the pause in my academic progress which meant that my life was soon being steered in a very different direction.

When I went back and looked over the dreaded maths paper, I realized what I had done – I had missed a decimal point. As I said, it seemed the worst day in my life. But it turned out to be the best day in my life, because it forced me to take a year off before going to university. I had got an A in biology and a B in chemistry, but a D in maths. I reapplied to go to medical school and got accepted for the following year at Newcastle University provided I got at least a B in my maths retake. That was something I managed without any more alarms. I was all set. Or so it seemed.

It was November 1984 when my friend Fuzz, with whom I had kept in touch since our meeting on the bus, said, 'You've got a year off before going to university. You really are a very talented athlete. You should come and join me at Southampton Athletic Club, you should come and train with Kriss Akabusi and Todd Bennett.'

Now these were athletes who had just come back from Los Angeles as Olympic 400 metres relay silver medallists, for goodness sake. I had sat up in the early hours of the morning watching Kriss, Todd, Phil Brown and Garry Cook winning that Olympic medal. The lure of meeting them, combined with the fact that I no longer had any preoccupations with my exams, made me think, 'Why not?' Fuzz, who was a talented high jumper, recommended me to Mike Smith, who was the coach at Southampton, and he was happy for me to go along. The curiosity about what I might achieve in the sport was already there when Fuzz asked me to join the club. In the back of my mind, I was beginning to think, 'Maybe athletics is something I could do.' I had nothing to lose, and a lot to gain. So I agreed. I was on my way.

Immediately after my A-levels I had gone camping in France with my girlfriend of the time, Jessica. We were on the cross-Channel ferry and I remember picking up a magazine with a big advert featuring a picture of Ade Mafe. That summer, he had gone to Los Angeles and made the Olympic 200 metres final at the age of seventeen. I remember seeing this picture of this guy and thinking, ' He's a year younger than me and he's already done that. I wonder what his life is like?' I didn't real-ize it then, but a year later we would run in the same 4 x 400 team in the 1985 European Junior Championships at Cottbus and win the gold medal.

What subsequently happened to Ade is a good example of the fragility of an athlete's fortunes. There was somebody who seemed destined to become the greatest British sprinter, but two years later Linford Christie came along and destroyed that ambition. Ade had great talent, but never really fulfilled it. Fortunately he has done well for himself, and now works as fitness advisor for Chelsea FC.

The first time I trained with Southampton Athletic Club was a Monday night, in a dingy gym. Kriss and Todd were there, and they were obviously the leaders of the group, although they were very different characters. Kriss was more ebullient, but Todd was quietly confident. Everyone warmed up by play-ing basketball, including me – this spotty, gangly kid of eighteen years of age trying to pick things up. Todd was a very good basketball player, and I think that because of my build he assumed I would be good too. But I was one of the worst basketball players you could ever find. It was a highly competitive game, and I was rubbish. I felt really intimidated. Then we did a training session and I was amazed at how hard it was. Todd was an incredible trainer, and Kriss was very dedicated. I was star struck – I couldn't believe I was working with them.

It took me a while to become accepted in the group. Early on I remember having to drive to a school in Southampton where they used to train and not being able to find it. I eventually turned up an hour late in the yellow Mini I had at the time, and everyone was laughing at me. I felt a complete idiot. There is an unwritten hierarchy in the world of athletics and to move up the ladder one had to run fast. At this point in my athletic career, however, I had not had the opportunity to do that. And in the eyes of my training partners it was not for me to turn up late.

Gradually I found my place in the scheme of things, and those days down in Southampton, from the winter of 1984 until I left in 1987, were very happy ones. I was part of a great group – apart from Todd and Kriss we had others such as Paul Sanders and Paul Harmsworth, also internationals, and Fuzz and Tony Lester. I probably enjoyed training then more than I ever have since. Athletics is an individual sport, but if you train with a group of people it's great fun. Looking back I can see I was young, naive and enthusiastic – and consumed by this exciting new environment I found myself in. Over the last few years I've tried to recapture these feelings, but as time goes by it becomes harder to re-create that freshness and appetite, that wonderful naivety which means that, in the words of the slogan, you just do it.

Training was hard. We'd meet up Monday night, Tuesday night, Wednesday night, Thursday night, Saturday morning and Sunday morning. Todd, Kriss and I would meet up Monday morning, Tuesday morning and Thursday morning as well. With the benefit of hindsight, I realize my body wasn't up to the strain of that regime – but at the time I loved it. I didn't think about how to run the race at all. The gun went, I went off and just ran as hard as I could and hung on. I didn't know about relaxation and pacing or anything like that. On my last 50, 60 metres I would have lactic acid coming out of my ears.

It was round about this time that Kriss gave me the nickname of Bambi, because my legs would always go at the end of each 400 metres I ran and I would be just like the character in the Disney film when he takes his first wobbly steps. Kriss has also been credited with thinking up my later nickname – Sex on Legs. But he didn't make that one up, although he did adopt it with great enthusiasm. It was something we both saw on teletext – 'Roger Black, otherwise known as Sex on Legs' – coincidentally as we were both being interviewed by the *Mail on Sunday*. When the article came out, it was full of how Kriss liked to call me Sex on Legs. I suppose if I had to choose a nickname, I could think of worse.

It helped that Kriss noticed my talent pretty quickly. We built a great empathy very early on, and he took me under his wing when I had my first indoor race at the Cosford Games in January 1985. Kriss was running there as well, although he was doing the 800 metres to build up his strength, and he said he'd drive me up. So I arrived in my Mini at the little army house where he lived with his wife Monika, and then we travelled up together. Because he was one of the stars, Kriss had a hotel room booked for him by the British Amateur Athletic Board. I was a nobody, obviously. I was left to arrange my own accommodation when we arrived in Cosford. We went to the meeting, and ran the early rounds, and then Kriss made sure that I was looked after and sorted me out with a good bed and breakfast place.

The following day I won the 400 metres at The Cosford Games, beating a well-known British international, Ainsley Bennett, and my winning time of 48.06sec was a British indoor junior record. But a little of the gloss was taken off when *Athletics Weekly*, reporting on the meeting, talked about a new up and coming talent called Richard Black!

It was at this meeting that I first saw Daley Thompson, double Olympic decathlon champion and world record holder, plodding across a field full of snow next to the stadium car park. Over the coming years, he was to become an important part of my sporting life, but at the time I was merely taken aback at the sight of a snowbound legend.

When Kriss and I were driving back, he said to me, 'You're special. You don't realize it yet but you're going to be a great star.' The funny thing about my relationship with Kriss is that it started with him being the big brother and me being the young athlete. Later I won the European Championships and he changed events from the 400 metres. But he was still big Kriss. It was only when he really achieved his potential in the 400 metres hurdles, winning the European title in 1990 and beating David Hemery's twenty-two-year-old British record in the process, that our relationship became symbiotic, whereby he had as much to learn from me as I had from him. It's a funny old relationship because even now it can switch back to its old footing. Only the other day when he came round to see me, I found myself reverting to the role of pupil again. But there are times when he will drop by just to talk about something in his life. He respects my judgement because of the sort of person I am, and he becomes the pupil, so to speak.

I'm always being asked, 'What's the secret to great training?' Of course, in the world of athletics, you need coaches to work with, and that has worked fine with me, but for me, the answer is to have great training partners. I'm a great believer in the concept of synergy, that one plus one doesn't equal just two, but can often add up to more. I have been lucky in my career because between 1986 and 1993, my only true partner was Kriss. And I think the inscription he wrote in his biography when he presented it to me shows he thought that too: 'To my only partner. To Roger, the right hand that knows what the left is doing.'

When it came to big decisions which we both had to make about our careers we always took them in consultation with each other. We took our decision to train in California for the first time, together. It was a huge step, because Mike Smith didn't believe we should go there. Kriss and I knew we had to go. And subsequently I won the European Championships. In training it felt as if there was virtual telepathy between Kriss and myself. To the point that when he did stop training, even when I was training on my own, I would always imagine he was there with me.

On the face of it, it seems odd that we should be such good friends. On the one hand, you have this white, middle-class boy, someone with a lot of the traditional English reserve who has grown up in comfort. On the other, there's this black guy who was born an Ibo prince in Nigeria, but then lived in a succession of foster homes in England and went on to become an army physical training instructor, with a real extroverted character. There are sides to Kriss that most people will never see – and it frustrates him that many don't see his deeper side – but I do. Just as his wife will say there are aspects of him that I would never see which she does.

When Kriss walks into a room, you know he's there. When he opens his mouth, you know he's there. He laughs a lot, he is unashamedly loud. But he has this incredible discipline, something he got from his time as an army PT instructor perhaps, and despite all the difficulties he has had in an unsettled childhood, he is someone who has moved forward in life. He never complains, he never moans, he gets on with life to the point where, if he wants something done he does it himself. And when he does something, he does it 100 per cent. He's an all-or-nothing person. He showed that in taking up the hurdles in mid-career. It was very hard for him but it was something he had to do. I respect him for that. Sure, Kriss talks the talk but he always walks the walk as well.

That attitude also shows in the way in which he has embraced Christianity. He was at the Commonwealth Games in 1986 when he reread an old Gideon Bible he had taken from a hotel room years before, and the message began to take a grip on him for the first time. In April of the next year – 14 April, at three in the morning, to give his exact timing – he woke up and wrote an account of a dream he had just had in which Jesus appeared to him after he had been swimming against the current for a long time. It was so vivid that he regarded it as his baptism by the Holy Spirit. He was in California at the time, combining training with studying theology. When he joined us on the track that morning, it was a case of 'Hi guys. Last night I met Jesus.'

Our response was, not surprisingly, along the lines of, 'What are you on?' But every day, Kriss would turn up at the track, and every conversation would be about God. It led to some very stimulating discussions during warm-up – far from the usual topics discussed by athletes at such times! He had the mickey taken out of him relentlessly, of course. There were a lot of people training at the time, including Daley Thompson, but Kriss would just debate and debate – he loved the whole process. Because he is so loud and outgoing, people sometimes underestimate his knowledge and intelligence – but he really knew his stuff. He was always questioning himself, and us. And I know that for him it has been a great sadness that I, as one of his closest friends, have not turned to Christianity too. I know the same thing has caused difficulties with many of his relationships, certainly with his wife. In those early days his concern was that unless we converted to Christianity he feared that we would end up in hell. I know that thought caused him great distress. His opinion has become less drastic recently but I shall just have to wait and see if he's right, I guess. There's a part in all of us that wants to have faith. The nature of the athlete is to have faith in themselves. I think Kriss realizes now, though, that you have to let people find their own way.

A lot of people he comes into contact with find him somewhat overpowering because he is such a strong individual who just likes to get things done his way. And, of course, like all of us, Kriss has a selfish side too. But with me it was different, because he wanted to get on in athletics, and I suppose he needed me to progress, just as I needed him. We helped each other so there's always been that partnership side to our relationship. Even though he hasn't run for a few years, it's still there. Maybe it comes back to the fact that in the world of athletics there are very few who have performed at the top level, so it creates a bond between people that can often overcome any of their personal failings. You will put up with those because you have this thing in common and you know what it has taken to get there.

Kriss has dined out on how he ran the final leg in the 1991 World Championship relay victory many times since. A run lasting forty-five seconds lasts forty-five minutes in the telling – and fair enough. It was such a wonderful thing to happen to him – the right person at the right time.

Now he has established himself as a television performer, presenting programmes such as *Record Breakers*, and that looks like being another thing we have in common apart from athletics because I am developing my career in that direction too. Kriss and I have been invited on to many programmes together, because we provide this wonderful blend – black guy and white guy, different backgrounds, different characters. It works because we still have the same kind of understanding we shared on the track. Even now, if I walk into a room with Kriss I automatically shrink into the background, even though he hasn't run for five years and I am the Olympic silver medallist. On the other hand, if we're in an environment where I'm more comfortable, Kriss is the one who shrinks into himself. Although not for very long! Put us together, and there's no environment we can't cope with.

What we do is compensate for each other's shortcomings. In my case, it's the fact that I don't like to be too outgoing. He can make conversation with anybody; I'm not as extrovert as Kriss. If I try to be, I feel very false. I'm happier when there is someone else who can take the lead, whereas Kriss loves to be the centre of attention. But the secret of why we work together so well is that we understand each other's strengths and weaknesses and we never compete with each other.

In the earliest days of my career, Kriss's help was of a more directly practical nature.

After the excitement of my first Cosford Games I went on to win the AAA Junior Championships, and was then selected – at the age of eighteen – to run the indoor relay for Great Britain versus West Germany. As I went to the line for the opening leg, I saw there were blocks in every lane. I'd never used blocks before. That was a measure of how far I had come in such a short space of time. That was how green Black was.

I said, 'Look, I don't use blocks. I don't know how to use them.' But I was told by the officials, 'You have to use them under international rules. This is live on television.' It was indeed, and my family were watching back home. I just didn't know what to do.

Fortunately, Kriss was running one of the later legs and when he saw the commotion – I think the West Germans were beginning to suspect some elaborate gamesmanship was taking place – he was able to jump on to the track and set up my blocks for me. He just arranged them as he would have done for himself, and then said, 'Look, go like that, and that will do.' And then he got off the track and I went on and ran. Naive or what?

That incident, and my subsequent international run against Italy in Genoa, where I beat Ainsley Bennett again over 400 metres, began to get my name into the national press. As Neil Wilson pointed out in the *Daily Mail*, that first British race was not just my first experience with blocks – I had never even run with a baton before.

When we were walking off the track in Genoa, Ainsley took me aside and said, 'You're the best 400 metres runner I have ever seen.' He was a big star at the time, and that generous encouragement was important to me, because to be accepted by my peers gave me a growing feeling of confidence.

Another of my peers, Todd Bennett, had a tremendous year in 1985. After my run in Genoa, I went to the 1985 European Indoor Championships in Piraeus with him and Kriss, accompanying them on the drive from Southampton to Heathrow. I got knocked out in the second round; Todd went on to win the 400 metres title in a world record time. And if I had been in awe of him on the drive up to the airport, I was even more so on the drive back.

Todd was a local Southampton boy, only 5ft 7in tall but hugely powerful and determined as an athlete, and immensely dedicated in training. He had been coached by Mike Smith for many years, and was clearly the senior figure in our group. His world record, coming a year after he had won an Olympic silver medal in the relay, was a fantastic achievement. But that was ultimately his day. He never really capitalized on it, and he never got back to the top level after injuring himself just before the 1986 European Championships, where I think he would have won the 200 metres if he had been fit.

It cannot have been easy for Todd to see this young athlete coming into his group and making his mark so quickly. When I won the European Junior Championships in 1985, my time matched Todd's personal best. A year later I was European and Commonwealth champion. But to Todd's eternal credit, he was always gracious about it. Now when I bump into Todd I still feel enormous respect for him. Kriss and I were confident enough to broaden our horizons, but for Todd it was all a bit too late. By nature he is a quiet, diligent person who just gets on with things. And he was from an era of athletics when you simply did what you were told to do.

What Todd and Kriss and Phil Brown and Garry Cook had done in winning the Olympic silver medal in 1984 had started a tradition in British 400 metres relay running. You had four great characters, four genuine friends – and that showed. And if you ever came into the 4x400 squad, you had to become friends. When Derek Redmond and myself came on the scene in 1985 it was just such a joy. I remember the first time Derek and I were invited to train with the squad at the Alexander Stadium – the fab four were jogging together while we trailed a few yards behind them – and Derek turned to me and said, 'One day we'll be up there too.' Even he couldn't have dreamt how soon that day would come.

On 15 June 1985 I had what felt like my first experience of 'fame'. It was after I had run 45.91sec at the Southern Counties Championships – the first time I had beaten 46 seconds. I was walking through Crystal Palace past a TV shop with my friend Fuzz when I saw my race being replayed. We just stood outside watching, and it felt incredibly strange. But I remember being very frustrated soon afterwards when I didn't even get a mention in the local paper for winning the European Junior Championships. I wondered then what I had to do to win recognition in the public's eyes. And the truth is, as I discovered, you've got to win something big, buddy. Something really big.

Those championships, which took place in Cottbus, East Germany, were the focus of '85 for me. The most vivid memory of that time was travelling to get there. We flew into Berlin and then we had to get into a coach and cross the Berlin Wall through Checkpoint Charlie. That was an eerie experience – going through no man's land. It was the first time I had been behind the Iron Curtain. I have been back since the Wall came down, but every time I go along that road I always remember that first visit on the way to the European Junior Championships. With hindsight it was an incredible team – John Regis, Jon Ridgeon, Dalton Grant, Ade Mafe and Colin Jackson. Elliott Bunney was there too. He won, although he didn't go on to fulfil his potential. Junior athletics is a riot, you're very young, your hormones are roaring – it's just fun. The junior days are not serious so the transition from junior to senior is very difficult for many people.

In Cottbus it was hot. It was the first time I had ever run in serious heat. I went on to win the gold medal and break the British junior record of 45.36secs, which was quite a perfor-

Practising block starts at a very early age with my twin sister, Julia. I'm the cute one on the right.

The twins, aged seven.

Singing in *The Mikado* (back right). Our efforts as gentlemen of Japan don't appear to impress the girl in front!

BLACK'S DILEMMA

Portsmouth Grammar School athlete Roger Black could face a teasing dilemma this time next year. Black, one of the hottest track properties on the local scene at the moment, may have to choose between a career in sport or medicine.

BY STEPHEN BREACH

The 17-year-old Gosport-based sprinter, who is expected to take the Hampshire Schools Athletics Championships by storm at Southampton today, is hoping to follow his father into the medical profession, but that could depend on the breaks he gets in sport in the next 12 months.

Black, who cleaned up in last week-end's Portsmouth Grammar School Championships at Burnaby Road, is a gifted athlete, but he has clashing interests.

Just minutes after receiving the trophy for the most outstanding athlete of the championships at the impressive Royal Navy stadium — he completed a hat trick of victories in the 100 metres,

admitted: "I only really do athletics to keep fit — my main sport is rugby."

Last week-end's times were up to national standard and Black's great strength is his sprinting which helps him on the rugby field as a nippy wing half.

So what does the future hold for the son of a Gosport doctor? "I have considered a career in sport, but whether I

"It all depends on me. I like athletics and like winning but to be honest I don't get that much satisfaction out of it."

Black is not attached to any local club and both Fareham and Portsmouth have tried to persuade him to join their ranks.

"I ran for Fareham three times last season, but did not get any real satisfaction. That's why I'm not interested in signing up for anyone."

Black's rugby record is impressive. He has represented Hampshire for the last two seasons and two years ago was called up for an England trial.

team game and that appeals to me more. Athletics is too individualistic."

Black is currently studying for his A levels at Portsmouth Grammar School. He will finish this time next year and then the heartsearching could start.

"At the moment all I'm concerned about is studying for my A levels, but I've obviously got to look to the future.

"My father is a doctor and I would like to be the same. I suppose the next stage will be University and what happens in sport will simply depend on the breaks I get in the next 12

Portsmouth Grammar School Sports in 1983 – the day I came of age and left Justin Allen and Mike Wedderburn for dust.

The Team Solent 4x400 metres – Kriss Akabusi, Paul Harmsworth, Todd Bennett and myself with Mike Smith in charge.

Winning the Commonwealth 400 metres title in 1986 – my big breakthrough and quite a shock for Darren Clark of Australia.

California 1987 – Kriss Akabusi before taking a loser's dip in the ocean.

A truly legendary 4x400 metres relay team – myself, Edwin Moses, Derek Redmond and Daley Thompson, Mount S.A.C. Relays, 1987.

Posing in the Californian sun with Phil Brown, Derek Redmond and Kriss Akabusi, 1987.

'The A Team' in Minorca,1991 – the boys on tour were Jon, Fuzz and Kelvin.

Kriss and myself with Danny Harris – the most talented of us all.

On my knees in Minorca after a 52 second 400 metres – too much beer and a very dodgy paella!

(Right) Dipping on the line with Thomas Schoenlebe in the European Cup final in 1987. He won this one.

(Below) The one that got away – my chance to become World 400 metres champion goes on the line to Antonio Pettigrew of the USA.

(Above) Defending my European 400 metres title in 1990 – the end of two years of pain and frustration.

Celebrating becoming World Champions in Tokyo in 1991 with Derek, Kriss and John
– the happiest moment of my career.

Still celebrating our win with the boys at Christmas 1991. It's not every day you
become a World Champion, so we kept on celebrating.

Pre-Olympic training in Monaco in 1992 with (l-r) Mike Whittingham, Mike MacFarlane, Marcus Adam, John Regis, Kriss Akabusi, Sven Nylander and Jonathan Edwards.

Outside Buckingham Palace with my MBE and my parents.

mance. It took a big chunk off my personal best, over half a second, and that was the real beginning. That was the statement of intent. That was the first time I really felt I had made a mark. And to top it all off, we won the relay as well.

A trip to China in 1995 was another memorable experience in my year off from studying. It was the last England under-23 great expedition. We had two big meetings in Beijing and Nanjing. It was boiling hot, and my 400 metres partner was Derek Redmond. He won both races, which started off our rivalry. But what I remember most about that trip was that after the races were over we had two days before going home, and plans had been made to go to the Great Wall of China and the Forbidden City.

It summed up the attitude of many athletes when most of the people on the trip seemed to be interested only in complaining about the standard of the hotels and the food. They just wanted to go home. There was a mutiny on the team bus. The main bulk of the athletes wanted to take a vote on going home early. Jon Ridgeon and I were at the back of the bus, and we stood up and said, 'Guys, you can't come to China and not go and see the Great Wall or the Forbidden City. So there's no point in even thinking about a vote because we are going to see the Great Wall and the Forbidden City.'

I just couldn't believe it. It was a case of, 'We've done the competition. Now let's go home.' People didn't seem to realize this was probably the only opportunity they would ever have to visit these places. When we eventually got to the two sites, I remember thinking, 'Bloody hell, how could anyone not want to see these?'

A lot of athletes appear to have a very narrow-minded approach to life because they centre their existence on just athletics. Many don't appreciate the opportunities we have in our sport for travel and sightseeing. One of the things I always try to do in a foreign city is go to an art gallery. I always try to see something. But those athletes did have a point. The food in China was desperate.

By the end of 1985 I was working harder than I had thought possible at my athletics – and having more fun than I had ever imagined.

One long-running joke at my expense came about after Kriss, Todd and I had been running a coaching course for some children. We went to lunch at a local pub and I ordered scampi and chips – no big deal – and I asked, 'Do you have any tartare sauce?' Kriss and Todd, for some reason, thought this was the most upper-class thing they had ever heard. Whenever we ate together for the next two years, regardless of what was on the menu, the question would always be asked, 'Would Lord Black care for some tartare sauce with his cuisine?' I recently had lunch with Todd who still found it amusing to place sachets of tartare sauce on my plate even though I had ordered steak and kidney pie!

Kriss would delight in telling us that when he was in the army he once sat in an officers' mess and, while waiting for the food, started eating his bread roll after spreading on it what he thought was strawberry jam, but it turned out to be cranberry jelly. In truth, his culinary habits were often very bizarre. A few years later when Kriss and I were attempting to follow a strictly non-fat diet according to instructions on ideal nutrition for athletes, I recall coming down to breakfast at our hotel and seeing him tucking into mustard on dry toast. According to Mr All-or-Nothing, they were the only permissible things on the menu!

But for all the mickey-taking, there was great fondness between us all at Southampton. Having said that, no one had the mickey taken out of him more than fellow 400 metre-man, Paul Harmsworth. Paul would turn up to training straight from work in his suit, get changed, touch his toes and join in with the group – but he had none of the natural co-ordination you would expect in an international athlete. Most people have an in-built co-ordination – as the right leg comes forward, the left arm moves forward as a natural counter-balance. But Paul didn't have this natural balance. At times, he appeared more like a marionette than an athlete, and we ribbed him mercilessly about it. Someone once called him Bill and Ben the Flowerpot Men, and he never heard the end of that.

All athletes regularly go through drills designed to improve co-ordination. There is the heel-flick, where you have to scuff the ground with the ball of your foot and then bring your heel up towards your backside. There is the 'high knees' exercise, where you have to practise bringing your knee up so that your thigh is parallel with the ground as you run. And there is an exercise which involves rolling the feet to improve the mobility of the ankles and the calf muscles. The only problem for Paul was that, in his case, the co-ordination never arrived. Which only made his achievements in the sport the more remarkable. In 1987, he won a European indoor bronze medal over 400 metres; the following year he ran 45.5sec outdoors, earning a trip to the 1988 Olympics in Seoul as a member of the 400 metres relay squad.

In 1995, years after he had retired, I spoke to him at the club he now owns in Soho called School Dinners, which is very popular with men who still hanker after the traditions of their schooldays, such as plain English cooking and the occasional caning – which is administered by the restaurant's waitresses. I had not submitted to the lash that night – although I believe my brother-in-law sampled some of the punishments available. But amid all the hilarity, Paul had turned to me with great seriousness.

'Do you know what, Rog?' he said. 'You really piss me off.'

'Why?' I asked.

'Because you've got more talent in your little finger than I ever had. But I know I've fulfilled my potential. And you won't.'

'Yeah, but what about all the injuries?' I countered.

'Sometimes you've just got to bloody go for it.'

And I remember thinking, 'Actually, you're probably one of the best qualified people to tell me that.' I couldn't complain. He had more right to say it than anyone because he had indeed gone beyond his own potential. What Paul was able to do throughout his career was to step out of his comfort zone. He placed no limits on himself and, although he simply didn't look like an athlete he turned himself into one. That conversation really affected me and I made a commitment to remember it.

By the end of 1985, I had established a link with someone who became my weights trainer down in Gosport where I was living with my parents and who proved to be an invaluable help to me all the way through to my Olympic medal win.

Joe Picken was a physical training instructor who had been in the Royal Navy for many years, but he was working in removals when I met up with him. I knew who he was because he lived near us, and I knew his daughter, who went to the local high school. I used to do a run round the beach near our house, and one day, as I was doing a loop round the village when I passed his removals van, he stopped me and said, 'I hear you're doing athletics now. You're a spindly lad, you need to get stronger up top. I can help you, if you want some help.'

'Sure,' I replied. And I started doing weight training with him in what was little more than a converted shed at the bottom of his garden.

Joe's a big man, and a very likeable one, but he has an odd sense of humour which some people find hard to get the hang of. A lot of it comes from his time in the Navy – there were always plenty of jocular references to 'all present and correct' and 'ship-shape and Bristol fashion'. He liked to sing old naval songs and sea shanties while we worked, or sometimes he would whistle and go into some mad routine as I was trying to do my bench presses.

Weight training has never appealed to me – lifting inanimate objects up and down repeatedly is not my idea of fun – but I've spent a lot of time working in the gym with Joe because he provided the companionship and jokey atmosphere which managed to eliminate the boredom of training. When I did abdomen exercises with him, he would to say to me 'Work your Bobby Charltons, lad,' because he always remembered when Bobby Charlton took off his shirt after the 1966 World Cup final had gone into extra time, and revealed what a good example of a well-developed abdomen he had.

Sometimes people would ask, 'Why bother to go there? Why not go to a proper gym with better equipment?' But I have never liked working weights in crowded gyms. When I go to California we work out in this enormous, plush gym. And I hate it. You don't need fancy equipment to get fit, or carpets, or music, or jogging machines. All you need is a heavy, inanimate object. With Joe, I have always used rusty old weights, some of which have come off scrap heaps. But that suits me, because I don't want any luxury about me when I'm training. Many athletes complain about facilities in this country, and I have always said to them, 'Yes, we could all do with better facilities. But in the end, provided you have what it takes, all you need is a weights bar, all you need is a road to run on.'

Joe is very special to me. He has always had total faith in me and my ability, and in my early years, I used to have a ritual of popping round to Joe's for a cup of tea and a chat before a race. Despite his somewhat bizarre manner he was always totally committed to me and during my darkest days, when many people would be writing me off, he would always tell the doubters 'Don't you worry about Roger Black. He will be back.' After I won my Olympic medal, in my first TV interview I said, 'Joe, you can open your bottle of whisky now.' Because soon after I started working with him I had bought him a bottle of Scotch and he had said, 'I'm going to open that when you win an Olympic medal.' He and I had waited a long time for that moment.

*

All in all, my first year of taking athletics seriously was more successful than I could ever have imagined. During the summer, to prevent undue interference with my training, I had managed to switch my medical course from Newcastle to Southampton, where the university had been kind enough to create a special place for me. But once I went there in the autumn of 1985 I realized I had made a big mistake. A year earlier I had hardly thought seriously about athletics. Now I could think of nothing else. It soon became a real struggle trying to combine training with my course at Southampton. I had no time for socializing. I was struggling with my work because I wasn't really motivated and we were working with a lot of dead bodies at the time. I remember one day sitting in my college room and thinking, 'I really don't feel part of this.' I felt so guilty, because the university had made this special place for me. But I said to myself that I could always go back to medicine, whereas I would never have another chance in athletics. And I didn't want to be an 'if only' person. You see them all the time in the world of sport. 'If only I hadn't had this injury, I would have won the title myself . . .' I didn't want to say to myself one day, 'If only I had concentrated on my talent instead of staying at university, I might have been an Olympic medallist.'

During my A-level year, when I had first considered a future in the medical profession, I had written to the man who had so famously combined studying as a doctor with top class athletics, Sir Roger Bannister. On 27 June 1984 he kindly wrote back to me advising me to give 'full priority' to getting the grades I required to reach St Bartholomew's, where I would be able to join an active athletics club. 'If it is of any interest to you,' the first four-minute miler concluded, 'I did no athletics whatsoever from the age of fifteen until I went up to Oxford and started again. There will be plenty of time to do the special training which your coaches consider that you need once you are installed as a medical student in London.' His response was greatly appreciated. But I was finding out very quickly that the world of athletics had changed, and the days when you could combine two careers as Sir Roger had were long gone.

I was faced with a choice. I could spend the next five years reading medicine, cutting up dead bodies, studying macro- and micro-biology and amniocenteses to obtain my degree as a stressed out, alcoholic chain-smoker. Or, I could become a full-time athlete, train three or four hours a day, spend three months out of every year in sunny California, run for my country in the Olympic Games, have fame and a degree of wealth and, more importantly, have 10,000 women screaming at me whenever I walked out into an athletics stadium. Tricky one!

So I sat down with my father in the dining room at home and told him I was finding the whole thing very difficult. Remember this was a doctor who was very proud that I was following in his footsteps. But he was unbelievably under-standing. All he said to me was, 'You must do whatever you feel is really right. Whatever decision you make I will support you.'

I made an appointment with the Dean of the university and I felt very uncomfortable. She said she regretted my decision, and told me there were a lot of people who would have loved to have been given the chance I had. But when I won the European Championships the following year, I got a fantastic letter from her. And in 1992, I am proud to record, the univer-sity gave me an honorary degree.

I remember one family acquaintance who was distinctly unimpressed by my choice. He was an estate agent and I had rung him up to ask if there was a possibility of doing any part-time work now I was leaving my course – and he ripped into me. He said, 'I don't know how your father could have let you leave a position at medical school for sport. I don't know how your father could even have thought of it.' I was shaking as I put the phone down. When I won the European Champion-ships a year later, I remember recalling that conversation and thinking to myself, 'Who's sorry now?'

I left university and got a job in the parts department of the Mercedes Benz factory in Southampton. It felt great. I would train in the morning with Kriss and Todd and my bosses let me come and work when I wanted to. I cleaned all the nuts and bolts, and I was never happier. Because I had a clear purpose in life now – I was focused on athletics.

5

CALIFORNIA DREAMING

Early in 1986, Kriss and I decided that if we wanted to improve ourselves in the athletics world, we should go warm weather training in California, where we had an invitation to work at the University of Irvine. Mike Smith felt we would do better to remain in Southampton and made his feelings known. But Kriss and I went out anyway, not least because the invitation had been issued by the world's most famous athlete of the time, Daley Thompson. 'Come out and join me,' Daley had said. What aspiring athlete could ignore that summons?

It was not the first time I had met the great man. A year earlier I had been introduced to him in Portugal while on my first warm weather training trip. There are very few people in this world who have natural presence. Daley Thompson had – and still has. At the time of our meeting, Daley was hugely famous. He had just defended his Olympic decathlon title at Los Angeles, and raised a media storm with his post-competition comments about Princess Anne, and with his T-shirt featuring the slogan: Is the world's second greatest athlete gay? So to meet him was awe-inspiring. Later that day I nearly died with him as well.

We were both in the back of a car being driven by another decathlete. On a winding cliff road he lost control of the car, which skidded towards the edge. There was an instant moment of fear before we came to a halt. We had survived. Then I realized, 'My God, Daley Thompson was in the car. This would have made the news all over the world.' We were both scared stiff, but once we recovered, we were able to laugh about it. We have been able to laugh about a lot of things since then.

The times I've had with Daley are some of my happiest. If you want to be one of the boys, if you like playing games, whether it's cards, or bowling, or tennis or golf or whatever, Daley Thompson is just great to be around. He is never happier than when he's playing cards with the boys. And nor am I, so there was an immediate connection. In our early days in California our game used to be three-card brag. (Now it's poker. And Daley usually wins, because he usually wins at most things he does.) So after training, Kriss and I would drive to the huge house Daley had on the waterfront to play cards with him and his friends. Imagine, Daley Thompson and Kriss Akabusi at the same table (this was before Kriss became a Christian). It's going to be loud. Very loud. Daley would win a hand, and he'd jump on the table and rub the cards in your face shouting 'Read 'em and weep, boys!' or 'Cowabunga baby!' The most competitive man you could ever meet. I well remember one night when we decided the person who lost the most money would go skinny dipping in the ocean, which was freezing cold. Kriss lost that bet. And we've got the pictures to prove it.

If I'm playing tennis with Daley, I want to win but mostly I want to have a good match. Once the game's over it doesn't matter to me. Daley wants to win everything. That's why he was so great, but it's also his downfall in a way. I think Daley can be difficult if he doesn't win, but this is purely frustration within himself because he sets such high standards.

I never got caught up trying to compete with Daley – only idiots ever tried to do that. But he would suck people into starting to think, 'Yeah, I'm going to beat you! I'm going to beat you! Yeah, bring it on!' And you knew it would always end up with the same result. He loved having people to do that with.

I used to play tennis doubles with a friend of mine who was

a tennis pro against Daley and another decathlete. Every Friday we would have a game, and then go to a restaurant. And my friend would control it so that we had close matches, knowing full well that if he actually played properly we would win every time. But if you beat Daley . . . Well, it got to a point when my partner and I said we'd rather lose than win, so that we could have fun at the restaurant. And that's what we did.

Daley's fallen out with a lot of people in his time, and there are many who are not enamoured of him. His run-ins with the press, whom he avoided almost without exception, have been numerous. But I have seen him walk away from people who were friends of his as well. I think with Kriss and I he always knew that we didn't want anything from him. Except his friendship. And he returned our friendship.

Kriss and I had this instant camaraderie with Daley. You always had something to laugh about. He'd help us with training, we'd help him, though our training routines were governed by the events we pursued. By the time Kriss and I went down to the track Daley would have been there for an hour and a half before us. He'd have to train from nine o'clock in the morning through to three, four. Whereas we'd turn up at 10.30 and go until two. It just shows the wisdom of choosing one event rather than ten.

Daley has always been generous about my music. When I was composing songs and playing in a few clubs in California in the early '90s, he would act as my No.1 fan. He would sit and watch me play, and he knew all the songs, so he'd say, 'Oh, play that one, play that one!' He'd take the mickey in a nice way, because all the songs I've written are, as he put it, very depressing! He didn't have any musical talent himself, it wasn't one of his areas of excellence, so it was neutral territory where he didn't feel he had to compete.

Our friendship was not based on athletics. I was in California with Daley for a week in early 1997 and it reminded me just what fun the man is. It was so great to be able to play cards with the boys as we used to without complicating anything, or analysing anything.

Daley is a classic example of an athlete finding life difficult after athletics, which he misses more than I ever will. His whole life was being with the boys, playing cards, training, and being competitive. I really want to try and avoid that. That, though, is why Daley was the consummate athlete. He could only ever have been a decathlete, because that meant he could play all day. Since retiring he has been in big demand, appearing with the BBC commentary team and working on the promotions side for a couple of large sportswear and watch companies. But his decision to go into football as well – in recent years he has played for Wimbledon reserves – was about carrying on playing in the wider sense of the word. He really loves to play – but he lives to compete.

California was a huge adventure for Kriss and I. We had no money, and we shared a room in a cheap motel, the Kirkwood Motel, which has now been demolished.

We were so naive. I remember we wanted to get a cheap rental car and we were told that all the rental places were on Harbor Boulevard. So we got on a bus and said, 'Harbor Boulevard, please.' The driver asked, 'Whereabouts on Harbor?' 'Just Harbor Boulevard.' When we got there the guy said, 'Harbor Boulevard,' and so we got out. What we didn't realize was that Harbor Boulevard is more than ten miles long. It runs from Disneyland all the way down to the coast. So there are Roger Black and Kriss Akabusi, walking north, thinking, – 'Well, we'll see a rental place within five minutes.' No. Ten minutes. Nothing. Fifteen minutes. Nothing. We're getting hacked off now. And we walk, and walk and walk and walk.

I live just off Harbor Boulevard when I am in California now, and I sometimes drive down that stretch of road Kriss and I travelled. I've measured it, in fact. We walked for seven miles. And even though I have long legs, for most of the time I was about twenty paces behind Kriss, whose army days had clearly equipped him better for route-marches. Eventually we arrived at the aptly named Nickel Rent-A-Car – classy, no? (Unlike the Kirkwood Motel, it is still standing.) We went in and we couldn't afford anything. So we got the oldest, most decrepit jalopy you have ever seen. We were so proud of ourselves. This car drank petrol like nothing you've ever known, and it must have broken down about five or six times in the four weeks we had it. But – it only cost us five dollars a day. And we felt like California dudes behind the wheel.

It took us a little while to get used to the local ways. Mike MacFarlane, who had reached the 1984 Olympic 100 metres final two years earlier, had come out to join the group along with fellow sprinters Donovan Reid and Ernest Obeng. On our first night together we went to a local restaurant. When we'd finished we paid the bill and walked out. The waiter came running after us, 'Hey guys – what's your problem?'

'What do you mean, what's our problem?' we asked.

'Was there something wrong with the service?'

'No, it was fine,' we assured him.

'Well, you didn't leave a tip.'

We didn't realize it was obligatory to leave a tip in America. I'd never been to America. Mike and some of the others had been to the Olympics the year before, but obviously they hadn't eaten out a lot. This waiter was getting really irate. But Mike MacFarlane wasn't having any of it. 'You got a problem, man? What's your problem? How dare you be so rude to us? So we didn't know you had to leave a tip. Have your f—ing tip.' He was livid. The aggression required to be a world-class sprinter was clearly demonstrated! And as we walked out I couldn't stop laughing.

As I have become more well known at home I have come to value hugely being in California. It is a place where nobody recognizes me and I can concentrate on my running without being bothered by anyone. The weather, though, is the main reason to go there, because as a 400 metres runner I need to be starting to run fast in April and May, and it's easier to run fast in heat. There were other advantages too – not least the quality of training companion.

Meeting Ed Moses was a wonderful experience. He lived and trained at Irvine, and the curious thing was that the world record holder at 400 metres hurdles never hurdled when we were there, never even went on to the track. He just used to run round and round this grass field alongside. He was very laid back. He wasn't part of the group – I mean, he was Ed Moses, the world's greatest hurdler – and he had his little ritual. He'd come down to the track with this mat which he would proceed to place on the grass field. And he'd sit on this mat stretching for about two hours. And then he'd run. And then he'd come over and say, 'Hey, what's up guys?' And that was it. I asked him about not practising his hurdling. He just said 'I don't need to. I can already hurdle. It's easy.' What Kriss would have given to have been able to say that!

Ed's only hurdles practice came when he was wiping the floor with all comers in races. He was a most beautiful runner to watch. To this day, when I'm running round that field I get this vision of Ed Moses which I try and emulate. He would just churn out these repetition circuits, with huge strides, floating across the field. It was amazing to be in his presence. And it was also a great help. Because after I won the Europeans, when Kriss and I were in California in 1987, we took Ed out to dinner. And he told us about the way things would be for us on tour, how we should get to know the race promoters and establish a personal relationship.

But probably the best piece of advice I got at that time on the subject of business came from Daley Thompson. He told me, 'When you sign a contract, remember two things: you should walk away happy. And you should always know someone else is probably getting a better deal.' What he was saying was, if you are really not happy with something, don't sign it. But if you sign it, don't moan further down the road that you've been ripped off. If you sign it, accept it.

My early days in California in a sense reflected my early career. It was a relatively carefree existence, and once I had finished training, the options were simple: go out, have fun, have something to eat, go to the movies, play cards, play guitar. That was it. That kind of relaxed way of life is something I have found increasingly difficult to maintain, but for the last ten or eleven years I have always managed a week, sometimes two, away with the boys. Call me old-fashioned, or sexist, or whatever, but that's really important to me. I'm never happier than when I'm sitting round a table with a few beers playing cards with my best mates. And fortunately Elsa totally understands that and insists that I go away once a year with them.

We have had some great times over the years. Soon after the Tokyo World Championships in 1991 I had my usual annual holiday with my two closest friends from school, Kelvin Hackett and Jon Ayling, who is a former Hampshire cricketer, and Fayyaz. We went to Minorca, and it was there that I discovered how quickly you can lose form when I had a bet with Kelvin, who is not particularly athletic.

We got very drunk one afternoon and then went out for a paella. There is a track in the middle of Minorca, and the bet was made – as bets usually are in such circumstances – that I couldn't get round 400 metres in under 50 seconds, there and then, and he couldn't get round in 70 seconds. Three weeks beforehand I had run 44.60 in the World Championships. I struggled round in 51.5. So he won the bet because he managed to jog round despite the heat of the midday sun and after a plateful of paella. It brings you down to earth when you can't break 50 seconds, even in a pair of trainers.

It becomes increasingly hard to get the time, but it will be a sad and sorry day when I can't find a week to go away with the boys. It's fundamentally the three of us – Kelvin, Jon and myself – plus one other, and that one varies. Kriss Akabusi joined us for a couple of years, giving me the opportunity to play against him in our annual tennis match. I used to play quite a lot of tennis when I was younger. Kriss, since he retired from athletics, has had hundreds of tennis coaching lessons. And his big goal is to beat me. But he's never beaten me. And he never will. It's a great opportunity to watch a grown man cry, which is quite pathetic. I think the only goal left in his life now is to beat me at tennis. He's spent so much time and money trying to achieve it, and he has all the equipment. He turns up with three rackets, I turn up with the old racket I've had for five or six years. And for some reason he just cracks under the pressure of competition. If asked, he would certainly object to me playing what he calls 'girlie tennis'. But I have always preferred to beat his brute force with finesse.

I used to play a lot of tennis in America with Daley and John Regis, and it just got silly because we are all quite good players but we can't just have a knock around, we are naturally comp-etitive. And so what should be just a nice game of tennis would turn out into a 100 per cent serious match. All it takes is a twisted ankle and you are out of training for three weeks. So I stopped playing tennis, I just had this one game a year with Kriss. But I told him I was not going to play in 1997. It is a measure of how serious I was about 1998 that I pulled out of that match. I was doing everything possible to mini-mize the risk of injury. And he was really pleased that I did, because it showed I was serious about trying to win the European Championships in 1998.

When I finish with athletics I will play a lot of tennis. I played only at school level, and I'm nothing special. But I'm good enough to beat Akabusi. He hasn't got the temperament for it. He gets frustrated and he gets bored. Daley, of course, is the best player of us all. But if you want people to play games with, Daley and Kriss are perfect. They've been very support-ive of me since they both retired. But I think both of them are looking forward to the day when I hang up my spikes and rejoin them to play seriously.

A sense of play is an important part of being an athlete. In a way it is an extended childhood. Many athletes acknowledge the fact that you keep yourself young by thinking young and acting young. At the grand old age of thirty-two, however, I have become a little more responsible. I suppose there is a natural evolution to these things. When I go to California now I do a lot of yoga and I don't risk any other sports – I can't afford another serious injury at this stage in my career. I also do a lot of research for one of my other main interests, motivational speaking. It's a subject I have become deeply involved with since my traumatic year of illness in 1993, and I do a lot of reading and attend seminars with my friend Sven Nylander, the Swedish 400 metres hurdler.

Other California experiences have proved less edifying, however. In 1993 I was left a little shaken up when I got booked for speeding on the I5 freeway on the way to San Francisco – perhaps the straightest, most boring stretch of road in the world – near a little town in the middle of nowhere called Coalinga. I was with Elsa and another friend of mine when I was stopped – apparently I was doing 100mph. This policeman came at me with a gun pointed at my face – it was the most frightening thing – saying that he could throw me straight into prison if he wanted to. I said I was sorry, and that I didn't realize I had been going so fast. Fortunately I had my California driving licence on me. He told me that if I hadn't I would have been in a lot of trouble.

Four weeks later I had to go all the way back to Coalinga, which was five hours' drive from where we were staying, for a court appearance. Mike Whittingham drove me there in case I got banned and he had to drive me back. I was sitting in the courthouse with all these people who were up for various crimes, among them a US army officer in full uniform who had been caught speeding on the same section of road as I had been. He was facing a fine of 1200 dollars, and when the judge asked him what he had to say in his defence, he read out a prepared statement explaining that he had been in a rush to get home and he had to go off soon to serve his country, and as an ex-serviceman he was sure the judge would appreciate the pressures he was operating under, and he didn't get paid that much anyway, but then as an ex-serviceman the judge would probably know all about that too . . . When he had finished, the judge said to him, 'Son, you're right. I was a member of the armed forces once. And you should know better. Double the fine.'

So I was sitting there thinking, 'I've got no chance.' But I played the Englishman to the full, stiff upper lip to the fore, saying I didn't realize I had been going so fast. And because it was a first offence he halved my fine to 600 dollars. Sometimes it helps to have an English accent.

There are also occasional boys' nights out when I am in California, but very few athletes drink heavily. Come to think of it, the throwers manage to put away a fair amount of beer. But for most, drinking is simply not part of the culture.

I haven't given up the cards, though. And I try to get to Las Vegas twice a year so I can play poker. New York has been described as the city that never sleeps but surely that title should go to Las Vegas. The bright lights, theme hotels, Elvis impersonators and the constant sound of slot machines make it the perfect escape from reality. People will bet on anything in Vegas. I was foolish enough to get caught up in the wave of British patriotism whilst there for the Frank Bruno v Mike Tyson fight in 1997. The MGM Grand Hotel was heaving with the strange mixture of British fans chanting 'Bruno, Bruno' and gold-laden American gangsters supporting 'Brother Mike'. My bet on Bruno to win in three rounds was placed more out of loyalty than belief but it was worth it just to be in Vegas for the big fight.

I always wanted to try and hold my own at the poker tables in Las Vegas. During my first few visits I would stand behind the ropes watching the many different games taking place, feeling intimidated by the speed of play and betting. My poker experience consisted of regular Tuesday night games with friends in California, as much social as it was financial, and very different to sitting round a table in Vegas with complete strangers whose sole intention is to fleece you of all your money. Eventually I plucked up the courage, read a few books on poker psychology and took my seat at the cheapest table of seven-card stud at the Mirage. Six hours later I got up from my seat slightly poorer but feeling a lot richer for the experience. I haven't had the courage or the desire to move up to the more expensive tables probably because what attracts me to poker is the fact that you can bluff and still win – something that unfortunately is never possible in the world of athletics – but I now take my trips to Vegas very seriously, often playing from six in the evening to six in the morning (there are no clocks in the card rooms so night and day don't really exist in Vegas). I love poker for its test of one's nerve and wits and to date have just about managed to hold my own against the regulars eager to bankrupt some out-of-town big shot who fancies his chances. I remember a cocky young cowboy from Texas who sat at our table one night, stetson on head, whisky in hand, with two women to impress on each arm. He got lucky for the first hour betting agressively and consistently winning money on good hands. It was, however, only a matter of time until the distraction of the women and the drink combined with his bravado caused him to lose all his money to the regulars who had seen the likes of him many times before. In Vegas poker good luck cannot last for ever, it is patience and skill that must prevail. As the song says you must 'know when to hold them' and 'know when to fold them'.

Unlike in athletics anyone with enough money to start can line up (or sit down) at the Poker World Championships. It is a tempting thought but I am sure that many a fool has sat down with the big boys only to get quickly knocked out in the first round.

6

THE DRUGS DON'T WORK

Can you win an Olympic medal without drugs? Yes, you can. I've done it. But only I know for sure that I've done it. I'd put my hand in the fire for my training partners Kriss Akabusi and Jon Ridgeon. But I can't know for certain. The only person I can be sure hasn't taken drugs to improve their performance is me. With drugs there is obviously the issue of the damage you may be doing to your body or your future health. (If you're really worried about damage to your body, don't train for athletics, because it is a punishing business!) The main issue, for me, is about the rules of the game. It's about nothing more than cheating and people cheat in all walks of life. You know the rules, you know what you can and can't take. To me it is not a medical issue, it's a moral issue.

I think the suggestion made before the 1996 Atlanta Olympics by the former British Olympic doctor Mike Turner that 70 per cent of athletes are involved in illegal doping is a gross exaggeration. But there are clearly athletes out there who are taking drugs. I don't know how they get round that fact in their own heads, because I know I couldn't. I couldn't stand on a medal rostrum if I'd taken drugs. I do believe there are athletes who have taken drugs who convince themselves that they haven't. Because I think people can do that. I'm not talking about the East Germans who may have been administered with drugs unknowingly in the past. I'm talking about Americans, Britons and other Europeans. You've got to assume that at least some of them have taken drugs – and it's as if they are in denial.

But the old argument, 'Well, everyone else is doing it' is a total affront, because not everyone else is doing it.

I will take anything that is legal. Only the other day I was asked to test a special oxygenated water that was apparently going to improve my performance. I've been taking protein and carbohydrate powders for years even though I don't like the taste, because I believe they help me recover. I'm not cheating, because there's nothing in them that breaks the rules. There's a clear line, and anyone can find out where it is drawn

I have never thought of taking drugs. In twelve years, no one has ever approached me to take drugs, my friends would say, 'Yeah, because you are the last person they are going to approach.' That is because I'm independent in the sport, and always have been. If anyone ever did that to me, I'd say, 'I'm sorry. You've just made a very big mistake. Because I'm going to turn you over.'

The former American sprinter Darrell Robinson once admitted to me and Kriss that he took drugs, claiming he was ten times the athlete when he did. But I have heard other views which suggest taking drugs – whether it be steroids or human growth hormone – is not a certain way to improve your performance.

In 1997, a conference in London heard further revelations about the systematic use of drugs in the old East German athletic federation. Among those whose performances must be tainted is Thomas Schoenlebe, the leading European 400 metres runner apart from me in the late 1980s and early 1990s. At the time, many people asked me if I didn't feel very resentful about the likelihood that he had been taking drugs when he was racing against me. Truthfully, I hardly gave the matter much thought. But it is easier for me to acknowl-edge because even if Schoenlebe was taking drugs, he never beat me when it mattered. He couldn't beat me in 1986 or 1990. And when he won his world title in 1987, I was out with injury.

It's true that I would have been European record holder for periods of my career – although not for that long, because

Derek Redmond broke my British record with 44.50 in 1987, and David Grindley lowered that mark to 44.47 at the Barcelona Olympics in 1992.

But I've said it many times, and I mean it: records mean very little to me. If Schoenlebe had beaten me to win the European title, yes, I would have been upset. But as things turned out, he never took anything away from me. If you told me Michael Johnson took drugs, it would be different. Because if that was the case, he would have prevented me becoming Olympic champion, taken from me the ultimate prize.

There seems to be a general cynicism within athletics, or maybe it's lazy journalism, that means that exceptional performances are all-too-often tainted with the suspicion of drug assistance. A lot of people who suspect that Michael is on drugs ask, how can you win the Olympic 400 and 200 metres titles in those times, so close together? Michael would acknowledge that himself. His problem is people have pointed to his relatively modest performances in 1997 and said, 'Ah, you see?' I think that is unfair in itself – he did after all win the world title, and he has been running consistently well for more than eight years.

I choose to believe that Michael is clean and base my position on the question: Why can't he be that good? He trains hard, he could be. I believe I am exceptional at what I do, but I don't think I am extraordinary. I think Michael Johnson is. He is one of the most dedicated, disciplined people I have ever met. If you put that together with talent, then you have the potential for extraordinary performance.

Reading his book *Slaying the Dragon* – which I did lying on a hospital bed in January 1997 after having some cartilage taken out of my knee – was proof to me that he wasn't taking drugs. I remember thinking as I finished reading, 'Gosh. He must be clean. Because if he isn't, then he is living in constant denial.' You can't put out a book like that and be taking drugs. If you are, God help you. You can't tell people how to achieve their dreams, when in brackets it's 'Oh, by the way, I took drugs.'

If you read Michael's book, you can see where all the mental strength and discipline come from. He is meticulous about every aspect of his life. Not that I would want to live like that. I'm very dedicated about what I do, but it does not consume me, it never has done. Which is probably why I'm not Olympic champion – although I think in that year I wouldn't have been anyway. And I'm happy to admit that.

The speculation over Michael is an example of the constant contradictions that surround us in this sport. I don't *know* whether Michael Johnson, Frankie Fredericks, Merlene Ottey, Linford Christie, Carl Lewis, Daley Thompson, Ed Moses have taken drugs or not. I have no idea. I have nothing to hide. I've done it, clean. That's why I have told the authorities to test me whenever they want. Blood test me. I've no problem with it. Rights of privacy? Never mind all that. If there's a drugs problem in sport, we should do everything we can to find out the cheats.

At least, that had always been my attitude. But in the last couple of years, adopting such an open stance has become less straightforward because when the Diane Modahl case came around it changed everything. I can no longer invite any and every test with a happy heart, because Diane's overturning of her doping ban on appeal, after it was found that her urine sample had been stored improperly and rendered unfit to give a valid reading, has brought new doubts into the whole business. Diane would say her case has proved that the drug-testing regime is not as infallible as we were led to believe. She's absolutely right. That case has changed the world of athletics.

Now we are down to a two-year ban for a first offence of drug taking. Why? Because it's been shown that mistakes can be made, and the potential legal costs if athletes challenge drug findings in court are astronomical. Procedures are always in place to improve drug testing – the laboratories would claim that mistakes cannot be made and 99 per cent of the time I am sure that is true but this is of no comfort if you are the 1 per cent left over. That percentage of doubt plus the human error factor in storage, transit and paperwork mean that any athlete found positive can proclaim their innocence – as most seem to do nowadays.

People often ask me about the rights and wrongs of the Diane Modahl ruling. How could someone like Diane, one of the nicest people you could ever meet, take drugs? But being nice is irrelevant since nice people can obviously take drugs too. I believe Diane is absolutely innocent. I'm English, I like her. I'm biased. People in other countries who don't know her would say she did take drugs before she was sent home from the 1994 Commonwealth Games. They don't know the story. To be innocent but be found guilty must be 'living hell' as Diane has described her experience. It is not just your athletic achievements that become subject to suspicion but in effect your whole character and respectability. I remember speaking with Diane's husband in 1997 and being struck by his anger, bitterness and despair at how both his life and Diane's had been so cruelly affected by somebody else's mistakes. It's a whole situation that doesn't bear thinking about.

The argument that has been advanced by some people that we should just let everybody take anything they want and then see who comes out on top is the ultimate in cynicism. But it's an interesting subject. Why do people take drugs? I think it's because their desire to be the best or better is so important to their identity that they will do anything. I do not have that inside me. Any win in those circumstances would be the chemicals talking, and I would know it. If, however, I was somebody for whom being the No.1 in the world mattered 100 per cent, then I could see how I might take drugs.

I have witnessed at first hand the temptations that play on people's weaknesses. The fact stands that I have let the former British 400 metres record holder David Jenkins, who was jailed for drug smuggling in 1988 and who also admitted to experimenting with steroids during his time as an athlete, play a major part in my career.

Jenks was one of the people Kriss Akabusi and I met when

we went out to California for our first training trip early in 1986. By then, Jenks had retired from a career which had brought him the European title at the age of nineteen in 1971, a silver medal in the relay from the 1972 Olympics and the distinction of being the first Briton to break 45 seconds for the 400 metres.

I first met Jenks at a barbecue at his home near San Diego. Phil Brown and Derek Redmond were over there at the time and Jenks was helping them out. Kriss and I and Daley and all the boys were invited down. I was so eager to meet him. I've always been like that. I've always been someone who wants to learn from people who have done things well in the past. If I'd known that day how much help Jenks would give me in my career, culminating in the Atlanta Olympics year, I would have been amazed.

I didn't speak to him for long on that occasion. There were a lot of people around, and I don't think he was particularly relaxed around any of us, to be honest. He always had a reputation as a hyperactive character. But something happened, there was an immediate bond there, and I remember thinking, ' That's somebody who I will make the effort to speak to. He's been there, he's done it, and he's made mistakes, and I want to learn from that.' I didn't know what was going on in his personal life. At that time he would have been involved in drug trafficking. I had no idea.

I remember vividly a conversation we had about drugs later in 1986 when he said to me, 'You never need to take drugs.' As we were speaking he probably had the drugs in his garage. And he could have easily said to me, 'Try this.' But he made a big point of saying that I could do what I wanted to do without having to resort to drugs. In hindsight, I think what Jenks was telling me then was, 'Don't make the mistakes I made.'

He has told me that he took drugs during the build up for the 1976 Olympics and then on and off until 1982. He never ran his best races on drugs. He has subsequently said to me, 'If you stand on the line, and you're clean, and you're healthy, you can have a mental edge to the man who stands on the line and has taken drugs.' I'm not convinced of that. But he did say it to me.

David Jenkins was arrested in April 1988 on charges of conspiring to smuggle and distribute anabolic steroids. It was claimed that his smuggling ring controlled 70 per cent of the American black market in steroids worth $100 million. The drugs were manufactured in Mexico and Jenkins arranged for them to be illegally imported over the border. The American authorities feared that the drugs, which are known to have side effects including liver cancer and heart disease, were making their way into colleges and high schools. Jenkins pleaded guilty and served ten months of a seven-year sentence imposed in December 1988 before being released on condition that he conduct lectures to young people on the dangers of steroid abuse. He claimed after being arrested by undercover FBI agents that he had decided to pull out of the operation. He had been caught on what would have been his last job. He maintained that he had kept all knowledge of his activities secret from any of the athletes he mixed with in California. It was, he said, a large-scale criminal operation and he was not going to risk blowing his cover for the sake of selling a few bottles of pills to athletes.

I first heard about it while I was in California. Kriss and I were playing cards round at Daley's house when two policemen arrived at the door asking questions. They had Daley's name and address because Jenks had helped him find the property. It was a bizarre experience, with the two officers looking from Daley to Kriss to me and asking, 'Which one of you is Daley Thompson?' We thought that was funny, because Daley was massively famous at that time, and the idea that Kriss, or even more ridiculously, I, should be mistaken for him seemed absurd. But the atmosphere soon changed when we heard why the police were calling. When we found out Jenks had been arrested and it was related to drugs trafficking, it was very difficult to know what to think. Our first reaction was, 'Bloody hell, what's going on?'

It wasn't until Kriss and I got back to our rooms that the

magnitude of it really hit. The stigma attached to Jenks's name in the world of athletics would be terrible. And rightly so. What he did was abhorrent. It was disgusting. Especially if you think of the kids that would have taken those steroids.

You didn't really admit to being associated with David Jenkins. I thought long and hard about it, and a lot of people said 'You ought to have nothing to do with him.' And many did have nothing to do with him. But in the end for me it came back to that conversation we had had when he had told me I never needed to take drugs. I felt that he was somebody who had made many mistakes and had got caught up in things – which I don't condone, but I couldn't just turn my back on him. And Kriss couldn't. And Daley couldn't either. I kept thinking, 'I wonder how he is?' I didn't know the details. But I didn't care what other people thought. I didn't care that people would associate us with him. We were not involved in any of the business which got him into trouble. We just knew him as David Jenkins, former athlete, a person who would talk for hours about athletics. And I still valued what he had to say.

I learned a very big lesson then. Guilt by association – it does not stand up. I knew people were thinking, 'Roger Black, Kriss Akabusi, Daley Thompson go out to America for four months. Who do they hang around with? David Jenkins. Oh. That's a strange one, isn't it?'

We got tarred with the same brush, there's no doubt about that. No one actually came out and said it meant Roger Black and Kriss Akabusi and Daley Thompson were taking drugs, although it was implied in at least one newspaper article. But Jenks never, ever did anything to me. Apart from tell me not to take drugs.

When we went back to America in the spring of 1989 myself, Kriss, Daley and a couple of other friends drove for about three hours to visit Jenks at his prison in the middle of the Mojave desert. Visiting him in prison was a statement by all of us. We were high-profile athletes, going to see a steroid trafficker in prison. We were clean athletes, but deep down it had nothing to do with athletics. We were visiting a friend. He claims that he got enmeshed because the money was there and there were dodgy people and he couldn't get out. He admits he got greedy. I think we could understand how he had got caught up in it.

It was a surreal experience. We were all sitting there, and Jenks turned up in his prison gear, trying to put on a brave face. We spent about an hour and a half with him. We were there to try and cheer him up. Daley was at his best. It was as if nothing had happened. We all thought it was the right thing to do, to visit Jenks. I think he was embarrassed by us coming, 'This is what it has come to. I'm in prison, and I've lost everything, and you're visiting me' – but I think it meant an enormous amount to him. We made all the obvious jokes about prison life: 'Pretty white boys need to keep their backs to the wall . . .'

It was only half a joke.

The most poignant moment for all of us was our departure. We put on this façade of 'ho, ho' and Daley was laughing and joking, and underneath all that there was this consciousness of the seriousness and severity of what was actually happening. We were visiting a fallen idol. We left in silence. As we walked away, we turned to look and he was standing up at the window looking at us. Simply staring at us.

The drive home was a sombre one. But it was so important that we went. For all of us. It made me realize that it is possible in friendship to be very forgiving.

Jenks did his penance. He put his hand up and admitted he had taken drugs himself. He does feel there are several people from his era who judge him and were happy to condemn him who would do well to look to themselves and what they did at the time.

Although we had been in touch for a number of years, our relationship didn't become a close working one until some time after Jenks had served his sentence. It was very difficult for me, because I have always been very anti-drugs. But I remembered a scene at the end of the film *Dad*, with Ted Danson and Jack

Lemmon, where the father says to the son, 'I want to give you some advice for the rest of your life – be forgiving.' We spend our lives not forgiving people. I think I am quite a forgiving person. With Jenks there was a choice – either you could disown him, or you could say, 'Who am I to judge him?'

He did what he did out of greed – no more and no less than that. I think it was obvious to everyone that he was a very vulnerable person in certain ways, and I could see how he had been seduced by the potential to make an enormous amount of money and then got caught up in something. There was a demand for steroids, he supplied it. Then again any drugs pusher could say that. What he did was terrible.

Clearly there was a moral issue involved too, but it was just not strong enough as far as he was concerned. Jenks is a very complex character. He is not proud of what he did, but he has come through and learned an enormous amount from his time in prison. That was a period of great pain for him and there was only one way to go from then on. I think he came out a far better man. I know he feels that, because I have spoken to him about it. He's now an extraordinarily successful businessman – more successful, I think, than any of us can comprehend. He has the best-selling protein powder in America.

What David and I have in common, and what we have talked endlessly about, is the 400 metres. He still had an enormous contribution to make to my career. There is part of me that feels that any athlete found guilty of taking performance-enhancing drugs should be banned for life – to allow a cheater a second chance two years later is offensive, morally, to the many athletes who train hard every day and play by the rules. Nothing that happened to Jenks has remotely changed that. Unfortunately, as a result of the Modahl case, I have to believe that mistakes can be made and an innocent athlete can be found guilty. So a ban for life if you test positive for drugs can no longer stand.

As I write these words, I could be taking drugs. You, the reader, can never know for sure. That is the tragic thing about drugs in sport – all discussions about testing and bans become academic. It is only the individual athlete who knows the absolute truth.

7

TWO TIMES A CHAMPION

David Jenkins was not to play a major role in my career until 1996, but by the summer of 1986 he had become someone to whom I turned for advice at key moments, and he played a part in helping me to achieve the double flourish of becoming Commonwealth and European champion in my first senior year. At the time, that achievement was like a big wave which swept me forward. In retrospect, it looks more and more extraordinary.

The last 100 metres of the 400 metres can be described in many ways. People liken it to having a fridge thrown onto your back. Or a bear jumping on to your back. It's what makes 400 metres running unique, because the surge of lactic acid is so strong and the loss of power and strength from your body is so obvious. And that's why athletes from other events respect the 400 metres runners. You have to have both speed and strength – you have to have endurance. My running strategy, if that's what it could be termed, consisted of going out fast and seeing how long I could put off my legs buckling – the Bambi nickname was a good one for me. The theory was, 'I'll buckle at 300, then the next race I'll buckle at 320, and then eventually I'll put it together and my body will adapt.'

My first big event of 1986 was the UK Championships, where I finished third behind Phil Brown and Brian Whittle. I was in the lead at 300 metres and then died a big death at 340. Lots more Bambi references were made. I was still running only

45.5s in the early part of the season, which was nothing special. But then in the AAA Championships I came second to Darren Clark of Australia, who at that time was one of the best runners in the world, having been fourth at the 1984 Los Angeles Olympics. I ran 45.16, which was a significant improvement; and I think then I knew I could beat Darren at that year's Commonwealth Games in Edinburgh, even though he was the huge favourite.

Meanwhile, my first conflict with Mike Smith was developing. I was suffering from tight hamstrings. We trained very hard in between races, and I felt I wasn't getting much chance to rest. Kriss and Todd could deal with it, but I wasn't strong enough. I sat down and thought, 'Who can I talk to about this?'and that's when I started phoning Jenks. On 24 June, I wrote in my diary:

> Jenks phoned me. He feels that rest is vitally important. Surely Mike is wrong to set us these hard sessions and expect us then to do three 200s tomorrow. It's crazy. If I'm to run fast on Friday night we must sort this out or I am not going to reach my full potential.

The balance of training and rest is crucial in athletics, and the careers of too many athletes have been destroyed because they haven't had the confidence to do nothing when it is necessary. The belief is, 'I get better by training. No pain, no gain.' What many people have found out is that you actually get worse by training because your body doesn't get time to recover, so you never really run to the best of your ability. Jenks really believed he didn't rest enough in his career. Steve Cram too has said the same thing to me.

Here's another diary entry, from 17 July:

> Jenks phoned me tonight and thinks I can win the Commonwealth Games if Clark is unable to handle the rounds. He says that I mustn't train tomorrow, so I

won't. There's so much he wants to tell me but he is unable to do so over the phone. He says I mustn't do the opening ceremony.

The schedule in Edinburgh had the 400 metres semi-final and final on the same day, with a three-hour gap. It was a very windy day and many runners were really paranoid about this, including Darren Clark. But fortunately I didn't really give it much thought. In his semi-final Darren took it really easily because he was worried about the final. But he eased down too much, to the point where he got the outside lane in the draw for the final, while I was two lanes inside him.

When it came to the final there was a really strong wind into everybody's face from between 50 and 300 metres. But because I was so naive, I didn't respect the wind. The others must have thought, 'Right, it's going to be really windy in the first 300, but as we come home for the last 100 we'll have the wind behind us.' But I didn't give a damn about where the wind was. I just ran my normal race because I only knew one way to run – go out hard and hang on. So Darren and all the others took it easy to 300, and by the time they got there I was seven, eight metres ahead. If you watch the race again you can see Darren's face reacting like mad when he realizes the situation. And he starts running, but it's too late, because by that stage I am becoming a wind-assisted Bambi in the last 100 metres! I crossed the line something like five metres ahead of the rest of the field. And that was it: Roger Black had arrived.

I didn't think anything. I just did it. How I would love those days to come back. But I felt for Darren. He was crucified by the Australian press.

Mike Smith was delighted, and Kriss was really great about it. Kriss had taken me under his wing a year earlier, and when we were getting ready for the race it was almost as if he was more interested in me than in himself. Between the semi-final and the final he kept telling me that he thought I could win it.

He didn't feel *he* could. In fact he came fourth, and that was the day he decided to turn his attention to the 400 metres hurdles. He has told me since that he knew then he was never going to beat me over 400 metres. He had to make a decision. I guess he made the right one!

Kriss's ability to make a decision and go with it is a lesson for everybody. What he achieved was incredible. In America the following year Daley and his training partner Greg Richards were trying to teach Kriss to get from hurdle to hurdle in thirteen strides. He could manage with fifteen, but the thought of thirteen was daunting for him. He couldn't hurdle. But he worked so hard on his technique with Mike Whittingham. So hard.

Lots of athletes seem to say nowadays, 'I'm going to switch to the 400 metre hurdles.' They have no idea how hard Kriss had to work to do that. It took him two years before he became proficient, but he never gave up and he never cut corners. I remember one morning's session he did with Mike Whittingham which Kriss completely messed up. We all went home. The following day, when we met up for training, it transpired that Kriss had gone back the previous afternoon on his own to do that same session again.

And although at first everyone said, 'He's a useless hurdler. He looks terrible,' he went on to win a European title, and Olympic and world championship bronze medals, and became the first Briton to run the event in less than 48 seconds, beating the British record David Hemery had set in winning the 1968 Olympics. It was a reward for sheer dedication.

We won the relay as well at the Commonwealth Games in Edinburgh, but it was an awkward situation because Todd Bennett was disappointed about the 200 metres, where he had been beaten by the Canadian, Atlee Mahorn. Todd was No. 1 in our group, and I had won a major championship, something he hadn't done. Suddenly I'd become the centre of attention. I found that a little bit difficult to deal with. It marked a change too with the friend who had got me into athletics, Fayyaz. He was in the high jump, and I was rooming with him. But whereas it had all started as a bit of a laugh, all mates together, now I had won the gold medal and my place in the athletics world had, inevitably, been altered. The Commonwealth Games proved to be a turning point not just for me, but for several of those closest to me in the sport.

Going into the European Championships a few weeks later was a challenge of a different order because, as both Mike Smith and I were only too well aware: I was up against Thomas Schoenlebe of East Germany. Everyone felt deep down that Schoenlebe was going to be too hard for me to beat. He was running regularly under 45 seconds, something I had still never managed, although I did run 45 seconds dead in Zurich the week before competition began in Stuttgart.

The Commonwealths were where I made my mark and proved to myself that I was more than just another athlete, but the Europeans were where it all clicked. That was where I became a championship performer. To be in the same team as the likes of Daley Thompson, Steve Cram and Sebastian Coe was just incredible, but the final surpassed all my expectations.

The day before the first round of the 400 metres, Kriss, Todd and I had gone down to the stadium and chosen a lane on the track to walk round in order to familiarize ourselves with the layout and the feel of the place. As I walked, I felt a conviction that something special was going to happen to me in this place. They were testing the scoreboard at the time, and at that moment, as if by way of confirmation, the word 'Europameister' – 'European champion' – flashed up. I took it eagerly as a good omen.

I reached the final without undue alarm, and when I got there, as I had in Edinburgh, I just ran off as quickly as I could and hung on. The monkey jumped on my back in the final 100. The fridge too. But I carried them through the line and won in a British record of 44.59sec – taking nearly half a second off my personal best. Schoenlebe was just behind me with 44.63sec. I remember writing this afterwards: 'I'm the bloody European champion and British record holder. And there's so much more to come from these Bambi legs.' And all at the age of twenty. As David Coleman said in his TV commentary in Stuttgart, 'He's done it all in one race.'

Kriss clearly remembers a conversation we had afterwards where I said I could run under 44 seconds without undue problem. 'All I've got to do is run half a second faster,' I said. And at that time I really believed it was that simple.

Two days after I won the title in Stuttgart we won the 4x400 metres relay. The event had already departed from plan well before we even set foot on the track because Todd Bennett had been injured in the 200 metres and was unable to run. So the team that went out to warm up for the final was Derek Redmond, Kriss Akabusi, myself and Phil Brown – to run in that order.

We went to the warm-up area, and twenty minutes before we were due to be called up we became aware of a kerfuffle going on at the other end of the room involving Phil Brown and the national coach, Frank Dick. We were all bemused, and then Phil came over and said, 'I'm not running.' He had a hamstring problem. and he didn't believe he could carry it through the final. So suddenly Brian Whittle, who had been warming up half-heartedly as first reserve, was told he was running in the European final. And the order had changed to: Derek to Kriss to Brian to me.

Moments like that can either break you or pull you closer together. And it pulled us closer together because we believed that whatever team we ran, we could still beat the West Germans, who were our main rivals. For me, being thrust on to the anchor leg took a bit of adjusting, because historically that was the Phil Brown leg – always, no matter how he was running in the individual event. And the third leg, traditionally, meant Todd. But suddenly these two were out and we had a totally different team.

The incident which assured the victory a special place in people's memories happened when Kriss came in at the end of the second leg and accidentally took one of Brian's shoes off with his spikes as he handed the baton over. And poor old Brian had to run the whole 400 metres wearing only one shoe. In fact it was lucky old Brian because that is still his main claim to fame. He will always be remembered as One-shoe Whittle. As he handed over to me I was within striking distance of the West German anchor runner, Ralf Lubke, and came through to win the gold medal. It was the icing on the cake of an extraordinary four weeks for me. The European 4x400 final was on 31 August. The Commonwealth Games individual final had been on 27 July. Within those four weeks my world had changed. As a result of my achievements I went on to become British Athlete of the Year. When I came home to Gosport the town put on a civic parade for me. I was dead against the whole thing because I thought, 'No one's going to turn out, or there'll be just a couple of old ladies and a street-full of kids shouting out "Wally!!" or worse.' It would be so embarrassing, especially as they wanted to drive me down the high street in an open-topped car with the Mayor of Gosport. But it was already all organized – with a brass band and everything.

As I wrote at the time: 'What could have been a very embarrassing day turned out to be a great experience. Thousands of people turned out to welcome me home.' The streets were packed, lined with banners saying 'Well done, Roger.' And there were flags waving all over the place. It was quite something in a place where, a few weeks earlier, I could have gone down to the local pub unrecognized. In a place where, a year before, I had been so frustrated that my local paper had not even mentioned the fact that I had won the European Junior Championships. Now I was front page, back page, middle page – and it was the beginning of a close relationship with my home town that culminated in my being made honorary Freeman of Gosport in 1996. It highlights how difficult it is to get noticed in our sport. You have to win things. Big things. European junior champion and British junior record holder is great, but to Joe Public it doesn't mean anything.

Something else that becomes very obvious to you is that, when you achieve at a certain level, you become a commodity. Companies which beforehand were only giving you kit start talking money. Your race fees go up. Certain athletes are important to the marketing of the sport – getting bums on seats, getting people to turn on the TV to watch. In commercial terms, certain athletes matter. The majority, unfortunately, don't. The attitude is: if they are not in the race, get someone else in. But you know when you matter to the people who run the sport, to the television people. Obviously some people are needed more than others. In world terms, a Carl Lewis or a Michael Johnson, an Ed Moses or a Linford Christie. But I had suddenly become relatively important.

I felt it immediately. Suddenly Puma and Adidas were battling it out for me, wanting to get me on board. I didn't have a manager at the time, so Kriss was involved, and Daley helped me a lot in choosing a shoe company. Medals make a big difference in the sport. Gold medals make a huge difference.

Once you reach a certain level in athletics, a lot of your life is taken up with travelling from hotel to hotel around the world. When you start out you are young and impressionable, but eventually you get your first invite to the world of the élite athlete. That status was effectively conferred on me in 1986 when I was first asked to compete in the Zurich grand prix – which has built a reputation over the years as the three-hour Olympics and is effectively the test of whether you have made it or not.

Walking into the lobby of Zurich's Nova Park Hotel is a daunting experience to the uninitiated. You see opponents of whom you are in awe, and other big stars who you have only read about or seen on television, people such as Carl Lewis and Said Aouita. Suddenly you are there, and you are part of it. And while you are thrilled to be there, you don't know anyone except for the odd Brit. So you end up forming your own little cliques.

You know you have become an established face – and it takes a few years – when you know all the athletes' managers, rather than just the athletes, on first-name terms. You've been around a bit by then.

The beauty of a meeting hotel lobby in the hours before a grand prix gets underway is the variety of people who gather there. You have got fifty Kenyans trying to persuade the promoter to find them a run in the 5,000 metres A race. Or failing that, the 1500 metres B race. You have got the Russians drinking vodka in the bar. And you have got the Russian women. A few of them would always wear leather trousers and too much make-up – becoming Westernized, but a bit too Westernized to the point of going over the top. And you've got the Americans, all living out of suitcases, for whom the lobby is base camp. There always seems to be a sofa-full of young athletes in the corner simply mucking about and laughing at some private joke or other. Athletics is a childish sport in many ways. It keeps you young, because you have to be young to do it. When you get physically old, you still have to stay mentally young to compete.

Not everyone fools around, of course. I don't recall anyone who can claim to have had a really good laugh with Carl Lewis, who would usually stay in a separate hotel from all the other athletes, surrounded by Santa Monica Track Club groupies and minders. But he did turn out to be more approachable than I would have expected when I had an opportunity to talk to him properly.

In 1991 I was flying on a plane specially chartered to take athletes between two European meetings, and I happened to be seated next to Leroy Burrell, who was then holder of the world 100 metres record, while Kriss was sitting next to Carl Lewis. You often have this misconception of star athletes because of the way they are on the track. These two American sprinters were huge stars at the time, and the natural tendency when you end up sitting with such people is to think, 'We are not worthy.' But I had a great chat with Leroy. We were discussing

California, where we both spent a lot of time, and I was saying how it was a place I could remain unnoticed by the general public. Funnily enough, the world 100 metres record holder said exactly the same thing – such is the low profile of athletics in the United States.

Carl Lewis revealed himself to be immensely knowledgeable about athletics. I wouldn't have expected my achievements or Kriss's to even have registered with him, but he knew everything about our performances – times, races, everything. And Kriss and I were sitting there thinking, 'This is the great Carl Lewis talking – about us.' It is all very unreal for me sometimes, being part of this game.

8

DOWNHILL, AND UP AGAIN

It's easy to get to the top. It's hard to stay there. After the excitement and success of 1986, my physical and mental resources were to be tested in a way I could never have imagined, causing me to split with the man who had guided so much of my early running, Mike Smith.

I returned to winter training as Commonwealth and European champion, but that swiftly became an irrelevance. Nothing brings you back to earth quicker than a wet, windy evening running up a hill in Southampton. We got back into the routine. But it was then that aches and pains started to plague me, and I began to notice discomfort in my right hip. I kept running through it, but it was always there. That little, niggling problem was the first of a succession of setbacks lying in wait for me over the course of the next two years.

I went back to California with Kriss a little richer. The previous year we had been on fifteen dollars a day, but we could stretch to a bit more this time. So we got a better apartment, hired a nicer car – this time we knew how to get there. The jalopy days were over. But, in athletic terms, I was about to career off the road.

When I returned from California in 1987, I felt the British public expected me to win the World Championships scheduled for that summer in Rome. And not just the public, the British athletics establishment as well. But my hip problem was still there. And although I was still running quite well with it, the discomfort was gradually getting worse and worse. Every time I started, the hip would 'clunk in' and 'clunk out' again. I started having a lot of physiotherapy on my hamstring and hip but no one could really do anything about the pain. For the first time in my life I was running with pain and all the mental stress that that brings.

My mental strength was further eroded by something which happened early in 1987. A large, loping American called Butch Reynolds came along and started running 44.2, 44.3 seconds regularly. Looking back, I realize I let that affect me more than it should have done – I was too aware of Reynolds being around. Athletics is a particularly volatile sport – you can think you've established yourself, but there is always someone new arriving to threaten all that.

Everything came to a head in a domestic meeting which was staged early in the season at Crystal Palace. I was warming up but it just wasn't happening. My mind was on my hip and my leg, and I pulled out of the race. It was the first time I had ever done such a thing at that stage – and the last. I never want to go through that experience again. Things had reached a point where I was actually scared of competing. I knew that I wasn't able to run well enough to do myself justice, so I didn't take an individual place for the World Championships though I said I would run in the relay.

I had to sit and watch the person I had beaten into silver position at the previous year's European Championships, Thomas Schoenlebe, become world champion. Britain went on to win a silver medal in the relay through myself, Kriss Akabusi, Phil Brown and Derek Redmond. But my main memory of the Rome World Championships was of working with the British team doctor.

After the championships I had a series of traumatic injections into my sacro-iliac joint, which was apparently unstable and was thought to be the cause of my problems. Within the space of a year I'd gone from being this young, healthy, not-a-care-in-the-world athlete to just one of the countless number for whom the injuries had started arriving. In retrospect, this was the first serious test of my belief in how good I was, and of how much I wanted an athletic career.

At the time, however, it was just awful. My mother would drive me from Gosport to Guildford for the injections and she'd drive me home. The injections didn't work. It felt as if I was in the wilderness. I laboured on in training but the back of my leg was constantly in pain and any attempt to sprint was nigh on impossible. The frustration was intense. The injections had not worked, local physiotherapists seemed unsure of the cause of my problems and as I began to run out of people to turn to, I became almost desperate to find help.

Then Frank Dick, who was the national coach, told me to go to Germany and see someone called Dr Hans-Wilhelm Muller-Wohlfahrt, whom he'd heard about through another athlete he was advising on physiological training, Germany's Wimbledon champion Boris Becker. Subsequently, many of Britain's leading athletes turned to Muller-Wohlfahrt in times of distress, including Linford Christie and Colin Jackson.

I went to Munich, and Muller-Wohlfahrt gave me a series of injections of calf's blood and honey in my back and leg which were supposed to help ease the inflammation. All this treatment was not cheap, and I was having to fund the bulk of it, including air fares, so it was even more galling when none of it seemed to work. I went into the winter of '87 still training in pain, and knowing that I wasn't 100 per cent.

Then in November my right foot started to hurt. I could train with the pain up to a point, and suddenly there'd be this feeling of a red-hot needle jabbing into my foot and I had to lift it off the track instantly. The worst of this was the unpredictability of it. I'd start again, and begin to think that things were going to settle down and then – red-hot needle time. While all this was happening, many people were beginning to feel, 'For heaven's sake, just get on with it. You've won the Europeans and the Commonwealths, you've found it's not as easy now, and you are losing it mentally.'

That has always annoyed me throughout my career because I know when I'm injured and I know when I'm not. When an athlete's injured, I accept it's difficult for other people because they don't know how you feel. You can't describe the pain, and some people think you should just run through it. Many athletes have bottled it in similar circumstances, but I don't think I ever have. In hindsight, the problems I was going through were a logical product of the way my career had gone, but at the time it was very frustrating for other people because, naturally enough, they wanted to see me running fast.

For a coach, too, it's frustrating, because their reputation is bound up in the performance of their athletes. If an athlete is not performing, the coach begins to feel insecure. As my problems continued, I felt that my coach, Mike Smith, was beginning to doubt me.

The primary benefit of joining the group at Southampton AC had been the set up itself, and the early days of working with Mike's group were probably the happiest I've had. I loved training. I never thought about how much training I was doing, I just went with the flow and I went with the group. It was a fantastic environment for training. In implementing any training programme, the most important thing is the people you surround yourself with. We had people like Todd Bennett and Kriss Akabusi, supported by Paul Sanders, Paul Harmsworth and around twenty other athletes hoping to move up to a higher level. Together we trained much better than if we had been on our own. We were motivated to keep with the group and to move forward together. In a curious way, our competitiveness with each other became suspended: if we were doing a session of six 300s, Todd would take the first one, Kriss would take the second one, and in the early days I would just run behind them. Then, as I got better, I would take the third one, then Todd would take the fourth. When you are taking the lead the pressure is on you and you run well and take the others through.

Of course you must have a good coach, somebody who knows what to say. But if you can share a goal and a dream with somebody then what you have is synergy – together you are more than the sum of your individual parts. There is a downside, though, if you stop listening to your body because peer pressure is there and you want to keep going with the guys.

Kriss had a different physical structure from me. He was aerobically very strong, but he didn't have the speed I had. Todd had enormous natural speed and ability to train and train and train. What he didn't do was rest, and as I was to find out, knowing when to rest is hugely important for people striving for the highest levels. Doing what the group does is fine to a degree, but ultimately you have to realize that you are not all the same and that you have to treat everyone as different.

Mike Smith is a great trainer. There is possibly no better trainer for 400 metres in the world. His life, from Monday to Sunday, is athletics. He created an environment where you can work constantly, and we did get through a phenomenal amount of work. But to be a great coach takes more than that.

We had no specific weight training programme and if there was a long-term plan, it was not always entirely clear to us. Ultimately if you are to survive in the world of the Zurichs and the Olympics, you have to have a clear strategy. There is another level to which coach and athlete have to aspire. It's very different from the world of day-in, day-out down on Southampton Common.

A coach–athlete relationship needs to function on many different levels, not just that of physical training. It was very clear early on that although Mike and I cared for each other a lot, we couldn't relate to each other – and that was partly because of the difference in our ages. Also, every day matters when you are training, and there were days when Mike would not be in the best mood. That was understandable, because he has always looked after large groups of twenty or thirty athletes, and catering for so many different people and different egos entails certain problems. All it takes is for one of those egos to upset you and the rest of the group feel the shock waves. It is far easier for a coach to work with one or two athletes, and I learned that it was better for me to be in a smaller group because ultimately Mike did not have the time to communicate with me as an individual in the way that I needed.

Mike's thing was his group and that was it, so athletes would come for a year, gain an immediate benefit and go. I had the feeling that Mike always thought that I was aloof, because of my background – medical student, all that sort of thing. He used to jokingly call me Lord Black. But I think he was always a little bit threatened by that.

As long as you are healthy and running fast you don't address these things. The time when you do, as I found, is when you are badly injured. At that point, all that mattered to me was me. And it was suddenly a very lonely existence, because the group simply went on without me. I have no bad will towards Mike Smith. As he has said, Iwan Thomas and I were the most talented athletes he has ever had, and he would say that much of the credit for my development belonged with the group of athletes with whom I was training, but he directed the group so therefore he must take the credit.

Mike obviously wanted me to be healthy again, but he didn't know how to help and he didn't have any medical network in place. He did not take it upon himself as the coach to guide me. It was a case of, 'Well, go and sort it out. Go to the local hospital. When you're better, come back to the group.' He was sympathetic as a person, as a friend. We got on very well, but that ultimately was not enough for me.

Kriss couldn't offer me the help I needed either. He had no idea about injuries, because he had a body that never got seriously injured. And although Todd had suffered an injury in 1986, he had never sorted it out properly. All this left an enormous void within me.

We are not all hard as nails. We do need a shoulder sometimes, we do need to feel needed. I was twenty-one, I was European champion, and I was in big trouble. My whole body was breaking down, and it was frightening. This is why I had decided to turn elsewhere, to Frank Dick, the national coach and others.

In February 1988, when my worries about my foot were beginning to undermine me as an athlete, I was booked to go on the *Wogan* show with Kriss because it was Olympic year. And I remember thinking as I was being interviewed, 'This is really strange, because I am on prime time TV talking about the Olympics but my foot hurts, my hip hurts, I don't know how things are going to turn out.' I was really insecure because I wasn't training properly, certainly not well enough to do well in the Olympic Games, and maybe not even well enough to get there. That was the truth, but I was unable to admit it then.

We went off to California soon afterwards, and the first three weeks were a struggle for me. My foot was getting worse, Kriss was training really well and I was just getting left behind and having to miss sessions. One day my foot got so bad that I walked off the track and went to sit on the hill which overlooks Irvine. As I sat there looking over to where the others were working, I just broke down in tears. When I stopped crying I decided to face up to my problems.

I had to confront the fact that the Olympics were only a few months away and my foot was killing me and I had to do something about it. I did not just have a little problem, something needed to be sorted out properly. I sat on that hill for about half an hour. As I turned round and walked back to the track, Kriss saw me coming towards him, but I told him, 'I'm going to go home.' He couldn't believe it, and he tried to get me to stay on and see how things went, but I knew that was no good any more.

So I returned to England. I went to see an orthopaedic surgeon who took X-rays of my right foot and told me I had something called osteochondritis, which involved flakes of bone in the ankle joint. He said it would require a very risky and complicated operation, which really scared me.

I was discussing the details with my father when the thought occurred to me: 'Why was only my right foot X-rayed?' Why wasn't the left one, which wasn't causing me any problems, done too as a check?

I had the left foot X-rayed as well – and lo and behold, it showed exactly the same picture of flaking bone. It turned out to be a congenital condition – not ideal, but clearly not the thing which was causing the pain in my right foot after all. I suddenly thought, 'Oh my God! I could have gone ahead and had that operation and it might have been the end of my career for something that was never needed.' From that day onwards I've never had enormous faith in the medical profession. I've always wanted to have every option covered before I accept a diagnosis. I decided to seek another opinion from Muller-Wohlfahrt.

I had been the first British athlete to see Muller-Wohlfahrt, although it had done me no good then. It had been very difficult as a twenty-one-year-old sitting in Munich on my own, not able to speak a word of German, and with my whole career in the balance. It was to take two more visits to Munich before I discovered the information I needed to take a proper step back towards fitness.

The first time I returned, in March 1988, I stayed for ten days while Muller-Wohlfahrt injected and tested my foot. It was a case of getting up early each morning and sitting in his waiting room for hours until he could fit me in. After that, I had to walk around Munich killing time until he could spare me another half an hour or quarter of an hour of treatment. It was a miserable experience, really, although Muller-Wohlfahrt was very kind.

I went back to England and started running on the foot – and it was just as bad. So I returned once again to Germany in April. Muller-Wohlfahrt still couldn't understand why the foot hadn't responded to treatment. Then suddenly he said, 'We haven't done the obvious here.' And he sent me for a special computer scan.

I remember sitting waiting to get a first look at the pictures that might mean an end to all the problems I had had. When they came they showed clearly that I had fractured my foot – a long, vertical fracture of the navicular bone. I remember looking at the picture and seeing this clear line straight through the bone. I went outside and sat down on a park bench and there was a huge sense of relief that at last there had been a positive diagnosis. When you are in limbo, having treatment and nothing is happening, you just get more and more frustrated. Once you know what's wrong you can start to take action. I walked the prints round to Muller-Wohlfahrt's office and showed them to him. He was shocked and a little embarrassed.

The treatment for a fractured foot is 'Get off it.' So I was immediately put on crutches for about four weeks. As for my hip problem – well, you start to ignore a hip problem when you have a broken foot. I was told I would have to return to Munich to have a metal screw fitted in my foot which would help the bones heal back together.

By now it was June 1988, and there was definitely not going to be any Olympics for me. Regardless of the fact that I was Commonwealth champion and European champion, I had always wanted to say I was an Olympian, because the Olympics are special. You wouldn't swap success there for anything. So it was devastating not to be able to go. My season was over.

After having the operation, I was put in plaster for a further eight weeks. As it turned out, I watched the Olympics like that while I was working as a panellist for ITV.

One of the worst things about the operation and its aftermath was that the foot was totally rigid when it came out of plaster, and it required a long period of intensive physiotherapy. I spent some time with my friend Fayyaz, who was out at Iowa State University by this time, and started getting my fitness back. By Christmas 1988, however, I was still only thinking about jogging. My foot did not suddenly get better, in fact it was terrible – it made a cracking sound when I moved, and it still hurt. I was thinking to myself, 'This hasn't worked.' And the doctors were saying, 'These things can take ages. You've got to re-educate your foot.'

I simply didn't feel I was part of the sport any more. Linford Christie and Colin Jackson had come back from Seoul with Olympic silver medals. Kriss had reached the Olympic 400 metres hurdles final. I remember going to Cardiff round about that time to watch a meeting – I was still on crutches – and feeling completely out of place. I had known Colin for years, but suddenly he seemed to have moved on beyond me. That's how it is in our business. If you are running badly you feel as if you are nothing, if you are running well you are everything.

Meanwhile, my problems with Mike Smith were getting worse. I remember vividly when the fractured foot was diagnosed Mike saying to me, 'Well, it would have happened anyway wouldn't it?' And I replied, 'I don't know. Probably.' What appeared to matter to him was that it wasn't his training that had got me injured. Understandably, he didn't want it to be his fault. Now I blame Mike Smith for nothing. But deep down when he said that, I felt that he was saying to me, 'Roger, I am good at what I do, but maybe this shouldn't have happened to you.'

By the beginning of 1989, I felt as if I was getting nowhere slowly. I was still struggling in my solo efforts to regain fitness and feeling increasingly detached from Mike and the group. But in February a chance meeting at a dinner changed my fortunes.

I sat next to a journalist called John Bryant, who had helped coach Zola Budd when she was living in Britain a few years previously and who was working for *The Times*. He asked me how I was, and I said I'd had this operation and was still having complications because every time I ran my foot became swollen and painful. And John told me, 'Look, there's an extraordinary man you should see called Ron Holder. He's a South African, and he works in kinesiology, which is the balance of the body. He's done great stuff with lots of Africans, including Zola Budd. Go and see him, because he's in England at the moment, working from a health club.'

And I thought, 'Why not?' I phoned up this kinesiologist and arranged to meet him at his club in London. He had been very quietly spoken on the phone, but when I met him he was completely different from what I had imagined – a big, dishevelled, cuddly bear of a man. If you saw him walking down the street you wouldn't think he was a brilliant doctor. Never judge a book by the cover.

At this point I was far from sure that I was going to be able to get back to competition. I sat with this man and told him my story. And before he even touched me he said, 'Look. I'm going to draw you a picture. I want you to watch.' He made a stick drawing of the human body, and said, 'If this bit is out of balance, what's going to happen to your hips?' And he did another drawing showing how, if your hips were out of balance, it would affect your whole body.

Ron doesn't merely tackle the symptoms, he goes all the way back to the cause. He says your body tells you everything, and he can identify physical weakness incredibly swiftly. What he told me was that ever since I had started playing sport as a child, my body had slowly but surely become out of balance. 'You've probably been like that all your life,' he said. 'With most people, it wouldn't be noticed. But as you start to do more and more training, everything becomes exaggerated and you put forces through your body that shouldn't be there. Hence, your hip was going to go first. And it was going to result in your foot breaking. And it doesn't matter how much treatment you have, if you don't go back and attack the cause you are always going to have problems.'

What Ron does is put you back into balance using a system of wedges made out of very thin pieces of paper – ideally, pieces of the Yellow Pages! He finds that the Yellow Pages are the only material that can be specific. One page can make the difference between being in balance and being out of balance. The first thing he did to me was put a wedge underneath my left foot which must have been two inches thick. Then he told me to go for a run, and it was one of the weirdest experiences I've ever had in my life. I came back, and he tested me again, and the wedge started to go down. I was gradually re-balancing my whole body.

If I'd never met Ron Holder, I'd never have run again. I can't say that about anybody else, but I can about him. Because at that moment in my career nothing made sense. And he made absolute sense. His treatment, I grant you, was a bit wacky. I've had conventional surgery, and I've been treated by people like Muller-Wohlfahrt, who is not exactly conventional. But compared to Ron Holder he's the most conservative doctor in the world. For all that, I felt totally comfortable in this man's care. After I'd seen him three or four times, I was able to start running on grass. I remember after the third or fourth treatment, striding on grass. It was the first time for a year that I had felt normal. Suddenly, I had hope again.

I still had in my foot the metal screw which had been inserted during my operation in Munich, but Ron said there was no point in continuing to try and treat me if it stayed in. So on 6 March 1989 I had another operation to remove it. After all I had gone through, that was no big deal.

The only problem with Ron was nothing to do with his treatment, but merely his availability. The human body needs a lot of re-balancing treatments because it is always changing. And unfortunately when you've got a twenty-three-year-old body that has been through physical hell it is going to take ages. I needed to see him every day and that was just not feasible. He lives in South Africa as well as England. And therein lay the problem. But there was no doubt that he got me back on the road.

It was around this time that I spoke about my situation to Mike Whittingham, a former international 400 metres hurdler who had been schooling Kriss in that event after his switch from the 400 metres flat. He asked what seems, in retrospect, to have been a simple enough question, 'What's your rehabilitation programme?' And I replied that I didn't know. I realized I didn't actually have one.

Mike had overcome a fair amount of injury in his own career

in the early '80s, and offered to help me regain my aerobic/anaerobic fitness through a structured programme which he would supervise. We just connected straight away, because he understood my situation and knew about the difficulties involved from his own experience. He didn't poach me – I needed him desperately at that point in my career. So I started meeting up with Mike – secretly – in Aldershot, where I would run on grass to avoid impacting too much on the foot. I was still in pain the whole time but I felt I was progressing and enjoying it. And my confidence came back.

I was able to go back to California in 1989, working on grass, feeling part of something again even though my foot was still not sufficiently better for me to accompany the others on the track. But my clear focus was to get a race of some sort in that year. And the meeting Mike Whittingham and myself had targeted was a relatively low-key occasion at the end of the season – the Jersey Games.

The secret to getting back from an injury is to take your time and get it right. So many athletes don't get it right because they don't have the patience. During my lowest moments with the foot injury, I remember a friend of mine saying to me, 'Well, it's going to get better one day. You just don't know when that day will be.' And he's right. You can't be injured for ever. At that time I still was young enough to know I would have years ahead of me if I got better. Looking back, that period was not the hardest for me. A few years later, when I had glandular fever, was worse, because then I really didn't know if I'd have time to come back. Now, with Mike Whittingham's guidance and the help of Joe Picken, my weights coach and the unsung hero of my career, I was slowly but surely coming back.

A diary entry from 14 April 1989 indicates that I was thinking seriously about restructuring my training environment:

Mike Smith cannot now become as big a part of me as he was before because he hasn't stood by me. He will still be my coach, but not my controller. I must use the right formula of myself, Kriss, Mike Smith, Mike Whittingham and Joe Picken. I must do what I feel to be best for me, and I can no longer rely entirely on Mike Smith's judgement – but I do need the group.

I hope Mike will be able to step back a little with me. Remember those who have stood by you, they are the only ones you need to involve. The rest mustn't have the pleasure of association with your success.

As I look through my diary I can see when I began getting better. When we started training together one-to-one, in June, Mike was beating me. But a little note on 23 July indicates that I was making up lost ground quickly: 'I'm picking up pace now. I'm leaving Mike behind.' As the season went by I was meeting Mike four times a week in a field in Aldershot, a field I ran around so many times that if I just close my eyes I can smell the different trees as I do a lap.

On 4 August, I wrote:

Mike Whittingham has been working with me one-to-one since 18 June. His contribution has been invaluable. We work well together and I know I'm getting it right. Mike Smith could never relate to me like this because of the size of the group . . . A CT scan yesterday showed the bone in my foot has repaired . . .

I went to the Jersey Games on 16 September, which was probably one of the most satisfying races of my life. I hadn't run competitively at 400 metres for a year and a half. I hadn't put spikes on for a year. When I got to the line after warming up, it was as if I was starting a new career. What I had achieved up to then was irrelevant. This was me coming back from losing everything. I ran the race, in blustery conditions, and won in 46.2sec. And that was it. I was back. For me that was a very emotional race. We had kept it very quiet, although I was billed to run. There was a reasonable crowd, but there were no other established runners in the field. As for press, there was only local coverage.

My sponsored car – a Mercedes – had been taken away a month earlier. And I was in debt. On top of all the money I had had to find for treatment and travel in the previous two years, I had also bought a house in 1988, which was very foolish. When young athletes say to me, 'I'm thinking of buying a house,' I tell them, 'Think very carefully. Because in this business if you get injured and you don't run you don't get anything. Make sure you can afford it if that happens.'

I couldn't. I had to borrow money from my father, and I was also loaned £10,000 by Sir Eddie Kulukundis, a Greek shipping magnate and theatrical impresario, and one of the sport's major patrons.

Sir Eddie is married to the actress Susan Hampshire, and is a man who, cynical people would say, bought himself a knighthood. Which is so unjust and so unfair, because he's a man who has spent enormous amounts of his own money for the only reason that he genuinely believes in giving young people a chance, and he is absolutely fanatical about athletics. He has helped so many athletes for years and years by giving them the opportunity to go warm weather training or supporting them during the hard times, as he did for me. Many of those will never make any money out of the sport, but Sir Eddie believes in giving people the chance that the sport has not been able to give them. This is a man who hired a huge house in Atlanta at the 1996 Olympics and paid for twenty personal coaches to stay free of charge. He cares about athletes and the sport is indebted to the man.

Emotionally, too, I was in debt because I was going through a difficult relationship – which went on for another year until the European Championships – with a girl who was also a British international athlete. But when I went to the line in Jersey, it wasn't about any of that. It was about, 'Am I an athlete? Is it still there? Have I got it?'

The Jersey race was one of many turning points in my career.

If I had put in a poor performance, you might never have seen me on a track again, but in fact I ran very well, and as a result was selected to run the relay at the Commonwealth Games in January of the following year.

On 25 September I wrote:

> I ran my first race for over two years at the Jersey Games. I recorded 46.2 in windy conditions, which is great, and I was subsequently added to the 4x400 squad for the Commonwealth Games, since 46.2 is the second fastest time by an Englishman this year. I'm very pleased, and once the injury has gone I'll be as good as I ever was.

But now I found myself in a dilemma because it was Mike Whittingham's support, friendship, sympathy and expertise which had got me back. Mike Smith had known that I was working with Mike Whittingham, and had been happy for me to regain fitness with him. But he was not happy for Mike Whittingham to be part of my coaching set-up, even though I had never once trained with the Southampton group during my time out. My mindset had changed. I'd learned that I could train on my own – I didn't necessarily need Kriss and Todd around me all the time. And maybe I didn't need as much training as they did. Maybe my natural talent was such that I had to be protected. The gulf between myself and Mike Smith had become huge. I felt he was very threatened by my involvement with Mike Whittingham, but I couldn't help that.

The whole business came to a head when myself and Kriss went round to Mike Smith's house and I said 'Look, I've had my injury, I've come back, and Mike Whittingham's been a great help to me. I want to train with you and your group but I want to have some involvement with Mike Whittingham, too, because the man is helping me and he's taken me through the hardest times.'

Kriss was training with Mike Whittingham, doing his hurdling with him, and then doing his stuff with the group.

And that's what I wanted to do. But Mike Smith refused to accept that arrangement. And I just sat down in a chair in Mike's front room and broke down in tears. 'Mike,' I repeated. 'I've been through hell and I've got back, and Mike Whittingham has helped me. I want to be in this group, I want to train with Todd and Kriss.' It was a rare outburst for me, and it was from the gut.

My distress shocked Kriss – who was simply trying to mediate – and it shocked Mike. I remember him looking at me and I think it was only at that moment that he began to realize what I had been through. He had not been able to relate to what it was like to be out for a year and a half, to go through two operations and to do it all on your own.

I didn't see why it was wrong to want to get the best of both worlds, because in the end it's about the athlete, not the coach. I was not a selfish athlete, I was not somebody who was ruthless. That's why I broke down, because I was saying, 'I'm trying to do everything the right way. I'm asking for help. Surely everybody's focus should be: how can I get this person to be Olympic champion?' My 25 September diary entry went on:

This last week has been traumatic, since I have had to sort out my situation with Mike Smith. Before the Jersey Games and we argued on the phone. It is as if he's happy to get involved with me once I'm OK and doesn't recognize MW's contribution. It became very emotional for me and I cried in the meeting with Mike Smith and Kriss yesterday.

It was as if they didn't understand what I'd been through in the previous two years, and to come back from this is hard. Too many memories, too many things done and said during my time off, that I find it hard to accept some attitudes. I'm the one who's suffered, I'm the one who's cried, I'm the one who's had to sort out my problems, so I don't see why others should now start dictating to me what I should do just because I'm fit again.

Mike Smith means well, deep down, and all will be OK so long as we both play the game . . . I will defend the European title. I'm slowly getting there. It ain't easy, but as Daley often reminds me, if it was easy, then everyone would be doing it.

But the game had become too much for Mike Smith and myself to continue with, and we just drifted apart after that. Effectively I had said to myself: 'Right, that's it. I can't live in both worlds.' It was a very difficult time for me, leaving the group. I wasn't leaving Kriss, because he was still seeing Mike Whittingham, but I was leaving Todd, and Paul Sanders, and Paul Harmsworth. I was very sad about that. It was tough for Mike Smith; it was tough for me. But I had to go through it to find myself.

After my race in Jersey, the Commonwealth Games scheduled for January 1990 in Auckland were the light at the end of the tunnel. Given the difficulties I had had since the previous Commonwealth Games in 1986, however, I suppose it would have been too much to hope for a clear run in the final preparations.

So, despite my earlier fears, I went to Auckland to take part in the relay. Before the Games began, I ran an individual 400 metres out there and recorded 45.56sec, a time that would have earned me fifth place in the individual final, but the main point was that it was just good to be back and part of the team again.

The huge disappointment for the England team was that we were disqualified in the relay, which was an absolutely ridiculous decision. I was running the last leg in the opening heat, from which the first three qualified. England, along with Australia and Trinidad, had nearly a fifty metres lead over the rest of the field. I was waiting on what I assumed was the right line to receive the baton. No official pointed out any irregularity. But it turned out that all three of us last leg runners were standing on the wrong line to receive the incoming batons, and our teams were disqualified from the final.

Only five went through to the final in the end. It was unbelievable, so ridiculous, and it showed me how narrow-minded some people are. Minor officialdom hadn't done its job properly because nobody showed us where to go. I thought, 'How pathetic. These are billed as the Friendly Games, and all three teams disqualified were unintentionally standing on the wrong line. We are talking a metre of difference here in a 1600m race.'

What really got me was walking back into the athletes' village and seeing one of the Scottish team management laughing about it and saying, 'It was absolutely right they got disqualified.' Scotland were virtually certain to get a medal, because anyone could get a medal without Australia and England in there.

'You are joking aren't you?' I exclaimed.

'The rules are the rules,' he insisted.

'Did you think we'd stand on the wrong line on purpose? We were obviously fifty metres ahead of the rest of the field. Surely you don't honestly think this is good?' And I thought again at that point that there are some petty people in this sport.

The crowd were prevented from seeing what would have been a great showdown between Australia and England in the final. and the Scottish team with Tom McKean, a world-class 800 metres runner but hardly a one-lap wonder, went on to win the silver behind Kenya. I mean, so what? However, I had bigger things to worry about than that. I was getting ready to win the European Championships.

9

THE ROAD BACK

People often ask me what has been my greatest achievement. In the grand scheme of things, it has to be winning the Olympic silver medal. But to me, winning the 1990 European title seemed as great a personal triumph, despite the fact that it was one of the worst races I have run. The achievement was not in the 45.08 seconds it took me to earn the gold medal. It was in the three years of effort required to bring me to that race. In the television commentary, Ron Pickering's words were, 'Roger Black has come back from the dead.' A little bit dramatic, but in athletic terms he was right.

In the four years from 1986 to 1990, I'd gone from the heights of being European and Commonwealth champion at the age of twenty to the depths of injury. And yes, I'd been to the Commonwealth Games, but that had only turned out to be a matter of getting disqualified in the relay. So my comeback rested on the 1990 European Championships. It was there that I learned the truth of something that David Jenkins once said to me, 'Everybody wants to win. But it's the person who needs to win the most who will win most often. And often once you have found out why you need to do something you will also find a way to do it.' I thought, going into that European Championships, surely no other runner could need to win like I did.

This was a moment when I was saying, 'I've been through it all. This is my chance to end that chapter and move on.'

A week before the championships, my foot swelled up. I sat

in my front room, with a lump the size of a tennis ball on the end of my foot, thinking, 'I don't believe this.' The next day it was fine. It was bizarre. As an athlete, your emotions are constantly prey to the way your body reacts to physical stresses. In that respect, your life is permanently uncertain.

A disconcerting thing happened to me. Soon after I had got to Split for the European Championships, someone stole my training shoes from my room. I think one of the cleaners must have nicked them. Now one of the problems when you have size 13 feet is that it's very hard to get replacement training shoes. All I had was some basketball boots. So I had to do my warm-ups and warm-downs either side of my races in basketball boots. And back at the hotel, I was looking out for a cleaner with large feet – apprehend that man!

But even that couldn't put me off.

There were no other Europeans running that well then – although it never did to underestimate Thomas Schoenlebe, the East German whom I had beaten at the 1986 European Championships – so a lot of people assumed I would win. And I suppose if I had just run normally I would have done so comfortably. But I remember lining up for that race and feeling, 'I've got to win this for me. This is what the last three years have been about.' And when the gun went off, the desire to win was a little bit too strong.

Extra effort doesn't always pay off in top-class racing. When you run in the rounds at a major championship, you are generally more comfortable than in a final – ideally you should be expending about 80 per cent effort. It is an interesting balancing act. You can't afford to be complacent, but because you are running in a relaxed fashion, holding back a degree, you often find you are moving along very well. When you get to the final the secret is to retain that relaxation if you can. But nine times out of ten the realization that this is the race which counts means you try really hard, which doesn't necessarily make you go any faster. That was what happened to me in the European final. If I had kept the approach I had in the semi-final, where I had cruised through in 45.56sec, I would probably have won the race comfortably, but to do that requires an enormous amount of confidence which, at that time, I simply didn't have.

We were held up by the starter for a painfully long time before getting away. I was in lane two, and it soon became clear that the Yugoslav out in lane seven, Slobodan Brankovic, was going for glory in front of his vociferous home crowd. At that point in my career I was a reactive athlete, and I responded to Brankovic's rash challenge. By the time we got to 220 metres, the Yugoslav, who eventually finished sixth, was beginning to buckle. But I had built up a momentum which I maintained until it became clear that the speed was too much for my body to cope with. It was very obvious where that moment occurred. At 320 metres, I had a good eight metres' lead on the rest of the field. But with forty metres to go, the others began to catch me up very quickly. I was thinking, 'Oh no, I've totally misjudged this.' At that stage of a 400 metres race, it is not a case of who is accelerating most – no one is actually getting faster – but who is decelerating least. And I was decelerating so quickly I was virtually running backwards. But for my need for that gold medal – for so many reasons – I would have been lost. It was solely that hunger that brought me over the line ahead of the rest of Europe. Just as I had in Stuttgart four years earlier, I pipped Schoenlebe at the post, finishing five hundredths of a second ahead of him. Apparently he said afterwards, 'When Black is like this I cannot beat him.'

After the race I was so tired I walked the lap of honour. My reaction to the press was, 'I am a plonker. But I'm a plonker with a gold medal round my neck.'

I remember walking out of the stadium afterwards with Mike Whittingham. It was dark, and we were surrounded by people who didn't recognize us. And despite all the faults there had been with the run, I thought to myself: this medal is the right colour. For Mike and I it was a very personal moment, because it was the culmination of his help. Without him I would not have won that medal. Many people have played a part in my career – Mike Smith, Joe Picken, Tony Lester – but just as I don't believe I could have won my Olympic silver medal without David Jenkins, I could not have won my European title in 1990 without Mike Whittingham.

Mike would always be with me in the warm-up area before I raced. Each time you reach that wonderful moment when the athlete is totally ready. Before the final, I was totally ready in my own world, and just walking with Mike across a field to go to the call room. All that could have been said between us had been said. There was nothing more to say. But Mike must have felt he needed to say something. It wasn't, 'Have a good race, go for it, control, kick,' anything like that. What he said was, 'It's a beautiful sunset this evening, don't you think?'

I turned to him and said, 'Mike, I'm walking out for the European 400 metres final and the best you can say is, "What a beautiful sunset." ' I couldn't have cared less about the sunset, but that comment was so classically Mike. A few weeks later I gave him a huge framed picture of me crossing the line in that race, and underneath I wrote, 'To Mike, thanks for all your help. It was a beautiful sunset that evening.'

I've kept a lot of the cards and letters that Mike Whittingham has written to me over the years. We used to have a ritual whereby he would give me a postcard before important races. Before the 1994 European Championships, for instance, it was a picture of two wrestlers locked in combat. He once described me as a swan. On the surface it looks graceful and elegant, and underneath the surface it is paddling like mad to stay afloat. At times, that was absolutely right.

The emotion of winning that European title probably made it the most important of my life. No race after that was ever going to be as important. And I've gone on to do much greater things, but in 1990 I had done it. I had got back.

A couple of weeks after the final I wrote this:

I have retained my European title in 45.08 with another gold in the 4x400. The foot is still not 100 per cent. The hip is still blocked, but I can run. I still need to get them 100 per cent better somehow. I was unable to run really fast, but I can build on this for next year.

Personally however it's been hard. It is so sad that at a time in my life when I should be so happy because I have defended my European title, I am truly more sad than I have ever been before.

It was the old classic, I suppose. You put on one face to the world, you keep the truth to yourself. People are wrong to assume that if you achieve something, everything's wonderful. Just because you win a gold medal, it doesn't make you happy. That much I learned in 1990. The European Championships were a professional triumph for me – but an emotional disaster. They brought to a head a crisis which saw me break up with my girlfriend and become involved in another short-lived relationship which had alarming repercussions.

In the course of the year leading up to the competition in Split I had been having continual problems and arguments with my girlfriend, who was also a British international athlete. We were both young, and there were doubts on both sides. What made things even more difficult was the fact that she had a sports scholarship at a university in America. Athletics is a very incestuous world, and I was hearing things on the grapevine about what my girlfriend was supposed to have been doing. There was never any proof, but I wasn't secure enough in myself to be able to ignore the rumours. When you are physically strong and running well, you can usually dismiss these things. When you're not, your whole identity is threatened. In the two years I was out of action my confidence in myself dipped hugely. I felt detached from the world of athletics, and I was continually asking myself the question, 'If I don't run again, then what am I?'

But hard as I tried to concentrate my efforts on regaining fitness, I was stuck in this troubled relationship which was on my mind every second of the day. And in the course of my difficulties with my girlfriend I had lost touch with many of my close friends, and even with my family. I wasn't being true to myself. My parents noticed it. Everyone noticed. But you can't tell someone that they are in the wrong relationship. Because there are two things you shouldn't criticize a man about – his choice of woman and his choice of work.

My girlfriend and I were both at the European Championships, but the rumours there continued about other involvements. I was deeply unhappy about the relationship, and I knew that after two years I had to break out of it, which is what I did. She never did anything to hurt me directly. But it all ended up being very unpleasant and for a while I lost faith in other people. I cared about her and I still do. Sometimes, though, people get to a point in relationships where, in order to protect themselves, they have to get out, or they risk losing their identity and becoming someone they don't want to be.

That was exactly the situation I found myself in, and what tends to happen in those circumstances is that you look for comfort. I found a girl who was going through the same kind of thing and we became involved. Just to make things really simple, she happened to be the girlfriend of an athlete I had trained with in California four months earlier, Danny Harris. She also happened to be a friend of my girlfriend. A fine old mess.

But going off with someone else didn't feel right either, and our relationship, though intense, was shortlived. It also presented me with a somewhat difficult situation when I returned to train in California in February 1991. The essence of a successful training partnership is that you get on with each other – and there was obviously a bit of a question mark over that, to say the least, as far as Danny and I were concerned.

Danny lived near the University where we trained so I was concerned about what might happen when our paths crossed again. Mutual friends had warned me that his way of dealing with the matter might not be as diplomatic as I hoped. So I thought that I might well be in the position of having to physically defend myself upon arrival, something I had never had to do in the past. I had never had a fight in my life, if the truth be told. And Danny was a big, strong guy . . .

When faced with this situation, what does one do? Worried that the Queensberry rules were not going to be adhered to – I decided to have a swift course in self defence. There was one obvious person to turn to – Joe Picken, ex-Navy physical training instructor. So it was that my bi-weekly weights sessions with Joe in his rackety old gym came to involve a new warm-up routine. For the first ten minutes, I would be schooled in the dirty arts of hand-to-hand combat.

We had a ritual. Joe would not be around when I arrived, but then – like Inspector Clouseau's mad manservant – he would descend upon me with a terrifying roar and I would be expected to put into practice the moves which he had taken great delight in showing me. Joe used to shout, 'Come on! Hit me! Hit me!' But my response was generally pathetic; it was all I could do to stop laughing.

The number one lesson Joe tried to teach me was, 'If your opponent gets close enough for you to strike the first blow, then strike it. Don't give him a chance.' What I was supposed to do was to push the heel of my hand into his breastbone, and as his head came forward, get hold of it and bring my knee up sharply. It sounded highly effective. But I knew in my heart I would never be able to do such a thing – and I suspect Joe knew it too. My basic instinct was: when in doubt, run away.

What I was able to do very well, and very often, in the months before I went out to California was to visualize Danny Harris striding over the hill by the track and walking straight towards me with a look full of hate on his face. I really did think we would come to blows – as did Kriss and Daley.

When the dreaded moment finally arrived I was with those two and a few of the others doing stretching exercises beside the track. We weren't sure if Danny was going to come back and train with the group because a lot of water had gone under the bridge in the previous year. Then this huge hulk of a figure came jogging over the hill and down towards us, and you could just sense the anticipation going through the whole group. And to put it mildly, I was trembling in my spikes.

But despite all my fears, I think Danny understood that what had happened the previous summer had been something that was beyond all of us, and no one was without blame. More importantly, we both wanted and needed to run fast, and we could help each other in that respect. The worth of that outweighed any personal misunderstanding or mistrust we had. So when he turned up, he just said, 'Hi guys. What's the session today?' and joined in with the stretching exercises. As professional athletes we were able to set personal matters aside. And I'm pleased to say that the two of us are still friends. The love of a woman is one thing; the lure of a medal is another.

Danny won a number of medals in his career – but sadly, nowhere near as many as he should have done. He was without doubt the most talented athlete I've ever trained with. He had won the Olympic silver medal in 1984 at the age of eighteen in a junior world record time. He won the silver behind Ed Moses in the 1987 World Championships. And he was the man who ended Moses's 122-race unbeaten run in the same year. But his career was ultimately ruined by one tragic flaw – he had a cocaine habit. Danny tested positive in February 1992, and was banned for four years by the International Amateur Athletic Federation. Two years later, he returned to the sport under 'exceptional circumstances' – he had gone through a rehabilitation programme. But soon after his return he was caught again for cocaine and banned for life.

In the spring of 1990, when he started training with our group in California, he was awesome, but there was always a sense of uncertainty about him because rumours were rife about his drug-taking. We didn't socialize with him on a regular basis, so we didn't know how he conducted his private life. In the course of those weeks when we first worked together, though, he did admit to Kriss and myself that he had a habit.

He insisted he was able to deal with it. And Kriss and I

reasoned that if he could train to the level he did, he couldn't be taking large amounts of cocaine. But what did we know?

The irony of the whole thing was, cocaine was not making him a better athlete, it was making him worse. He would some-times turn up to training and be bleary eyed and unable to concentrate. Often he was late, and missed the warm-up, so he would just do a couple of quick stretches before joining us at the point in the session we had reached. His sheer talent and awesome power were apparent to us all, but he could never finish a whole session. Which was actually bloody annoying for me because if we were doing a session of say, two 500s, Danny would run the first one incredibly fast, but we'd come back and he couldn't finish the second.

He was a bit of a pain to train with because the essence of a training partner – and this was something which Kriss and I perfected – was to share the work. Say you have a session of three 300s, with fifteen to twenty minutes' recovery. The idea is to run them all around the same time. Consistency is the key. There's no point in going off and running the first one in 31.5 and the other two in 33.5 because you are so knackered. With Kriss, I would lead the first one, Kriss would take the second one, and whoever felt the stronger would lead the last one. So you got a rest when the pressure was off. Kriss and I became intuitive with each other. To the point that when he retired, and even to this day, if I go to the line on my own to do a run, I often say to myself, 'Are you ready Kriss?' Because we would have this routine of walking to the line, one behind the other, and saying, 'Are you ready Kriss?', 'Are you ready, Rog?', 'Two, one, go . . .'

I felt so angry with the sport for the way it condemned Danny Harris. Banning him was right because you are helping someone in that situation – hopefully creating enough motiva-tion for them to try and get off the drug. And the American federation did insist that he had to join a drug rehabilitation programme. But to condemn him as a drug cheat is nonsense. You can't compare using cocaine to taking a performance-enhancing drug. Danny was using something that was making his career worse for him – the fact that he was still performing to such a high level simply highlighted his sheer talent.

When Danny got caught for the first time, Kriss and I both felt powerless to do anything, but I did write to him. I told him I thought he was the most talented athlete I had ever trained with, and I hoped he could come through that period. He did come back – but then he did it again, got caught, and that was it. Life ban. He was a great athlete, but he had a habit he couldn't kick. He could have won everything and become a millionaire. He did make money – a lot of it. But he snorted it all up his nose. It just shows that having talent – even that sort of talent – is not enough.

10

CHAMPIONS DU MONDE

Soon after coming home from Split, I wrote:

> To win the Europeans for a second time was very different. The first time was unexpected, immediate, new and exhilarating. The second was expected, it required a longer preparation – and it was an enormous relief. Emotionally they were very different experiences. I don't need the accolades that go with success. I just feel a sense of personal pride.

Obviously things picked up financially after my win, which was great, because during the two previous years I had earned nothing. I took enormous pleasure in immediately using my bonus from Adidas for winning the European title to pay Eddie Kulukundis back. Without his help during a desperate time, I would have been under enormous pressure.

In athletic terms, I was on a roll. And exciting challenges lay ahead. On 26 May 1991, I wrote:

> I have just returned from three months in California and am running very fast. I feel nervous, unsure and excited about this season. Last year it was the comeback. Mistakes were allowed to be made. This year I'm back. It's as if it's the first real year. No injuries. No problems. No excuses.
>
> I've won the Europeans. I'm now entering the world stage. It is up to me to be the best in the world. It will take

a lot of mental strength to create the confidence required
to do so.

It was round about that time that Butch Reynolds was banned
for taking drugs. I had run against him in Malmo in 1990. That
had been the first time I asked a fellow athlete for an autograph.
This was the world record holder in my event, this was someone special, I'd thought. He signed my race number.

I remember thinking when he was caught for drugs, 'What
an idiot.' He has protested his innocence. And I've spoken to his
agent who genuinely believes he was innocent. I've spoken to
Butch a few times since, too. But you have to say, 43.29 seconds.
You have to wonder.

The build up to the 1991 World Championships was great for
me. I was running under 45 seconds nearly every time. Butch
Reynolds wasn't around, which helped. Michael Johnson was
just starting to run then. He ran 44.89 in London and I was
second. But he wasn't running the 400 metres in Tokyo – only
the 200. So I went to Japan with a real chance of becoming
world champion. On the eve of the race, I wrote:

Tomorrow I begin my challenge to become world champion. I know I can win if I perform to my true potential.
Anything else will result in failure . . . As Jenks once said,
these are rare days. To not do them justice would be a
waste.

I ran fantastically well in the World Championships. In the
semi-final I felt great. But there was one lesson I was still to
learn in my career, which I didn't assimilate until 1996. If I'd
taken it on board in 1991 I would have been world champion.
And that was the lesson of not being reactive, being pro-active.
Running your own race, not everyone else's. Not getting caught
up in it. At 400 metres, these things are crucial. It is a race of
balance. One slight mistake can be the difference between first

and second, and in 1991 I hadn't really mastered the event. Physically I was very strong. I was very confident. But I wasn't the complete package.

Prior to going out on to the track I realized I was dying to go to the toilet. We had to walk under the back of the main stand to reach our little room at the trackside, and that is normally the time when you should be collecting your thoughts and clearing your mind for the challenge ahead. I was trying to think, 'Focus, focus, focus' but there was this little voice in the back of my mind going, 'I am dying for a pee.'

The problem was that it was so hot and humid in Tokyo, I was drinking the whole time. We were constantly told to keep drinking water. Great! By the time I got trackside my mind was not on my race, it was on my bloody bladder. I was not concentrating as I should have been, and I knew that I had to do something about getting this off my mind. So I very quickly emptied my drinks bottle and refilled it myself and threw it into the bin. I hope nobody found it and took it as a souvenir.

I was standing there relieving myself into this drinks bottle with all the other athletes looking at me wondering, 'What the hell? Aren't you supposed to do that after the race?' And I also thought, 'This must look really suspicious from a doping test point of view.' Why is he getting rid of his urine right before the race? The truth was I was absolutely bursting.

The last thing Mike said to me before I went to the stadium was, 'Remember to dip.' And I replied, 'It won't come to that.' But it did – and I came second. I went off too quickly and I got pipped on the line by Antonio Pettigrew of the United States. The gun went, and I just ran too quickly between 200 and 300 metres. My real mistake was not having the confidence to stick to my own race.

I was happy with a silver medal because I still appreciated that achievement. If I look back now, I know that really was my one moment; 1996 wasn't, because I was not meant to beat Michael Johnson in the Olympic final. But 1991 was my chance to be world champion. I didn't take it – and I regret that. I did learn from it, though. I never ran a race that way again. In my opinion, Iwan Thomas made the same mistake in the 1997 World Championships. Everything is going well, but you just need to throttle back a little and come home a bit stronger. Hindsight is a wonderful thing. It's easy to look back and say it. Who knows, if I'd done it right, maybe I would have run 43.9 . . . if only, if only, if only.

I wasn't devastated by that defeat, although some people thought I ought to have been. It was very hard to be devastated when I had been through so much injury. My sense of perspective was, 'I could have not been here' – I was just happy to run again. It was still better to be there and come second than not to be there at all. But the best was still to come in these World Championships.

The great thing about being a 400 metres runner is you get a second bite of the cherry with the relay. And we had a strong squad: myself, a world silver medallist, Kriss Akabusi, a bronze medallist in the 400 metres hurdles; Derek Redmond, who was coming back from injury and running better and better with every race; and John Regis, who wasn't having a great season, but had proved himself the year before by running a 43.8 relay split in the European Championships. Along with John Regis, I sat out the semi-final, where Mark Richardson and Ade Mafe saw us through. And the team broke three minutes, which in 4x400 terms is exceptional. And the thought was, if we put in Roger Black and John, what can this team do?

We were always up against the might of the Americans. Their team included Pettigrew, who was world champion. But I knew I had the beating of Pettigrew. I should have beaten him in the 400 metres final. The other US runners were Danny Everett, who had got the bronze medal in the individual event, Quincy Watts, a relatively unknown and inexperienced young runner who went on the following year to win the Olympic title, and Andrew Valmon, who was fifth in the individual final. They had a strong team, but it wasn't unbeatable, and we knew that.

The night before the final we had a team meeting which Frank Dick, the national coach, and Les Jones, the team manager, attended. Frank usually worked out the order and told us what it would be. We agreed that Derek would lead off and hand over to Kriss, who would hand over to John, who would hand over to me. Because the basic thinking when you are choosing a 4x400 is that usually you put your best man on the last leg, put an OK guy on the first leg, and solid performers who can get inspired on legs two and three. And that's it really. It is always assumed it comes down to the last leg.

We all accepted the order without any great problem, and went back to our rooms to go to bed. As usual, I was sharing with Kriss, and as we lay there together, something was bugging us both. We didn't talk much. Suddenly, at about two in the morning, he turned to me and looked me in the eyes, and said: 'Are you thinking what I'm thinking?' I said, rather nervously, 'I hope not, but you look mighty cute in those pyjamas! . . .'

In fact we were both thinking about the next day's race. We knew that we had selected the right team to run a solid performance. But it wasn't in the right order if we wanted to win a gold medal – and we knew we had a chance of that. Sometimes in life you have to dare to win. You have to take a risk.

If we ran in that order, the logic of the race dictated that, the Americans would have a lead from the start and would probably run away with it. The 4x400 is very different from the 400 metres. In the individual event you all run in lanes and you don't really affect each other. In the 4x400, you directly affect each other, especially the runners in legs two, three and four, because they break from their lanes 100 metres into the second leg. Hence Phil Brown, who was not an outstanding individual runner, would become transformed when he ran the final leg in a relay, time and again beating runners who were far faster than him on paper. Now why is that? Because once you are chasing someone who's running in the same lane, you get inspired. You get dragged along. Your mind is not thinking about too much.

You just get in there, you battle it out, you scrap. Hence the success of the British 4x400 relay team – we are great fighters. It is really conducive to our spirit. I truly believe that.

We knew that what we had to do was to do what no one ever managed to do, and that was to be ahead of the Americans after the first leg. Put them under pressure; make them think – unknown territory to many Americans! And we knew the only way we were going to do that was to put me on the first leg. In fact, the way we had to run it was to put our best guys on the first three legs. And that meant me on the first leg, Derek on the second to hopefully extend the lead, or even if he couldn't extend the lead, we'd at least be in there with a shout. We could not afford to be out of contention by then.

We hoped John Regis would either extend the lead or keep us in contention. Imagine being an American athlete having big John Regis – with his chest so big it looks like two, his little ears and flaring nostrils – chasing your backside. The last thing you are going to be focusing on is your running technique! Imagine too having Kriss Akabusi in the same position laughing his way round the track. Maybe you can begin to see the method in our madness. Of course Pettigrew was world champion, but Kriss said, 'Roger, I train with you every day, I know that if I'm right behind you in training I can hang with you. It's not like running an individual race. So I know that I can do the same with Pettigrew. I know that I can deal with him if I have to.' And we believed that if we didn't do it this way, Pettigrew could have a five metres lead on me by the last leg, and I couldn't make that up.

We woke up in the morning and the first thing we did was find John and Derek and we sat down with them and said, 'Look guys, this is how we feel.' They were fine about it, happy to run second and third; they understood the logic of it. We called a meeting with Frank and Les. We walked in the room and said, 'We think we should change the order.' They really were not keen. I'll never forget Les's face. He was shocked. 'Oh, you can't do that . . .' Frank, to his credit, thought long and hard before agreeing with us. 'In the end, guys, you are the ones who have to go out there and do it. If you believe in this, this is the order you must run. Because in the end we just sit in the stands and watch you.' I thought that was very good management. He could have insisted we ran in the agreed order. It would have caused a bit of a rebellion and it would not have been very pleasant. But he didn't, and that was great. The moment that decision was made, you could just feel it shaping our destiny. And it proved to be a turning point for British 4x400 relay running.

The Americans had bragged before the final about breaking the world record. We were very quiet. We didn't say anything about the order, we just got down to the warm-up track later on that evening. John Regis couldn't warm up with us because he was running the 4x100, but as soon as he finished that, he put his track suit on and came straight across to us.

You declare your team at the last minute, and you have to sit in this wooden hut in the order you are running. As I sat down to run the first leg you could see the faces of the Americans, wondering, 'What's going on?' From that moment on we had won because we had already done what we had set out to do. Suddenly they were reacting to us, rather than the other way round. Americans are usually so – arrogant is a bit harsh – but they seem to think that they don't have to worry about anyone else in the 4x400. This time they had to think about us.

When a 4x400 team walks out, you don't really have to talk to each other, talking is done through the eyes. You only have to look at each other to create the feeling of, 'Here we go. We're a team here.' As I walked out to get ready to run the first leg, I looked Kriss, Derek and John in the eyes. No words were spoken. As I stood behind the line ready to lead off I wasn't running for Great Britain, I wasn't running for me. I was running for Kriss and Derek and John. That is the secret. That is what the 4x400 have that I believe the 4x100 have never had. John Regis would admit that. He would often say he felt that sense of belonging which is the essence of the British 4x400 squad. That is not an accident. That is something that, when I joined the squad, was passed on through the Garry Cooks, the Phil Browns, the Todd Bennetts – a genuine friendship – which went on to the Kriss Akabusis, to the Derek Redmonds, to the Roger Blacks, and is now handed on in this era to the Iwan Thomases, the Mark Richardsons and the Jamie Baulchs. We run against each other all the time, but we all get on with each other, because we know the 4x400 is bigger than any of us as individuals. I feel the responsibility to pass that down, and I feel it's in very safe hands.

For us on that day, the rest was history.

When I took off on the first leg I knew I had to put us in the lead or our gamble was doomed to failure. As I came round the final bend I had one thought in my mind, to hand over a lead to Derek, and I managed to do that. Derek made sure he got to the point where the runners break their lanes ahead of everyone else. He was seeking to extend our lead, but he began to run out of steam on the home straight and he was passed by Watts, who was demonstrating the talent which brought him a stunning victory at the following year's Barcelona Olympics.

Derek, however, managed to rally again and kept John Regis in close contention with the American's third leg runner, Danny Everett. Can you imagine what it must have been like to have Regis breathing down your neck? Everett knew he was there, all right. And Regis executed his job. He didn't have to go past, he had to do no more than hang on in. You don't want to be just in the lead on the last leg. You either want to be five metres in the lead, or right behind so your opponent has to think.

When Kriss set off on Pettigrew's shoulder, everything was still going according to plan. Kriss knew that Pettigrew would-n't run away from him. He knew when to act. And when he kicked off the final bend he hit it perfectly. He put his years of experience into that moment. And of course he went on to cross the line first and we became world champions. I wasn't watch-ing at that moment. I was crouching down, exhausted, by the side of the track, with my back to the action. I was looking at

Brendan Foster, there with the BBC, and his reaction told me everything I needed to know about how the contest had turned out.

There is no doubt that that was the single greatest emotional moment of my athletic career in terms of completely letting go of my inhibitions. It was pure joy. And to share it with three other friends was just fabulous. I went racing over to them shouting, 'Look at the time, boys! Look at the time!' We had smashed the European and Commonwealth records in 2min 57.53sec. I remember my mother saying that when she was watching the race it was one of the rare moments she saw me emotionally overwhelmed by a situation. Because usually I'm quite controlled and laid back about things.

The Japanese officials tried to stop us doing a lap of honour afterwards, but there was no way we were going to be prevented from enjoying that well-earned celebration. Even sumo wrestlers couldn't have held us back. We did the lap of honour, and then we had a television interview with the BBC. I was buzzing with the whole thing. So when it came to me, I said, 'Yeah! We kicked their butts!'

The words just came out really. Very unlike me – not my kind of expression. But when Kriss crossed the line the exhilaration of success was amazing, because the Americans hadn't been beaten for years and our plan had worked. Sometimes you get it right, sometimes you get it wrong. But there's no doubt that that Sunday evening in Tokyo was the most fun that I have ever had in athletics.

When we got home there was a great reception for us at the airport, and the public reaction was like nothing I had ever known. I think the reasons our win touched so many people were numerous. Obviously the excitement of Kriss coming from behind to just dip Pettigrew on the line was one. You couldn't have written a better script. Patriotism played a big part too. When people see individuals run well that's great, but when they see a team run, Britain running, not Kriss Akabusi of Britain or Roger Black of Britain, it has a special force. And I think it was also because of the fact that we were a genuine team, black and white together, even though there were strong individual personalities, it just blended.

At Sheffield a few weeks later we wore T-shirts saying, 'We kicked their butts.' My friend Fuzz had them made up. In hindsight it may have been a little bit over the top, but then you don't become world champions very often. We didn't really consider that it would offend the Americans. It wasn't done to offend. But I don't think they saw the joke.

The 400 metres is a very hard event, and I think the public have this impression that you go to races at championships eyeballing each other and trying to psych each other out because you all hate each other. The only time I really experienced that was in the very early days when there were a couple of German athletes who used to walk around and say things like, 'I will break you.' My response on those occasions was usually – but not always – a polite 'Pardon me?'

As you get more experienced, you get on the circuit around Europe, you get to know the guys you run against. I'm not saying you go out and have a beer with them. But people like Antonio Pettigrew, Andrew Valmon, Danny Everett and Quincy Watts are characters you can say hello to. Even in the 100 metres now most people get on, although of all events that's probably the one where there is some animosity. I remember the fight between Dennis Mitchell and Olapade Adeniken in Zurich a few years ago that left blood all over the carpet of the Nova Park Hotel lobby.

In the 400 metres, there is an underlying respect of the event, and therefore of each other. So in no way were we personally rubbing the Americans' noses in it, even if it did come across like that. From their point of view, though, I think they had reason to be unhappy with themselves. First, they had made a big mistake by not running Michael Johnson – who won the 200 metres in Tokyo – in their team. Secondly, the four who were chosen, Watts excepted, didn't run particularly well and they knew that. Obviously our celebration was really grating for them especially because they just expect to win all the time. You had to feel for Pettigrew, though. He was the world champion, and he was beaten by an old duffer on the last leg and made to look pretty average, really. But that's the beauty of the 4x400.

The great thing about that relay was not just the fact that British supporters were pleased for us, but that every single athletic nation was jubilant that we had beaten the Americans, from competitors to fans. The Germans, the French, the Canadians, the Jamaicans, the Kenyans, everybody. We were heralded by the rest of the athletics fraternity. We just milked it for all it was worth because we knew in the back of our minds that the chance of that happening again was pretty slim because of the might of America.

The 4x400 rivalry between us and America has continued, but we have never managed to beat them since. I think that justifies the jubilation of '91. It was an appreciation that such days don't come around very often, so let's enjoy them when we can. Which we did. And still do.

11

'ALL RIGHT BLACKIE'

Some time after the 1991 World Championships I was invited to speak at the Oxford Union to an audience that was, as I recall, predominantly female. It was a question and answer format, and one man stood up and said, 'Mr Black, you're intelligent, articulate, good-looking, talented – why you?' And I said the only thing I could in the circumstances, 'Some guys have all the luck.'

When you start to become well known, the thing you notice most of all is that people you have never met talk to you as if they know you, and they expect you to be how they imagine you. It can be very strange sometimes. The other day I was sitting in a pub with some friends and someone called out to me as they went by, 'All right, Blackie!' My friends looked at each other and said, 'Blackie? Nobody calls him Blackie.' This is not strictly true. David Coleman, television's voice of athletics, does in fact call me Blackie. I think, however, that he has earned the right to call us athletes whatever he chooses.

After winning the Commonwealth and European titles in 1986, I soon learned how high-profile success can change an athlete's life off the track. I got a car from Mercedes Benz, for whom I had worked the previous year. And suddenly, the function invitations started to arrived. When you become a 'celebrity', you become public property. I've been very lucky because the strain of celebrity has not affected my whole life.

Maybe that's because I've never won an Olympics or a World Championships, and I've had so many set-backs.

Nowadays a lot of my time is taken up giving motivational talks to companies, which is something that has interested me increasingly over the last four years. But when it all started for me it was a case of press interviews, TV appearances, charity dos, Olympic dinners, Commonwealth Games dinners, the Sports Aid Foundation, whatever. You have to be very careful, because if you say yes to everything, you end up missing training sessions.

There's a constant balancing act for a lot of the top athletes, because there are certain responsibilities I think we have both to our training and to our celebrity. The thing about celebrity is that even by doing little, you can do very much. Just giving your name to a charity can be the difference between whether they make £1,000 or £50,000. Simply by giving your name. Making one appearance which gets covered by a newspaper or television can be the difference for a charity between providing a school for disabled kids and not.

Different people do different amounts of work. Everyone always says, 'Oh, it's so good of you to do this, so good of you to do that,' but it's not a big deal, it is really not a hardship. However, I remember reading David Hemery's book where he talks about his return after winning at the Olympics in 1968. Looking back, he said the one thing he wished he'd learned was how to say no. It's hard to say no, because you're always going to upset somebody.

In the early days, it's *very* hard to say no, but as you get older it gets a bit easier. I've always believed it is better to be involved with a few charities properly, rather than lots half-heartedly. Ultimately your focus has to be on athletic performance. If you can't manage your time so that you can put the training in then you're letting yourself down. You're also letting down the charity indirectly – if you don't run well again, you're not of any real value.

The worst thing for me is that I get a lot of letters. Although

I read them all I don't remember the names and then a person will come up to me and assume I know them because they've written to me. They think they know me. That can be very difficult.

I've had something like that recently, when I met a girl who had written to me several times. She was queuing up for my autograph after an athletics meeting, and you could see there was something different about her. The emotion of meeting me was so strong, she hugged me – and she wouldn't let go. She asked, 'You get all my letters?' She was trying to convey the message, 'Look, I'm your number one fan.' But ironically, I hadn't got her letters, as they'd gone to the wrong address. I got a letter from her the other day when she found out I was engaged. She was not pleased at all – 'I am the one who loves you . . .'

The height of everything for me was probably in 1991. The screaming fans have now latched on to Jamie Baulch and one or two others. But in '91 I remember walking out at Crystal Palace with some American athletes and they could not believe the reception I got. People like Antonio Pettigrew, Darnell Hall and Andrew Valmon were there, and they looked at me as if to say, 'What the hell is this all about?' People were going crazy. It was all very flattering, but ultimately frustrating, because I knew that it motivated my opponents to try to beat me in races.

It did serve one useful purpose, though, because whenever an American won he would always turn round and say to me, 'Come on and do a lap of honour with me.' I remember Darnell Hall, who usually did win, saying, 'You're coming round with me, whether you like it or not.'

I was getting 100 to 200 letters a week at this time, which in athletics is a lot. And someone had to deal with them. I was having to pay a secretary just to reply. I sat down with my friend Fayyaz and we thought, 'Well, why not set up a fan club?' It had never been done really properly in athletics. So at the beginning of 1992 we set up the Roger Black Fan Club and it went very well, although the cost of doing it, which I was bearing, was a lot more than I had bargained for.

The period before the 1992 Olympics was a high-profile time, but I didn't perform particularly well at them, and then injury and illness took me out for more than a year. The harsh reality of the world of sport is that if you are not performing well, although the hard core fans will stay loyal, others are relatively fickle and they'll move from one person to another. So in 1993 I closed the club down because I could not justify it financially and I had nothing much to report to people anyway. The irony is that in '96 it would have been more than useful for it still to have been around.

Most of the letters I get from female fans are very polite – but some are seeking a lot more than my autograph, and they make their desires absolutely clear. They say things like, 'I really fancy you,' or 'I think you're gorgeous. I love your arse.' Getting straight to the point. I got one such just the other day. 'We are three students who have just moved into a new house. Come to our house-warming. It's all right. There's plenty of room, we'll all share one bed.' Women send in pictures in various states of dress or undress, although I've never had any underwear through the post, as some people assume. I have had several marriage proposals, though: 'I love you totally. We are meant to be. We must meet. I am the perfect woman for you.' That sort of thing.

When you get lots of adoring women writing to you saying they want to have your babies, people assume that most red-blooded males would jump to it and take full advantage. I've been in many situations which might have led on to something. I have met some gorgeous women who really wanted to know me, but I have never taken any of the offers up, because there's a deep suspicion and fear you have when you're in my position. I have absolutely no wish to be found out a week later in the *Sun* – nor have I ever got over the film *Fatal Attraction*, which has done more damage to the male psyche than anything ever before. You don't know if there are any boiling rabbits out there. You hear things from other people, and I've always erred on the side of caution. I don't want anything untoward to happen to my dog Jasper – nor do I want to end up in the kitchen as part of the menu.

It is nevertheless a matter of continuing annoyance to all my close friends that over the last ten years I have turned down so many wonderful opportunities. They constantly remind me of what a waste it has been – indeed, many of them have offered to take my place. But sadly none of them would be able to pull it off – with the exception of Steve Backley, who is constantly mistaken for me. Perhaps one day I will sit on a park bench in my old age, looking back on my life and mumbling to myself: 'What a waste . . . what a waste . . .'

Obviously Elsa was aware of this situation when she met me, but it hasn't been a problem. She has said that if she fancied someone, writing them a fan letter was not the way she would go about trying to gain their attention. The fact is Elsa is an attractive girl who many men would be more than happy to be with. She knows me well, and she's not at all threatened by the attention I receive.

Obviously there are times when we have arguments, and I feel like saying, 'Look, there's bloody hundreds of girls out there who would like to be with me.' And she always comes back with, 'Yeah, and there are thousands and thousands of men who would like to be with me, darling. They just don't have to write to me to let me know.'

It sometimes helps that she is from another country because she is oblivious to a lot of the showbiz trappings when we are invited out to functions. She hasn't been brought up in the English culture and many 'celebrities' don't mean anything to her. That's one of the attractions for me. I am not with someone who is totally thrilled by 'celebrity'.

I don't consider myself a big 'celebrity', but I don't pretend, 'Oh, I'm just like everyone else.' Because an athlete in my position is not like everyone else. You run for your country, you win medals, you get an MBE, you have dinner with the Queen or the Prime Minister. You are unusually lucky.

David Powell (of *The Times*) once did a piece comparing me with David Grindley, who broke the British 400 metres record in 1992, and characterized me as Boris Becker to his Pete Sampras, in that I had something which appealed to people in good years or bad, regardless of whether I was winning or not. I was pleased with that comparison because Boris is somebody whom I respect. He's not just a great athlete, he also has a personality, he really cares about things.

Athletics is a great leveller. It doesn't matter how big a personality you are, you have got to do the training, you have got to perform. In football, and certain other sports, you can live a wild life and any substandard performances are masked by the fact that you are in a team. But in athletics, that is not possible. Linford Christie is a huge personality, but when it comes down to it, he would agree that athletes' lives are pretty dull – because they have to be.

Glamorous women who write to me would be bored stiff by going out with me. They certainly wouldn't be able to go out every night. Fortunately, it works between my girlfriend and me because she's also an athlete, so she's not going to turn round and complain, 'Why aren't you coming out with me?'

People look at athletes and say, 'Well, there aren't many with great charisma,' but that's because the sport forces you to be very disciplined. You have to be, or you're not going to cut it. It's more important to me to win the medals, to run the races. And it's so bloody hard, and has been, to get back from the injuries, that I can't have the glamorous life.

I can get the occasional glimpse of it, though. In the autumn of 1997 I was invited to attend *An Audience with Elton John*, which was being filmed for television. Wherever you looked, it was – wow! There was Sting, there was Cher, there was Stephen Fry, there were the Spice Girls ... all invited personally by Elton. I spent most of my evening talking to David Gower – Champagne Gower is a great person to hang around with.

Then Elton started calling people up from the audience to come and wear some of his silly stage clothes. And I was sitting there thinking, 'These things are always fixed, so everyone who's going up knows.' And suddenly he calls me. So up I go, along with Ewan MacGregor, David Ginola and Linford Christie. And as Elton greeted me on stage I automatically kissed him on the cheek as some others who had gone up before had done. Of course Linford was led behind the screens to get changed by Claudia Schiffer. I got Stephen Fry – read into that one what you will!

It was quite an occasion for someone who was voted 1996 Sports Personality of the Year by a gay magazine, and who was introduced on the television programme *They Think It's All Over* as 'Roger Black, the man who has chased after more American bums than Liberace'!

Afterwards I got a real ribbing from a lot of people for kissing Elton. I mean, there was a very camp atmosphere to the occasion. Many of Elton's gay friends were there, and he got pretty rude at times. A few days later I was attending another function and the man who was driving me said, 'Oh, I saw the Elton John thing . . .' There was this pause. Then he looked at me in his mirror and said, 'What did you kiss him for?' The truth is it seemed rude not to. I was so pleased to meet him.

It was fascinating that evening with Elton to see the way people in the entertainment business view sports people. There were many other sports stars there, such as Greg Rusedski and Pat Cash. And Elton said on stage 'Deep down, we all want to be you. We all want to run for our country, or play football for England. We all want to be you, because deep down, we all want to be there.'

The two worlds are very different, because mine is not subjective. It gives you the comfort of knowing, 'If I cross that line first, it doesn't matter. You're going to love me. If I cross that line first, no-one can judge me on my colour or character. I get the gold medal.' But it still is an enormously hard world to live in. The music world is very subjective. I may like your song, but someone else doesn't. This is the reason I've never taken my music any further. Many sports people are scared to live in a subjective world.

Music has nevertheless played an important part in my life. I'm from a musical family. My brother is principal horn player for the Philharmonia Orchestra in London and my uncle was the director of music for the BBC and producer for the original Decca recordings of Wagner's *Ring*. My mother is very musical too. Early in 1992 I was writing a lot of songs and playing acoustic guitar – I was coming out of a troublesome relationship and you are at your most creative when things are not going particularly well. As they say, happiness writes blank.

One of the songs I wrote concerned the 4x400 team. A taxi driver in Auckland during the 1990 Commonwealth Games had said to me, 'You're the only British runner, all those black guys aren't really British,' and that had motivated me to write a song about the fact that we were black and white but all running for the same country. I wanted to reflect those things about the British relay win at the 1991 World Championships which people really liked – the feeling behind it.

I was once asked to play a couple of my songs at the London Palladium for charity with the other members of the World Championship winning 4x400 relay team as my backing vocalists. Since neither Redmond, Regis or Akabusi could sing in tune, they spent hours with a professional choreographer and on performance night were a sight to behold as they pranced around on stage wearing specially designed Lycra running suits dispelling the belief that all athletes have good co-ordination. I think we went down well although I recall the audience was taken aback more by my colleagues' antics than by my song-writing ability!

The thing I always wanted to do was to play in a bar and do a set for a couple of hours. I realized I was never going to be the best musician in the world, but I knew I was good enough to do what a lot of people did. I was used to playing the guitar to myself, but I had never been really at ease performing to other people. I had played most of my music during my training trips to California, where Kriss Akabusi and Daley Thompson were my only regular audience. I did play a few songs at a bar called the Sail Loft. If you ask Daley about it, he will say, 'God, don't let him sing. We'll all slit our wrists.' So it took some courage for me to play in front of a home crowd, as it were. I did two nights in what was then my local wine bar at Bishop's Waltham. The first time was unannounced, and it was one of the great nights in my life. But the experience of my second date at Bishop's Waltham indicated to me that I was on the wrong track, because I didn't want people to think that I was some sort of athlete trying to use his celebrity to become a pop star.

The problem was that after I had agreed to play at the wine bar for the second time, the local press got to hear of it. I'd been on for about half an hour when a press photographer came up and started flashing away, and I put my hand up and said, 'Look, I'd rather you didn't do that.' Of course, the picture that got published was the classic 'celebrity shielding his face from the camera shot' and the accompanying editorial was along the lines of, 'Who does Roger Black think he is?' At the time I was also doing some presenting for local television, and this was clearly too much for the new editor of the paper to bear.

A lot of people who were at the wine bar wrote in to the paper to say, 'No, you are totally out of order.' After that experience, though, I never played live again. I had almost achieved my goal by doing it once, but in the end I couldn't handle that environment, that subjectivity.

I knew a lot of musicians at the time and many people had been saying I should record my songs. There were distinct possibilities in the air and I was offered the opportunity to do it. But I turned the offer of the recording contract down, to the chagrin of several of my friends who couldn't understand why I wasn't going for it and trying to make a lot of money – if not with my songs, then with cover versions. I was never going to take up the last suggestion, because I hate cover versions of anything.

I'm a great believer that just because you can do something it doesn't mean you should do it. You have to be comfortable with why you are doing it. I don't pretend to think I'm an Olympic class musician. I'm good enough to write a few songs and sit around and play. But I am not at all motivated to do it as a business. Some people I know would have jumped on the bandwagon if they had been in my position, because celebrity can go a long, long way. When it comes down to it, though, I'm not a pop star.

One of the things a lot of performers and entertainers said to me at the Elton John evening was how much respect they have for athletes because of the sacrifices we have to make. In the past I have never seen athletics as being a matter of sacrifice, but I have to admit that I am changing my mind as I get older. I am looking forward to the day I retire from the track – which is not really a very nice place to be in. It's a very dangerous thing to say. But I am looking forward to the day when the weight can be taken off my shoulders.

I *do* let myself go for four or five weeks a year. Not least on the week I spend abroad each year, with my best schoolfriends, when we stay out very late and get very drunk. I do drink and I like the odd cigar now and again. But that's really it. You can't live it up or you won't make it. That cuts you off from a lot of people. Linford Christie lived it up for a few years, but then he changed – and became Olympic champion. He saw it. Underneath his celebrity there is a commitment to training, a clear focus and vision about what he wants to achieve which is second to none. He was a consummate athlete and I have had to be as well.

At functions or meetings, I have always tried to make a point of staying behind to do the autographs. Kriss and I have had the same attitude about this. We know that that one moment we take to sign a piece of paper can mean so much to some-body, and I've had letters from people saying they really appreciated me staying behind and signing because not everyone else did. There are times when I do have to be more selfish and I have to think about myself. Mike Whittingham often says to me I take on too much, but both he and I recognize the importance of signing autographs and I sign as many as I can because I still remember when I was the autograph collector. I remember waiting for hours to get David Gower's autograph at Hampshire Cricket Club when Leicestershire came down. And eventually he signed and it had a profound effect on me.

That's how it is for people when they wait for me. And that's great. It's really important to me. But of course ultimately someone has to be disappointed because you've got to leave eventually. People say to me, 'You ought to charge for signing your autograph.' And they go on, 'You must get arm ache. It must be awful. It must be a real pain.' And I always say, 'Do you know when it's going to be a real pain? When nobody asks for it.'

I'll never forget the first person who asked for my autograph back in 1985. I was at the Cosford Games with Kriss. I was not at all well known at that time, I had just walked in with Kriss. But then this kid wanted my autograph. I said in disbelief, 'You don't want my autograph.'

Kriss turned to me. 'Sign it.'

'But I'm nobody. I'm nobody.'

'To them, you're somebody. Sign it. Always, always sign an autograph. It's not for you, it's what it means to the person who's asking,' Kriss said.

It is so true. It's yet another example of how by doing very little you can do so very much. And thankfully I have not had to experience the downside of being well known; I am not sufficiently elevated to be a target for the paparazzi.

There are ways to grab attention and there are ways to avoid it. I don't go to pubs. I don't walk down the High Street making a show of myself. I don't go into a restaurant and say, 'Hi everybody!' On the other hand, if I go to a sporting event I know people are going to recognize me so I'm ready for it.

Ultimately, my life is my friends and family. Elton John has said he loves Britain because its people are so levelling. And all the people around me are levelling. If I do, or did, get too big for my boots my friends would tell me straight. But when people ask me if I have changed through being well known, the answer has to be, 'Well, yes, I have changed to a degree. But what has changed more is the way people are to me.' Because what you have of celebrity comes back to the fact that people know you. And people give you a position, whether it's positive or negative – they've already formed an opinion of you anyway.

I never cease to be amazed by the people who turn out to have an interest in the sport and in me. I did a radio show in 1996 and I was sitting next to Danny LaRue. So I said, 'Oh, Danny LaRue, nice to meet you, I'm Roger Black, I'm an athlete.' I never assumed he'd know who I was. It was just after the Atlanta Olympics, and it turned out Danny LaRue had watched all my races. The timing of the live television broadcasts, at two or three in the morning, was perfect for him as he arrived back home after evening cabaret. 'I'm a fan, you know,' he said.

One of the things about celebrity is that you get asked to do lots of things, from TV shows, to getting paid to have dinner with certain companies. Different people take it different ways.

A while ago I did a sporting quiz. There were six or seven sporting celebrities and we all had to host a table, and we were being paid to do that. We were chatting beforehand, Bernard Gallagher, Trevor Brooking, Annabel Croft, Mickey Skinner, Allan Lamb and John Parrott, about the things we had been doing and one of them said, 'Oh these things can be a real pain, can't they?'

John Parrott turned round and said, 'What are you talking about? You are getting paid to have good food, a bit of wine, meet some new people. And we are getting PAID to do it. It's a great life.' And I thought, 'Spot on. Absolutely spot on.' It's incredible the things you get a chance to do. You have a fun evening, and you get paid as well!

You get asked on TV shows from *Call My Bluff* to *Noel's House Party*, *Wogan* to *A Question of Sport* and *They Think It's All Over*, and you meet so many interesting people. I've never been able to understand those who knock celebrity. I always remind myself how lucky I am.

I was on a TV quiz show a while ago and rumour had it that one of the other guests wasn't happy with their fee. I found that attitude hard to understand, because the thing was fun. When we walked off from our show, the guests for the next show were waiting, so we saw Sir Cliff Richard, Sir George Martin, Adam Faith. It was really something.

There is a saying among sports people that you haven't really made it until you've been asked on *A Question of Sport*. The first time you do it you think, 'Right, that's it, I've arrived.' Mark Richardson announced the other day, 'I'm doing *A Question of Sport.*'

'That's great Mark,' I said almost dismissively because I assumed he had done it already. But then it suddenly clicked. 'Is it your first time?'

'Yeah,' he said. And I knew just how important that was to him.

I have done *A Question of Sport* every year since 1986. I was captain for three shows when Ian Botham was away, and I absolutely love it. You meet different people and you all have sport in common, you sit there and you answer questions about your own sport and you have a laugh. And you get paid to do it.

Doing TV shows is just fun, but television commercials are a bit more than that – and they don't come around that often. Daley Thompson did a series for Lucozade. Linford Christie advertised Puma. Sally Gunnell did adverts for Quorn. And after my Olympic success I signed a contract to do three commercials for Pot Noodles.

People might think I wasn't the obvious choice for that. But in fact I was, because the idea of the advert was to make everyone understand that it is actually not as bad for you as most people assume, because it has this image of being eaten late at night after the pubs close by students who can't afford anything else. I admit that my initial reaction was, 'I can't do Pot Noodles, it's full of preservatives.' I went straight down to my local supermarket and bought one to have a look at the ingredients – and there were no added preservatives in it. It was also the case that when I was young I used to genuinely like Pot Noodles. But the bottom line was you don't turn down a TV commercial, because it is worth an awful lot of money.

Athletes make their living in two ways – race fees and endorsements, and the major endorsement will be the clothing company, in my case, Reebok. You can supplement that with other contracts. I have had a six-year link with Lloyds TSB. But if you can get a TV commercial, it will pay you much more than you would get for running at the most lucrative meeting on the world calendar. If you are offered nearly as much money for two days' work as you might make in a year from running, you are going to take it.

So I had waited all my career and finally I had been offered a television advert for Pot Noodles! By looking at the Pot Noodle ingredients, I cleared my conscience, and I thought, 'If Gary Lineker can do crisps, then why not do this? If a kid is going to snack on something they could do a lot worse than a Pot Noodle.'

I did the justification to myself, and we started filming. There were a series of storylines with me and this Ned Noodle character, who was an actor dressed as a walking, talking Pot Noodle. There had been an earlier series of adverts where these two comedians made home movies about Pot Noodles. The latest idea was that they should hear of me getting involved in promoting the product and become upset that it was being portrayed as being not too bad for you. Their line was that Pot Noodles couldn't be good for you, because they tasted too good. So ultimately the storyline has them sabotaging my bit of the commercial and making off with the Pot Noodle, and I run after them.

On the day of shooting, we got to the final part where I was supposed to chase these two characters as they were making their escape in a car and leaning out of the window jeering at me. We had the whole production team there, there were about fifty people on set, including the writers. They were still look-ing for a suitable line to round the thing off because there was nothing in the script at that point.

At the time I had these three other tracksuited club athletes with me who had been acting as extras, and I had been chatting with them during the breaks. So the writers approached me cautiously and said, 'We need a line for when you are chasing after the car, and we've got a few ideas . . .'

You could see they were thinking, 'Right, this is the moment, guys.' Because if I wasn't happy with it, it wasn't going to happen. So they said, 'We had this idea where you're running along and they are taunting you with the Pot Noodle, and they are going, "Sil-ver! Sil-ver! Imagine it's a gold medal, Rog! Sil-ver! Sil-ver!" ' And the faces of the three other athletes when they heard this were really something. They were clearly think-ing, 'You can't let them do that! You're the Olympic silver medallist, you can't let them mock you like that!'

I was standing there, and there was absolute silence. All these writers and producers and actors were waiting to see how I reacted to this obvious line that they all thought was going to work. And I said, 'Guys, by agreeing to do this commercial and dress up in this silly outfit and communicate with a character called Ned Noodle, I think I have shown a degree of humour. And if we are going to make this funny, let's go all the way. If you're going to take the mickey out of me, then let's do it prop-erly. It's not just a line, it's the only line.'

So that was what we did, and it turned out to be very popu-lar. The only problem is that when I go to any school to give a talk now I hear that chant around me, 'Sil-ver! Sil-ver!' I was on *Call My Bluff* recently, and when I walked on to the set there was someone in the background going 'Sil-ver! Sil-ver!' I was coming home from Lanzarote the other day, just minding my own business, and from somewhere at the back of the airport there came the chant, 'Sil-ver! Sil-ver!' And I can just imagine it next season as I walk into the stadium . . . It haunts me wherever I go. But to me it means one thing – the commercial worked.

And it doesn't matter what taunts I get, or whatever anyone says to me. Although my Olympic silver medal looks silver to everyone else, it looks gold to me. I've won my Olympic gold medal. That's why I was happy to do that advert.

I haven't had the luxury of being Olympic champion. The harsh reality in the world of athletics is that your own personal achievement in coming second is fine, but it doesn't necessarily bring in a swamp of endorsement offers. Athletes assume that if they start winning medals everyone will want to snap them up for TV commercials, but it isn't that easy. It took me years, because all the ingredients have to be there.

The odd offer does come that you have to think twice about, and in some cases, turn down. I remember Mike Whittingham ringing me up soon after the Atlanta Olympics and saying, 'I think I might have something for you . . .' Now I know Mike so well that I can tell instantly when he is about to ask me to do something that he knows I won't want to do. He went on, 'The new adult Playboy TV channel would like you to be part of their launch.'

'Mike, although I'm sure I would enjoy the process, do you really think it's me?' I asked. The truth is, Mike and I know it's me – but you can't let the public know that, can you?

And although the thought of having a day surrounded by topless models was not my idea of hard work, ultimately I don't think it would quite have fitted my image. In the end I think they got Pamela Anderson to do it, which, I have to say, seemed a far better choice than me for the job.

One thing I won't do is nude photos. I've always been determined to avoid the Adonis complex. You see these athletes desperate to take their tops off to reveal rippling muscles – fine, but not for me. The depth of this conviction really came home in 1992 when a BBC producer asked me to strip down to my underpants.

I was asked to be a co-presenter with the former Liverpool footballer Emlyn Hughes in a television production for a transatlantic transmission entitled *Sports Mad*, which was to feature all sorts of weird and wonderful sporting activities. But as they never sent a contract – and especially as Kriss had been 'Gotchaed' by Noel Edmonds only two weeks beforehand – I was pretty suspicious before I even left the house. Knowing all about Noel's set up for Kriss on his *Noel's House Party* had put me on my guard.

So I arrived at the BBC to rehearse *Sports Mad*, complete with studio audience, production team, director, editor and scripts. The show was to focus on the zany side of British sport, and included items on pantomime horse racing, in which Emlyn and I would dress up as a pantomime horse, stone spitting, black-pudding throwing and nude hang-gliding.

We rehearsed my interview with the World Nude Hang-gliding Champion. There we were side by side on two hang-gliders and both fully clothed. Rehearsals over, we went 'live' to do the show. We got to the nude hang-glider bit and my interviewee appeared wearing only his underpants. The producer cued me in, 'Two minutes Roger, could you get down to your underpants please.' It was set up for me to do the full, 'No way, I am a strictly clothes on man – this was not what happened in rehearsal' scene. And then presumably Noel was supposed to come out with his 'Gotcha'.

The problem was that in the rehearsal, when I ran through the black-pudding throwing piece with Sidney Ecclesthorp, the World Black Pudding Champion, I had recognized him. After the interview I had taken him aside and said, 'You're Bobby Nutt, the comedian.' The reason I knew him was he used to be a close friend of the former British 400 metres runner Donna Hartley, another athlete trained by Mike Smith.

'Look,' I said to Mr Nutt, alias Ecclesthorp. 'You're Bobby Nutt and I know what's going on here.'

He, keeping up the thick Northern accent, tried to shout me down with, 'Nay, nay, lad, I'm Sidney Ecclesthorp.' This continued for a while until he walked off, obviously panicking.

It was an awful feeling. I knew they had gone to a lot of trouble to set me up. It had clearly involved much time and planning, and it must have been costly, but I'd sussed it before the 'live' show had even started.

I was in my changing room wondering what to do when Bobby came round.

'OK, you know I'm Bobby Nutt, but I don't want you to say anything, because I don't want the tax man to know.' He took one look at my face, I have no idea what my expression must have been like, and then he added, desperately, 'I pretend to be Sidney Ecclesthorp part time, and I don't want to be found out.' Not even half of me believed him, but I was facing my own crisis – what to do. It was a real dilemma. Eventually, I decided to play ball. It was to be a secret between me and Bobby, sorry, Sidney.

So it went ahead, and it was all very silly, and then we got to the nude hang-gliding bit, and the producer's order to strip, and – right on cue – he went mad when I said, 'Look, I am not taking my clothes off on television.' He was supposedly on a live linkup to America, and he said, 'All this has been agreed with your manager beforehand.' Of course he was really linked up the staggering distance of twenty-five metres to a cubicle next door.

It was a real conflict of interests, but in the end I just could not play it false, I could not pretend I did not know what was going on. So I ended up, fully clothed, doing this dummy interview with this hang-glider, and everyone was 'angry' with me, but before Noel turned up I was saying, 'All right, Noel?' to the camera. I still felt really bad about it. They did promise they would really get me one day – but they haven't got me yet. Now that I will be working for the BBC I consider myself a marked man.

I got some pointers towards effective interviewing – in a negative kind of way – when I appeared on Channel 4's *The Word* a few years ago. Terry Christian was the man quizzing me in his inimitable Mancunian fashion, and I could see four questions he had written down. I answered his first one, and he didn't appear to be taking any notice. Then I answered the second question, and in doing so covered the third and fourth. What would he do now? Well, he asked me the third question. And he asked me the fourth question. Then I knew for sure he wasn't listening to a word I was saying!

In the last twelve years I have met many famous people, including prime ministers. My first meeting with John Major was at an informal party in 1995. I was invited by a Tory MP, Sir Fergus Montgomery, who I had met once at an Olympic function. When I got my MBE in 1992 he had invited me and my parents to dine at the House of Commons after we'd been to the Palace, which we did.

There were a number of show business people at this party, and I ended up on a table with my sister, Eddie Shah, Jim Davidson, William Roach, who plays Ken Barlow in *Coronation Street*, Richard Branson, and John and Norma Major. The prime minister was in the middle of a leadership challenge from John Redwood, and an important vote was due to be held only two days later.

I remember thinking as I walked in, 'I'm amazed he's here tonight. The man must be under extraordinary pressure.' But he had promised to be there and he was there. He'd loosened his tie, he was relaxing, having a glass of wine and chatting to us about sport. It was one of those really strange occasions I sometimes find myself in when I think, 'This is just not real.' He was so impressive. My sister was nearly in tears when we left, because he was so nice. She felt very keenly the pressure he was under from the nation, and Redwood and his followers. But he had simply appeared to enjoy a night out with his wife, who he seemed very close to and who seemed fantastically supportive of him.

Richard Branson was equally relaxed, Eddie Shah was great company, and Jim Davidson had the whole table in stitches. When Major made some jokes himself, Jim Davidson turned to me and said, 'If the public could see him now more of them would vote for him.'

I just thought, 'I am so privileged to be in this position.' It had a very big effect on me that night, and on my sister as well. Major said at one point, 'You get penalized for being a nice guy sometimes.' I certainly think people in the world of sport have always felt that he was a genuinely nice man. Tony Blair's tribute to him when he took over as prime minister was absolutely right, because I think Major is basically a thoroughly decent man.

I met Tony Blair in January 1997, at a small dinner put on by Alan Pascoe, the former hurdler who now owns a big company promoting and marketing sport. The election was at least three months away, depending on when John Major decided to call it, but it seemed clear at the time that Tony Blair would be the next prime minister – and I was sitting next to him.

He had been travelling round the country earlier that day, and probably the last thing he wanted to do was be at that dinner, but the two of us had a great conversation about what it was like to be in an Olympic final, and the psychology of performing on the big occasion – because he was coming up to his Olympic final with the election. And again I remember thinking, 'This is weird, because this is going to be the next prime minister. And he's so young.' He was so easy to talk to, and so genuine. It had quite an effect on me. He admitted he wasn't particularly interested in sport. But he was happy to listen and to learn.

And he did. One of the suggestions that came up at that dinner was, 'Make the minister of sport somebody who actually loves sport.' And Tony Banks was appointed. Many people think he was a controversial choice, but one thing you've got to say for Tony Banks is, he loves his sport!

After that evening with Blair, I remember walking off to the car with Jonathan Edwards, and we both said how privileged we felt.

I was in America when the election took place and Blair won. I felt compelled to write him a little note, just to say, 'Congratulations,' and I remember thinking at the time that his life was about to change. I wished him the best of luck. I never expected to hear anything back. Ten days later – still in America – I received a handwritten letter from him. And I keep that letter with me for one reason. Never again will I use the excuse, 'I don't have time.' If Tony Blair could find the time to write a handwritten letter to me on 16 May, and send it to California – two weeks after becoming prime minister – how can I ever say I don't have the time? How can anyone say it? That was so impressive, and I think it summed the man up.

My experience of both modern-day prime ministers has been positive. Different politics, but very similar people. I have been privileged to see sides to them that most people don't get to witness.

I have also been privileged to have met the Queen on a number of occasions. After the Olympics, I was invited by the American ambassador to his final dinner before he left London.

The invitation read, 'Roger Black – Private Dinner with The Queen'. I thought there would be about 300 other people there.

I phoned up, and asked, 'I'd just like to say, this dinner, why have you invited me?'

'We really enjoyed watching you at Atlanta, and we'd really like you to come,' was the reply.

'OK, so how many people are going to be there?' 'Oh, about eighteen.'

'Sorry?!'

Elsa went out and bought an expensive dress for the occasion, and off we went to the ambassador's house. There was a lot of protocol and security was tight because the Queen and Prince Philip would be there. Everyone was standing around, really nervous. But the Queen put us at our ease. She was charming. At one point she and Prince Philip were chatting to Elsa and I over coffee, and the experience struck me as being hard to believe. The Queen said, 'I was unable to see much of your running in Atlanta because we're having problems with the TV up in Balmoral.' Which I thought was very tactful.

Meanwhile, the Duke of Edinburgh was taking the mickey out of Elsa. 'How can French people do athletics?' he asked. 'They're always smoking Gauloises, aren't they?'

More recently I was asked to another private luncheon with the Queen, and we found ourselves talking about our dogs. Jasper got an honourable mention, of course. And she told me all about the Corgis who, incidentally, had begged at our feet throughout our meal. At one point she requested a couple of Digestive biscuits which duly arrived on a silver plate and proceeded to crumble them up and feed them to the dogs as we chatted.

Those occasions – meeting two prime ministers and the Queen – they're things that will always stay in my mind.

The phrase keeps coming back: 'And all I do is run round the track.'

12

THE AGONY AND THE ECSTASY

My destiny in 1992 seemed quite clear – at least on the evidence of my diary. On 9 February I wrote:

I now know how to run the perfect 400 metres. Fast, controlled and relaxed to 300, then pick up my knees home. I will run it this year in the Olympic final.

Right competition, wrong year. At the Barcelona Olympics, I experienced perhaps my worst moment on the track. But that moment turned into one of the best moments of my life.

My experience has shown me that you need three good years consecutively to get the best out of yourself: one year to get back from injury, another to move on a level, which I did in 1991 when I broke 45 seconds ten or eleven times and finished as grand prix champion; and the third year when, if you stay healthy, you can do something special. With that in mind I was excited about the Olympic year of 1992. I was twenty-six – at the peak of physical ability. I felt this was my opportunity

I had this worry of achieving World, European and Commonwealth medals and then, years later, hearing my grandchildren ask, 'What was it like going to the Olympics, Grandad?' and having to say, 'Well, I never went to the Olympics.' 'But, Grandad, I thought you were a really good athlete . . .'

I trained well in the winter of '91. John Regis, who had won four medals at the previous year's European Championships, and Marcus Adam, the Commonwealth 200 metres champion, were now working alongside Kriss and I with Mike Whittingham. Both were great characters, and they had helped me improve my sprinting. But there were some warning signs. My hip injury was still there, which was annoying, and Ron Holder was not easily available to make the constant fine adjustments to my body's balance which I needed. I reasoned that it couldn't be that bad because I had won a world silver medal on it. My logic was, 'Look, no one's going to get this better, so I've got to run with it, even though it may hurt.' But the problem is that if you've got pain it's on your mind, and it just wears you down.

In February, however, I had a pleasant distraction from any gloomy thoughts that might have been gathering, when I was awarded the MBE. Essentially I do what I do for myself. I don't go out there and think about my country when I train. I basically set my goals, and I seek them under the flag of Great Britain. Every athlete will put their hand on their heart and say, 'I actually do it for myself.' Which is why it feels odd when you get the great honour of receiving the MBE from the Queen and you find yourself in company with those who have really put themselves out for others.

As I accepted the honour I thought of all those in the sport who, day in, day out, put so much in – the coaches, the helpers, the organizers. There were a lot of people who deserved this MBE more than I did – the Mike Smiths, the Mike Whittinghams – whom many would not have even heard of. And yet I was the one getting the recognition when what I did day in, day out was for the good of myself. But that's the way it is.

The fact that you can touch so many people by just running around an athletics track has always surprised me. One of the things which had the greatest effect on me in 1991 was a letter from a woman who said she wanted to thank me for making her husband's last minutes happy ones. He had died of a heart attack while watching the Tokyo relay. She said that if there was one consolation, at least he died happy. I mean, what can you say? There's an irony in that. I've always been aware of that when people come up to me and say things like, 'Thank you for what you've done for us.' You think well, yeah, that's just a by-product of a process really. That may sound very selfish. People may have this image of you out there doing it for your country. But even in the relay, you are running for the other three guys. You are always proud to wear your British vest and to see the flag go up. Always. But the fundamental motivation is a personal one.

I often think of a scene I witnessed while competing in April of that year in California at Asuza Pacific University, where Kriss was studying theology. During the 1500 metres race, one athlete was lagging far behind the others, and his coach was running alongside him, desperately shouting,'Do it for the Lord man! Do it for the Lord!' On this occasion, sadly for the back marker, no miracle occurred.

Receiving my MBE from the Queen was a very special moment for me and for my parents, who accompanied me. She was well briefed, and I remember her asking me if I had any races coming up. Only one that matters, I thought to myself. The Olympic Games was constantly at the back of my mind.

I felt in retrospect I should have won the 400 metres in the World Championships in Tokyo. I had been in shape but unable to concentrate 100 per cent on my performance. I didn't have the confidence to control it to 300 and thus died coming home. I knew I had to master my pace judgement if I was to do better. Five days before setting off for California training, I wrote: 'I realize that this is the big year. If I get it right this year I have basically done it all. A part of me is scared – but my need for achievement is greater than my fear of failure . . .'

I'm not convinced I was telling myself the truth at that point. But there was a part of me that knew that although I was doing enough to be very good, I needed to move up another level to find my true potential. I was starting to see I had to make a bigger input into what I was doing. I realized that if I was to become Olympic champion – or Olympic medallist even – it was going to take a lot more than I was giving it. There was a lot more to it than just training.

Despite the familiar problems with my hip I trained well in California and came back in good shape, winning the UK Championships at Sheffield in 44.84sec. It was a highly promising way to open the season. But as the weeks went on, my leg and my hip began to get progressively worse, and I started to worry. I got selected for the Olympic team, and we went out to Monte Carlo to prepare for the Games, where the problem was on my mind the whole time.

My training partners Kriss and John Regis were healthy and running really well, but I was still struggling, despite getting some very radical treatment out in Monaco from Mark Zambada, who was there at the time looking after Linford Christie and Colin Jackson. He has been my massage therapist ever since. I was so down on that trip that Mike Whittingham actually asked me, 'Do you want to go to the Olympics, or do you want to go home now?' It was a question that didn't have to be answered – but it did have to be asked.

I arrived at the Olympic village with my mind full of doubts over whether my leg would stand up to the pressure of competition. The team doctor, Malcolm Brown, decided I should have anaesthetic injections before I raced. So I would go down to the warm-up track, but instead of jogging I would go into a little cubicle with Malcolm and he would put needles in me – to take the pain away. In the next cubicle, the Cubans were sticking a needle into Roberto Hernandez, their 400 metres runner, and as the two camps looked across at each other I could only wonder if we were both wondering the same thing! On the face of it, it looked like something the doping authorities might have been interested in.

The cumulative stress of the situation got to me, and it resulted in my being knocked out of the semi-final, which was without doubt one of the most devastating moments of my career. I was world silver medallist and I couldn't make the Olympic final. What made it worse was that in the same race, a nineteen-year-old, David Grindley, had reduced the British record to 44.47sec. Suddenly my position as Britain's No.1 had been taken from me. I was numbed by the experience. Emotionally and physically drained.

My parents and sister were staying about thirty miles outside Barcelona. Although I don't usually feel comfortable with my family coming to watch me run, they had made a special visit because it was the Olympics. So the day after the semi-final I hired a car and drove over to see them. They weren't expecting to see me, and it was a very emotional occasion. It was a difficult time, because Kriss had won his bronze medal in the 400 metres hurdles on the same day as my semi-final, and his wife Monika was staying with my family, so there was a mixture of emotions around. My sister was in tears for me, and I cried too, which did me good. I reassured them that it was not the end of the world. I said I had been through worse than this, and that I had physical problems which I was going to sort out. I also told them I had some good news: I had a date that afternoon.

As I had walked off that track, feeling completely desolate, the first person to come and console me was someone I had never spoken to before – Elsa de Vassoigne. We had been looking at each other on and off throughout the Olympics without having the nerve to speak. We had, however, been communicating in the previous few days through the computer messaging system at the Olympics. She was writing to me in broken English, saying, 'Hello, Roger Black', and ending her letters the French way, with 'bisous' which translates as 'I kiss you.' So at the end of each letter she was writing this 'I kiss you', and I was thinking, 'Right. OK. Yes please.' Now this little French girl, who had been knocked out of the women's 400 metres semi-final before my race, chose to come up and give me a kiss on the cheek and say, 'Never mind.' A woman will always get a man when he's at his lowest. And she certainly picked her moment. In contrast to me, Elsa was very happy because, even though she'd been knocked out too, she'd run a personal best. And we arranged to see Barcelona together the next day. We visited the Cathedral, and the Ramblas, and the Sagrada Familia. It's a wonderful city – and there I was with this new girl I was physically very attracted to. And all the time walking round Barcelona, I was thinking, 'All these letters with "I kiss you, I kiss you." When's this kiss going to happen?'

It was very strange because, as I later discovered, Elsa had already decided I was the man for her – so she tells me – and although she is naturally a very forward person, she didn't want to come across too strong. We were in a silly situation where I was waiting for this girl to kiss me, because she had already told me she was going to, but any time I sort of hinted towards it, it wasn't happening. It was like something out of *Blind Date*. She was trying to convince me she wasn't just a French tart – which, of course, subsequently I found out she is!

I didn't get my kiss on that date. Not a proper one, anyway.

I found myself spending the next few days with Elsa, which was nice. The difficulty we had at first was that she couldn't speak English and I couldn't speak French. So we communicated in a couple of ways. One of them was through the dictionary. At first the whole thing was very weird, and as we left Barcelona I told myself, 'You can't hold down a relationship when you can't speak to each other properly.' So I left thinking it might be too much effort, to be honest. But two weeks later she turned up to compete at the meeting in Sheffield, and it went from there really. It's amazing how quickly you can learn someone else's language when there's an incentive like that.

The curious thing about having to communicate in the way we did was you find out if you actually like being with somebody when you can't really speak to them. It's a funny old thing. You can sit around with somebody and be really comfortable even though you can't converse. I suppose it was very good for me, actually, because I am prone to over-analysis, and in this case I was unable to over-analyse, because we were unable to have those kind of conversations.

For the first two years, there were times when we both thought, 'This is ridiculous.' But we kept on. Elsa was the one who made the biggest effort. She became fluent in English. I can get by in French now and we are able to have grown-up conversations. But she is always frustrated that she can't really express herself to me fully.

She is certainly my balance in life. She is more instinctive than analytical – and that's good, because sometimes I do take life a little too seriously, I suppose. Elsa is wild – she's probably perfect for me, because I'm attracted to the wild side in people. But athletics has prevented me from being wild, prevented me from letting myself go. It's always been a great pressure on me. You have to be disciplined, you have to be dedicated.

Elsa does not have the necessary dedication to win medals. But she never wanted to. She just wanted to get on the trips, and she's had a great career. When she was knocked out of her semi-final in Barcelona it didn't matter, because she is one of those people who just loves athletics and always gets the most out of it. She was never going to make the Olympic final, but she is this life force in the world of athletics. If there's ever a party going on, or she walks into a room, everybody knows her. And now she's not running much you see the real Elsa. She likes to party until five or six in the morning. And she smokes intermittently – whenever she can find someone to cadge a cigarette from!

For all that, she has produced some exceptional performances in her athletic career, never more so than when she booked her place to join me in Atlanta a week after I had won the British Olympic trials.

You have to be selfish as an athlete. I knew that 1996 was going to be my last Olympic opportunity, and I was desperate to maintain my good form. You've got to get a balance. Many athletes have failed because they have been emotionally drained by their partners. This is the great problem with being with someone who is not an athlete, because they don't under-stand. But Elsa does understand. She has always known when to leave me alone if I am at a critical point in my preparations. She goes back to France at such times.

So we have spent a lot of time away from each other – which, ironically, has kept our relationship going, even though it is tough in many ways. In 1996, we hardly saw each other at all.

I did not think Elsa would get to the Olympic Games. I was visiting my parents, waiting for her to ring me with result of the French trials, expecting her to come fifth or sixth because she was running badly at the time and was in no sort of form, and preparing myself to help her get through that disappointment and be a shoulder for her to cry on. It was very difficult, because I had broken the British record and was obviously in great shape, but I was just waiting for my partner not to make it. The thought of that was awful.

I was sitting on the beach at Gosport when she phoned me. This very depressed voice said, 'Oh well, I just did the final . . .'

'Well look, never mind, it was always going to be tough . . .'

'I know, I know.' Then she paused, and went crazy. 'I beat everyone, I beat the bitches!'

I was so happy for her, and also happy because we were both going to Atlanta together. She is a true Olympian, when she gets to the Olympics she just loves it.

She ran 51.92 in the 1996 trials but in the end the French only selected one woman in the individual 400 metres, their world champion Marie-Jose Perec, who went on to win. Elsa is one of Marie-Jose's best friends and one of the few people who can really understand her, because she is a difficult person. But for Elsa the main thing was to go to the Olympics, and she was in a strong relay team which, as chance had it, knocked out the British girls in the semi-final.

By that time I had won my silver medal, and I was feeling absolutely fantastic. And I met her on the warm-up track before her race and I remember feeling so proud that she had made it. She ran the final leg, taking over the baton in fourth place, just behind the British runner. And it was the first three who went through to the final.

I had been asked to give my thoughts on the race by BBC Radio 5, so I was sitting next to the commentator John Rawling, and as the runners came round with 120 metres to go, John was shouting out 'Can the British girls hang on,' and there was Roger Black next to him shouting, 'Come on Elsa! Come on!'

Elsa just dipped on the line to beat the British girl, and I was going, 'Yesss!!' So John said, 'For those of you back home listening, let me just explain that that was Roger Black cheering very enthusiastically as the British team were knocked out of the semi-final. I think he should explain himself.'

So I said no one could accuse me of being unpatriotic, but my girlfriend and I had come through some very difficult times in our careers, and love is greater than patriotism. As E.M. Forster once put it, 'If I had to choose between betraying my country and betraying my friend, I hope I should have the guts to betray my country.' The following day, France came last in the final, but that was irrelevant.

Atlanta was a wonderful experience for us. As we left, Elsa and I realized that as individuals we had achieved our goals. What frustrates me as an athlete is seeing people who don't fulfil their potential. I'm very disciplined and dedicated and feel I have come close to doing that. Elsa hasn't. But she doesn't have the mentality to do it, it's not in her blood. What she certainly has done is enjoy her athletic career. In many ways, more than most people. And she appreciates it for what it is.

I appreciate the variety of living with someone who is not just French, but from Martinique. The beauty of Martinique is that it is officially a Department of France, but it just happens to be stuck in the Caribbean. It is like France in the sun. When you have spent the first twenty years of your life on a Caribbean island, to deal with British winters . . . I guess she must love me. She reminds me of that often.

When I first went over to meet Elsa's family, my main worry was that my French was nothing like Elsa's English and I wouldn't be able to understand anyone. When I arrived I was paraded around the family – and a cousin of a cousin is family in Martinique. It's an island where everybody knows everyone. Every time I walked in someone's house they offered me some rum, which Martinique produces in abundance. So very quickly, on the first night, I had met *some* of the family and drunk a *lot* of rum. And I suddenly found myself conversing in pretty fluent French with everybody – at least, so Elsa tells me!

I loved going there, but I found some of their culinary habits a little strange. When I went round to Elsa's uncle's house, she was eating this bowl of hors d'oeuvres, and told me to have some. It was a kind of jelly stuff, which I tried. It was absolutely disgusting. Then I was told it was chopped-up pig's snout.

It was not the first disagreement over food which Elsa and I had had. A little problem with salmon a few years earlier had caused me to lose my temper with her for the first time. We had invited a couple of friends over for dinner and we had decided to serve salmon. So I made a start on getting it ready. Elsa, however, had been taught how to prepare fish at an early age, so she stepped in and said, 'No Roger. Let me do it – I know how.'

She wanted to take the scales off. I didn't. At which point I got cross, and said, 'I'm going to do it. I know how to do it.' But she was insistent that she should do it. So we had a situation which developed into a tug-of-war, with the fish in the middle. And in the end I threw it on to the floor. I went away and calmed down a bit, then apologized for what I had done, explaining that, at the time, the fish was either going to go on the floor or on her head! As I recall, we served it later without comment.

We are very different personalities. But the reason we get on generally is because of those differences. We are very lucky to have each other.

13

IF IT'S UPHILL ALL THE WAY, YOU SHOULD BE USED TO IT BY NOW

I had tried to ignore it, but it wouldn't go away. I could not carry on running in the state I was in. When I reflected upon my Olympic experience, I realized that I had to make a clear decision about how to improve my general fitness. Which I did – but unfortunately it was a wrong decision as well. From that first misjudgement I was to spiral down to depths I had not reached even in my lowest moments in the late 1980s.

My hip was a big part of the problem. It had been nagging away at me during the last three major championships I had been involved in, and I decided that it was finally time to do something about it. The problem was, no one could diagnose exactly what was going on. And I was running out of options because Dr Ron Holder, my re-balancing expert, was in South Africa for a lot of the time.

So, more out of desperation than anything, I had a hip-release operation in Birmingham. It turned out to be a very traumatic – not to mention unsuccessful – experience for me. I remember lying in bed afterwards thinking, 'This doesn't feel right.' Even at that stage I feared I had done the wrong thing. The rehabilitation took a long time – and the operation didn't work. In Birmingham I also underwent treatment to straighten my right knee, which involved replastering it three times at weekly intervals, each time under anaesthetic. It was a stressful means of dealing with the problem.

I got back into some kind of shape and returned to California in May 1993, but it soon became clear to me that I wasn't as strong as I should have been in training. I was exhausted when I ran, but it was not the natural exhaustion and surge of muscle-slowing lactic acid that usually occurs when one exerts oneself. I wasn't even generating lactic acid – I was just weak.

As an athlete, there are times when you have to be patient and say to yourself, 'It will click.' And because you train so hard you get used to being very tired. You don't know what it's like to feel really good. But I was feeling lethargic all the time. If my malaise was puzzling for me, it was even more so from the outside. And I sensed that some people were thinking, 'He's lost it.' I don't have any clear evidence of that, it was just something I felt. But then, as I discovered subsequently, negative feelings were merely another symptom of my underlying problem.

Mike Whittingham said to me, 'I think you should have a plan for the season. Take a rest and then get back to it. You are just a bit stressed out.' But I felt it was more than that. It wasn't just the case that I couldn't train properly, I hardly had the strength or the concentration to read a book. I was panicking. I wasn't twenty-one any more. I was twenty-six. And I had this growing fear that my career could be over.

In the end I had a series of blood tests and on 7 July 1993 I was diagnosed as having the Epstein-Barr virus, which is one of the glandular fever family. Initially I felt a sense of relief at the diagnosis. It totally explained the tiredness and the depression. But when I asked, 'Right, so what do I do now?' the only answer was, 'Rest.' Because the problem had to do with my immune system being unable to overcome the virus.

'But when am I going to get better?'

'It depends.'

'Well is there nothing I can take?'

'No. Just rest.'

That wasn't enough for me. I changed my diet, I went to an acupuncturist and I started taking infusions from a homeopath. I had a permanent sore throat and sweats, and I was tired all the time. But the worst thing was feeling depressed, which is not normally part of my make-up. It is something I avoid with passion.

My nature usually is to move on in life, but I found myself losing all confidence and self-belief. I started to use defeatist language when I talked to people. It was just a constant world of negativity and I became very detached, not just from the world of athletics, but from the world itself. I wasn't even seeing my friends – I couldn't make the effort. Walking down the high street was an ordeal. And yet, although I couldn't be bothered to go out, there were times when I couldn't stand to stay at home either. Watching television was a chore. On some days, I felt as if I was going stir crazy. I have subsequently sold my house in Bishop's Waltham – it holds a lot of negative memories for me.

I couldn't maintain my concentration for anything, not even listening to music. I was always yawning. It was an effort to hold a conversation. When I began to make a recovery, that was one of the ways in which I judged I was getting better, because I could have a conversation without losing the drift. I was alone at home a lot, because Elsa was in France suffering similar problems. She was also diagnosed as having glandular fever. And just to add to it, she had to undergo surgery for a stress fracture in her foot. A year into our relationship we were both being tested to the limits. I made trips to visit her but I didn't want to inflict my problems on her, and it was best that we were apart at that time.

Being ill is harder to handle than being injured, and harder to get others to understand. If you are hopping around on crutches and in plaster, people know you've got something wrong with you. They don't suspect that you might be feigning something or you are weak. Also, if you've broken something, you know it will mend. I wrote at the time in my diary:

The last few weeks have been very testing, the most testing of my career. All the time I know I haven't been feeling well but the nature of the athlete is to push on out of desire and fear and panic that the season is slowly passing by. Once the positive diagnosis was reached my mind was able to relax a little and not feel that it was the cause of all my problems.

Weakness in mind and body go hand in hand, each one controlling the other. This I have found hard. At times I have tried to be mentally hard in my approach but the lethargy and pain I have had in my foot has won on the day. Mental panic has been brought on also by other people's performances . . .

Watching David Grindley run so well and feeling powerless to do anything about it was having an effect on me as it does with all athletes when they are in the same position. Everything was compounding. I couldn't watch athletics on television. My diary went on:

. . . I've not been myself and I cannot put this 100 per cent on the virus . . . frustration and a modicum of bitterness has shaped my character recently.

I was thinking, 'I've had my operations, on my foot and my hip, I've had this, I've been through it, I've done my time. Give me a break, please. Don't give me this, this is just not on.' I knew that many people never got back from viruses. It can take years. A glandular fever virus for a non-athlete interrupts their life, but it doesn't rob them of their *raison d'être*. When you are a highly tuned athlete who has to perform at 100 per cent, it destroys you. And you feel pathetic. Because every day people are asking how you are, and saying things like, 'Well, you look all right.' But I couldn't do what I needed to do. I started to think, 'Maybe I shouldn't be doing this any more. Maybe this is a sign. I've had a good career. More high points than most athletes could hope for. Maybe I should start thinking about doing something else.'

I've always subsequently said that the sport owes me nothing. But at the time I was bitter. And there's nothing worse than a bitter athlete. You see them all the time, complaining about how unfair the sport has been to them. 'Oh, why me? This isn't fair.' And I always did my utmost not to be like that. It is a very cruel sport in many ways, because the degrees of skill involved in athletics are relatively small compared to other sports. If you are blessed with natural talent, you can go a hell of a long way in the sport. But as we have seen with Danny Harris, even if you have the greatest talent in the world you need more than just that to fulfil your potential. I had been blessed with an enormous amount of talent and I appreciated that. But I had also been given a body and a constitution that was fallible.

When you have times of pain or suffering, you either turn and face it and make decisions for the better or you let it overtake you and that's it. I started doing a lot of soul-searching at that point. I was doing my best to get out of the quagmire I had found myself in – but I was tending to over-analyse everything, which was less than ideal. I wrote in my diary:

> ... I've always thought I was more than just an athlete, but recently the effect the sport has had on me is immense. I'm not whole without it. I often hide behind my background and abilities off the track to justify my relaxed attitude to make me whole. Is this the sign of a narrow individual who has nothing else, or is it the mark of a pure competitor who has more ahead of him?

The way I was feeling was reinforcing the realization that I needed the sport a hell of a lot more than I had ever admitted to myself. So some positive things were starting to come out from this period of pain.

> ... my future in the sport is now dependent on my ability to search the reasons why I do it and how much I need to do it. The thought of life without athletics has, on the

175

surface, appealed to me. But beneath it, I'm scared to bits. I've felt alone lately. Kriss has retired, Jon's injured, and this has left me feeling isolated with Mike Whittingham my constant companion. Our coach–athlete relationship must evolve, and we need to reassess this.

. . . I've read two books recently. One is directly related to my situation, Seb Coe's *Coming Back*, and the other one is *An Evil Cradling*, by Brian Keenan. Seb had to deal with all this and come back from a virus and blood disorder. He had many other things in life, but athletics was the core of the man. Finally he made the decisions with his coach which led to his success.

Brian Keenan's account of his four years as a hostage in Beirut is remarkable. Each day he was forced to use his mind to exist, and thus delved into areas of himself that few of us ever have to. His strength of mind and character was tested to the full, but he came out of the whole experience more at one with his humaneness.

Since pursuing a life in athletics I have often pondered on my completeness as a human being. Athletics is just a sport, and has a short life span. I'm always talking about life away from the track, and how there's so much more to life. Ultimately of course this has to be true, or all athletes are confined to a life of misery after retiring.

But for those few precious years of participation, athletics is and must be everything. One day it will be the past and it will all be over. I'll know when that day has come, but at the moment my life is dependent on my running. We all have our day. I've had a few already but I feel there are more to come.

My success in 1991 made me well known in the eyes of the public – a Becker and not a Sampras, as *The Times* once said. I am fortunate to be popular off the track. I don't think I've got carried away with all that. But I'm aware that I was better known than maybe my athletic prowess merited.

... Now I need to rediscover my love and desire for running. I read recently: 'It's a foolish man whose happiness depends on something he has no control over.' I also read an article by Rob Andrew in which he wrote: 'Sport is cruel. You experience absolute highs, followed by absolute lows. A sportsman has to enjoy the former in the knowledge that the latter is lurking around the corner.'

I was also starting to be aware of another important truth. If I was to make big decisions about my life, I had to face up to the idea of telling people things they might not want to hear. I had to shed the tendency I had always had of trying to please everybody and not really saying what I felt. It was a growing up process that took an extraordinarily long time for me because I come from a background of always respecting people's opinions and doing what I'm told, of thinking it's better to do something rather than argue about it. That may surprise those who assume I have always known what I wanted and done things my way. It hasn't been the case. For many years I allowed myself to depend too much on others, and in hindsight that wasn't the right thing for me.

At this low point in my life I asked myself the question, 'Am I an athlete first who happens to have a life? Or do I have a life and just happen to be an athlete?'

Asking that one question really turned me round. Because I realized that as I sat there I was an athlete who happened to have a life. My athletics was everything, it was dominating my personality. I was allowing it to affect everything in my life. And the problem with that is, by definition, that the day you stop athletics is the day you die. And that's what was happening to me. I knew that I had to turn it round, get a life together and accept that being an athlete was just one part of it. To take that weight off my shoulders. And that's really what I did.

As a professional sportsman, what you need to do to maintain your ambitions must be the primary focus of your whole life, because every decision you make has to be the right one that will lead you towards your goal. The world of top-class athletics is so competitive that you have to make hard choices and be focused to the point of selfishness – which I always have been. The problem is, if you let it become all-consuming, if you get to the point where it tips the scales and is absolutely everything to you, then you are setting yourself up for a very big fall. If your running doesn't go well, you as a person don't function well. When the bad times come you fall out with your friends and family, you become depressive, you feel 'Without this I have nothing.'

I believe that you have to step back sometimes and have a better perspective of yourself as a human being. If you say to yourself, 'Without running I am nothing,' then when things aren't going well you are worthless by definition.

I learned the lesson then that to be competitive as an athlete had to be the most important thing in my life, but it could not be everything. Not just because it would diminish my life, but because when it's over I have the rest of my life to live and I am going to feel empty, as many ex-athletes do. I came to realize that, although athletics has 90, maybe 95 per cent importance in my life, I still have other things that can make me happy or that I can feel fulfilled by doing. I was accepting that athletics was the most important part of my life – I hadn't truly acknowledged that before then. I would say things like, 'Oh, I can do other things, I'm not just an athlete.' Now I accepted its importance, but I also acknowledged that as a human being it was foolish for me to base my whole happiness on that one thing.

I wrote the following on 4 August 1993, when I was in Brittany with Elsa and my parents.

I'm feeling better but I still get tired from time to time. My left foot is still quite a problem. The X-rays show it is not broken but it doesn't seem to improve. I've made a decision to go to Australia to get treated by a physiotherapist called Peter Stanton at the Institute of Sport in Canberra.

It was make or break for me. I had spoken to Jon Ridgeon and asked him what he thought. He said Peter Stanton was in his opinion the best physio he had ever worked with, and that he was going back to Canberra for further treatment. It was make or break for Jon too at this time. He had seriously injured his Achilles tendon soon after returning from our Californian break.

I made the decision to go to Australia for six months. That meant leaving Elsa, leaving Mike Whittingham, leaving everybody. It was a case of, 'I am taking this in my hands and I am going to get away from my environment where I am recognized.' I wanted to get back to the essence of when I started athletics. I wanted to start all over again, be nobody. And I knew I couldn't do that in England.

At the same time I had to get the best physio treatment I could. The problem with the system in this country is that you have good physios, but they can see you for half an hour, an hour and then you go back home. I needed somewhere where I could live and I could get five or six hours physio a day. I also needed to change my environment so I could get over my glandular fever. So I left on 21 September 1993.

I found a very cheap place to rent in Canberra where Jon soon joined me. If you say to an Australian, 'I spent six months in Canberra,' he'll ask you, 'Did you slit your wrists, or what?' because it is deathly dull. But it is the home of the Australian Institute of Sport – and if you are somewhere with a purpose it doesn't matter where you are. I felt I was moving forward. I was working with Peter and two other physios for five or six hours every day. They tried everything. They taped my foot. They stretched my hip this way and that. I was watching what I ate, how I slept. But they weren't treating only me, so I'd sit around with a book waiting until they could fit me in.

I read stacks of books. And Jon and I did everything we could to recover: we ran in water, we did stretching, we did weight training. I was there for two months before I did any running. I was doing it properly – and slowly but surely I began to feel better. I remember this grass field on which I would run – at first for five minutes, then it became ten minutes, and then I started to do 600 metres reps. Not like I had done in the past, but at least I was able to do it and I wasn't getting a terrible reaction from it.

They were really happy days for me in Canberra. Elsa came and joined me for two months. For the first time in a while I felt able to be myself again, I started to get my confidence back, and believe that maybe I could get back for 1994. And I started thinking of winning the European Championships for the third time.

On 30 November 1993, I wrote:

I've been out in Australia for two months now. I've had intense physio. I've had cortisone injections. I've had new orthotics made. The hip is so stubborn, it will not free up. But it is manageable so long as I concentrate on my hip position while running. I am not training hard, I am just feeling my way. My feet have to be taped up for twenty minutes every time I run to stop them over-pronating.

It's going to be hard, but I can make it back. My mind is a lot better. I'm focused and I'm getting ready. At least I have the chance.

Jon's career is really now in the balance since he snapped his Achilles again the other day. It is so sad to see him maybe finished after all his perseverance and hard work over the years. He is in a very difficult situation career-wise and financially . . .

Both of us were financially stretched. I was OK, but when you have these years out you don't make any money, you just spend money on getting better. I was paying every penny of flying to Australia, renting a house and employing physios. It adds up. And I wasn't getting any assistance on that.

At that point I really believed that Jon was not going to run again. He convinced me that that was the case. But Elsa, who is very perceptive and knows Jon very well, said, 'If he has a chance, he'll always take it.' And that proved to be the case, as he came back in 1995 and 1996, eventually reaching the Olympics.

Kriss was always my 400 metres running partner, but Jon Ridgeon, whom I had met in 1985, was someone I was quite clearly compatible with. Our backgrounds and educations were very similar, we were both European junior champions, and Jon without a doubt was the most talented young British athlete around at the time. In the course of his career he has had a series of terrible Achilles tendon injuries, culminating in 1993 with the tendon snapping in two and him accepting that it was all over and retiring. He was training in Australia when it happened. He walked across a gym from one piece of equipment to another and that's all it took. Snap. He flew back to Canberra, where I was training at the time, and he addressed the situation as it stood. His greatest quality –and he is similar to Kriss in this respect – is his ability to just get on with life.

When I look at Jon Ridgeon I look at somebody who is, in my mind, the epitome of success. He is a truly successful person, because he has had more setbacks than any athlete I know – more than me, and I've had my share. And yet at no point since I've known him has he felt sorry for himself or complained about it. I live in an environment of athletes who, if they have a little hamstring pull, feel it's the end of the world. None of them has a clue what Jon Ridgeon has been through.

Imagine what it must have been like for him to be world high hurdles silver medallist at the age of twenty, then get injured and see his great rival, Colin Jackson, become world champion and world record holder – somebody whom he had always beaten. To then see other people – myself included – go on to achieve things, get status and win medals, while you are injured for most of the time must be devastating. But he's never once lost his sense of fun or of getting on with life, even though all he's ever wanted to do is run.

Jon and I are very close because we have shared crucial

moments of each other's lives. And in 1993 when we sat down together along with Elsa and he decided that was the end of the line, I absolutely believed he would never run again. Because there comes a point when you have to weigh up your life, and to go through the pain of coming back from injury is an enormous sacrifice which requires that you put everything else on hold. Everyone was saying to him, 'Jon, stop please stop for your own sake. This is just crazy. You have had four or five operations. Just accept it.'

When Jon left Australia in 1993 he quickly established himself in the outside world, working first in advertising and then going into television, where he worked as a sports presenter and reporter. But Elsa always said, 'He'll run again. I can see it in his eyes. He is not going to let go.' And she was right. All he needed was a glimmer of hope, and when he got it in 1995, when he began to be able to train seriously again, he was back. So much so that he made the 1996 Olympics and ran close to his personal best in the subsequent meeting at Zurich. And so cruelly got a different injury – in his heel – after Atlanta.

To say Jon did not get the medals is of course wrong. He collected plenty in his early years, symbols of his great talent. But he never collected the medals he deserved. If Jon never runs again he will be left with a disappointment of not fulfilling the enormous potential that he had as an athlete. Fortunately I will never feel that disappointment but more than once in my career I have feared that I would never be able to say that.

In Jon's case, it has often been his love of athletics, and his love of training, which has been his downfall. Because he is an all-or-nothing person, like most successful people are, like Kriss is. You can argue that Jon probably trains a bit too much. He would argue not. And I think that fundamentally, he has a body that hasn't helped him.

We have had this discussion more than once. I've got the medals, but in my mind he is someone whom I see as the epitome of success. You are not really judged on your gold medals.

I know it's easy for me to say that because I've got my medals. But I know in the eyes of most people in the athletic world he is greatly admired. He's got the desire to reach his full potential and that's what keeps you going. It is like a flame inside you that burns brightly when things are going well and barely flickers when things are going badly. For him, it's been flickering for years, but he has never put it out. Others might have done it long since, but he can't bring himself to.

In the last twelve years I have seen athletes give up the struggle against injury for much less than he has put up with. It is such a cruel injustice that someone who had all the talent had all those injuries. One day you would like to think that he could see a reason for it all. I came back from adversity and was able to achieve again. That privilege has not been granted to him, but if there is any justice in the world, Jon will hopefully go on to fulfil his potential.

Jon is blessed with a character that allows him to appreciate life. He enjoys nature. Often when we were training together in America or Australia he would jump into the car on his own and drive off into the desert for twelve hours. And he'd come back and wax lyrical about some geological feature he had seen. He read Geography at Cambridge, and he just loves rocks and the landscape around him.

When we were in California in 1997 there was a comet that you couldn't see properly if you were in Los Angeles. So Jon got in the car at nine o'clock at night and returned eight hours later. He had gone out to spot this comet. When he reached the desert, it was cloudy. So he saw nothing. But when he arrived back early the next morning he wasn't put out at all. He accepted nature for what it was. And he went off the following night, did exactly the same thing, saw the comet that time and came back chuffed to bits. Happy. A guy who appreciates things, whose idea of a perfect holiday is hiking in the Himalayas – which I suppose you could argue is not conducive to an athletics career.

While I was out in Canberra, Kriss was trying to tell me I had to 'get out there' and 'get on with things' after my problems. I wrote then:

Kriss wrote me a long letter the other day all about having faith and having belief. It was meant well, and he is right to question my belief in myself. But he cannot understand how it feels to have a problem like mine or like Jon's. Faith is important but medical common sense is as well. I guess you need to balance the two and my scales have been heavily tipped towards the latter.

Athletics requires one to have no limitations. But a structurally weak body requires one to acknowledge one's limitations.

If you don't, you are simply going to break down. People like myself and Jon Ridgeon have that constant balancing act: you want to have no limitations, you want to think positive, you want to smash through those barriers, but at the back of your mind you always have to be careful that you don't break down. That is the constant battle that I have had throughout my career. And standing up and saying, 'Go on, do it, go and train harder' in some cases is just foolish. I have not had the luxury of being able to train really hard and get away with it. I've had to learn what I can and can't do, and even now I haven't completely mastered that.

On 23 February 1994, I wrote this:

I've moved on in leaps and bounds since October. My body still gives me problems but I can run with them. The left foot is much better due to the taping and the orthotics and the exercises.

My hip is still very sore but that's life. In January I confronted the reality that my hip will never be 100 per cent and I have a choice. It can stop me running or I can run with it. Only the clock can tell me if I can get better.

Jon Ridgeon was injured; Kriss had retired; I hadn't seen Mike Whittingham for six months. But I knew that if I was to win the European Championships later that year I really needed a group to be around. Fortunately Mike had arranged for me to go to France in April and train with Stephane Diagana, the French 400 metres hurdler.

I had had my first race back in Australia, a 400 metres relay in which, coincidentally, Darren Clark was making an appearance as part of his own attempt to come back from injury.

I was still very much aware of the dangers of becoming too wrapped up in athletics to the point where it became counter-productive. I wrote down something I had noted in a book called *The Pursuit of Excellence*:

> When you free yourself from dwelling on outside pressures and expectations, when you know that you will continue to be a valuable human being regardless of numerical outcomes, worry is less likely to intrude and disrupt your performance or your life.
>
> This is when your focus is free to flow naturally. Worry is one of the greatest inhibitors of skilled performance. If you can learn to view competition in a less worried way, or if you can find a way of focusing that is more absorbing than the worry, you will be well on the way to consistent performance at your optimum level.

I was starting to learn these ways of looking at my performance in 1994, but not really seeing it totally.

I went to France in April to work at the Institute of Sport, and Mike joined me out there. It was very strange having to grapple with my French, training in a new environment. The French don't really train like the English. They are very technical. We tend to train hard; they sort of ponce around. But it was nice to be with other athletes and to move on. Mike was acting as much as a friend as a coach now. Our relationship was evolving, and he was a great support for me during this period. He has always been very supportive during the bad times. Many coaches in similar situations fail to cope, but it is almost as if he is at his best during the bad times. He has always managed to keep pressures off me and allowed me to pursue my running.

I wrote:

The season is nearly here, and although I feel fast I have not done the speed endurance that I'm used to doing at this stage. Sometimes I feel that I'm just not meant to be hanging on here. The last year has been so hard. I've made decisions and sacrifices and I've done well, but I'm not the same physical or mental athlete that I used to be.

I've really had to dig deep to give myself a chance. I can't pretend that everything's great. This year will be like no other – my mental strength will be the only thing that will get me through it. Although physically it just isn't there any more, I am still fast, and if I give myself a chance mentally I could surprise myself.

I was very introspective at this time. I was wondering what it was that kept me hanging on to athletics:

Is it money, is it fame, is it self-worth, laziness, fear of losing my identity? I don't really know. Sometimes I like to step away from it all and see it for what it is, just a sport. But then I think of Jon Ridgeon and Derek Redmond and I know that as long as I have a chance I must persevere.

When it comes down to it, what has always kept me going is the appreciation of the talent I was given. I know I can do so much if I can just be healthy, and there are other athletes out there who don't ever get the chance. Either because they don't have the talent I have, or because their injuries are even worse. Derek Redmond, I believe, was probably the most talented 400 metres runner Britain has ever seen. Others would argue it's

186

Planning the season ahead with Mike Whittingham.

With Elsa.

With Sven Nylander in California 1995 – always in step with each other.

(Above) Receiving my honorary degree from Southampton University. How ironic, don't you think?

(Right) An expression that shows how focused and how determined I was to win the Olympic trials in 1996.

(Below) Winning the Olympic trials in 1996.

In full flight in the 1996 Olympic 400 metres final.

With Iwan Thomas, Mark Richardson and Jamie Baulch and our Olympic silver medals for the 4x400 metres in 1996.

On the medal rostrum in Atlanta with Michael Johnson and Davis Kamoga – so happy, so proud, so complete.

Another tough photo shoot for Reebok.

That celebration dinner with the boys – cheers Du'Aine.

Tuesday night is poker night in California – Lee, Sven, Brad, Ian, Mark and Paul.

With Joe Picken after Atlanta. He'd waited a long time to open his bottle of scotch.

Happiness is a sunny day with guitar in hand.

Completing my journey.

me, or Iwan Thomas, or whoever. But in my opinion it was Derek. And he didn't win at the major level because of injury.

David Grindley was phenomenal in 1993, but he got injured just before the World Championships and he has never been the same athlete again. When I look at these people I know that, yes, I've got problems, but if I just get past them I can still be very good. I have come through partly because I have had good people around me, and I have not been scared to put my hand in my pocket to help sort problems out. But I guess I do have the ability to keep going once I've made a decision. You can read all the self-improvement books in the world, but how many people would have arranged to go to Australia for six months? How many people would have come back and then gone to France? How many people would have just kept going?

14

BETTER AND BETTER

I entered the 1994 season knowing there was one main question to be answered. The AAA Championships on 10 June offered automatic selection for the European Championships to the first past the post. Was I up to it?

While I was in France I had discussed whether I should commit myself to running in the AAA, and the suggestion from my fellow athletes was that I would be much better delaying to give myself more time to show my form. But I said to Mike, 'If I don't race there, then where would I go?' The European Championships took place relatively early in the season, and there were very few other suitable warm-up opportunities on the circuit. I decided I should do it. My first 400 metres in a year and a half was going to be at the AAA Championships. I thought maybe I only had one or two good races in me that year, but if I got into an environment where I was going to have to rise to the occasion, who knew what might happen?

In my diary I wrote:

The season begins in one week. I know I'm in good enough shape to run 45.5sec at the AAA, and that will be good enough to win it because other people are struggling. It's fear of the unknown that's so frustrating. It's been a year since my last 400 and the memory is not a good one.

Training has been very sparse above 300 metres, but I am running fast and mentally I'm ready to dig deep and tap into my resources of natural talent. This is the second time in my career that I've made a comeback; maybe it is a third comeback if last year is to be seen as a failure to recover from my hip operation.

It's a lot harder than my task in 1990 due to the loss of confidence during the illness and the fact that I achieved so much in 1991. And money has become a factor again. The home is paid off now, but the taxman is calling . . .

So I went to the AAA Championships, which were held that year at the Don Valley stadium in Sheffield – and won in 44.94sec. I was shuddering with the effort as I crossed the line, but it was a tremendous feeling. Behind me, in a time of 45.36sec, was Britain's European indoor champion, Du'Aine Ladejo. 'I didn't like the loss, but I loved the race,' Ladejo said afterwards. 'I take my hat off to him.' It was a gracious response from a man who, as I was to learn, could not always be relied upon to behave with dignity.

Later I wrote:

After a year of trouble I have surpassed my expectations. This was my watershed, a test of how I really am. It was so natural and so easy. I'm excited and eagerly anticipating the next race. My training has been different but it just proves there are many ways to reach the top. It proved that, to quote David Coleman when he was commentating on the race, 'When he's healthy, he's so good.'

Ian Botham has said, 'Form comes and goes, but talent is always there.' I think I've just proven that. I'm so happy and proud of myself. I'm so pleased for Mike, whose faith has been rewarded. Many people thought my illness was in my head, but I knew I was ill and that when healthy my confidence would return. I've proved this and will go from strength to strength.

Four weeks ago I was sitting in a café in Paris, feeling terrible and lacking self-confidence. One race has changed my whole being. It's amazing how athletics does this. I'm trying to enjoy this moment. If I can't enjoy the good times, then all the bad times have meant nothing.

I have received more publicity from this one performance than ever before. It's the human story that people can relate to . . . I will enjoy this season and be relaxed about it.

After the Olympics of 1992 I had signed a two-year contract with Reebok, which was quite a bold step for them as I was injured at the time, but they wanted someone who was a name in Britain. You don't like to sign contracts when you are injured, but Reebok stood by me in '93. They took a risk, and I was very pleased for them when I came through the following year. The gamble paid off for them even more, of course, two years later in Atlanta.

On 7 July, while sitting opposite Edinburgh Castle on the eve of running a 200 metres at Meadowbank, I wrote:

I'm a third of the way through the season, I ran 45.08 in the European Cup and 45.30 at Gateshead. I've been feeling a bit tired recently – I trained three days in a row this week and my legs don't like it. I've argued with Mike about this.

What was happening was that I was falling back into my old ways – 'I'm back running now, so Mike can tell me what to do.' Our relationship was starting to get tested, and it was to get tested even more the following year. But at the time, the 1994 European Championships were looming ahead of me.

As the Championships drew closer, Du'Aine Ladejo was the only other person who was showing any form. We had given a joint press conference for the AAA Championships, and he clearly revelled in all the attention. It was there that someone suggested that we be pictured back to back with pistols. I suppose that was where the big Ladejo–Black rivalry was born, although I never saw Ladejo in the same light as David Grindley or Derek Redmond at that time. Du'Aine had won the European indoor title earlier in 1994. But at 400 metres, indoor athletics doesn't mean a thing, because the best guys don't run indoors. Simple as that.

There was a long build-up for the Championships, and I was hanging on to my form with increasing difficulty because I hadn't had the background of training I would normally have had. But Du'Aine was getting stronger and stronger. He hadn't broken 45 seconds – but he was the man in form, and he'd beaten me a few times. There was a lot of publicity surrounding us, and he was a very good self-publicist. He was saying things like, 'If Roger doesn't win this race it will be the end of his career. But if I don't win it doesn't really matter because I've got another ten years ahead of me.' I remember thinking, 'Welcome to the unpredictable world of athletics, my friend.'

In Frankfurt on my way to Helsinki for the Championships I wrote:

How ironic it is that the first person I see as I enter the airport lounge is Thomas Schoenlebe. We are still both here. His days appear to be over but you never know with him. Old adversaries going for three golds and three silvers? Who knows . . .

I was tired going into the Championships, but basically Du'Aine ran a better race and he beat me. We were level going into the finishing straight, but he pulled away to win in 45.09sec – not particularly fast, but too fast for me on the day as I recorded 45.20. It was only the second time in my career that I had set a championship goal and come second. I had really wanted to win it – to win the European three times would have been staggering. But I didn't and I had no excuses.

After the race I squatted down feeling pretty dejected. I

walked off the track and I knew the press were waiting for me, but I couldn't speak to anyone for a while. I seem to remember spending a very long time undoing my shoes. I felt I had to get outside the stadium, so Mike and I wandered a little beyond the entrance – and I just burst into floods of tears. At that moment, my experiences of the last year and a half caught up with me, and I just let out all the emotion. Many people expected me to be devastated. Because it's one thing coming second, but coming second to another Briton who you know deep down you are better than, isn't easy. I myself was expecting to be devastated, and I started to wonder whether Du'Aine was right in what he had said before the Championships about me not coming back if I didn't win this race, but then Mike and I looked at each other, and I just stopped crying and realized, 'It's not as bad as I thought it would be.' I looked around and I thought, 'Oh well . . .'

I had been beaten on the day by a guy who ran a better race. But I thought, 'European silver medal after glandular fever . . . haven't really prepared for this . . . would like to have won it, didn't have it in my legs . . . not a bad achievement really.' I learned then that you've got to recognize when you've achieved something. Winning it would have been magnificent, but I'd still achieved by being there. And I remember thinking to myself with Du'Aine in mind, 'If I'm healthy, you'll never beat me again.' And he never has done. And he never will.

We finished up by winning the 4x400, so I walked away from the European Championships feeling very positive, even though I was subsequently too tired to do the Commonwealth Games. When I had had a little time to reflect on the season, I wrote:

I haven't sat down to write about my feelings since Helsinki. My immediate feelings were of disappointment at not retaining my title, but ten minutes after shedding a few tears I was able to face it and be proud of what I'd done.

I had tried too hard to win off the bend. But once it was over there was a sense of relief at feeling it didn't change my life. The relay win was a bonus and I came away from Helsinki with much to be thankful for.

That year marked the beginning of a strange relationship with Du'Aine Ladejo. Two years later he annoyed me, and all the other 400 metres runners, with his behaviour at the Olympic trials in Birmingham. Most of my compatriot 400 metres runners were desperate for me to win that race – not so much for me, but so that he wouldn't win it. The sport often cries out for personalities, and Du'Aine Ladejo is certainly a personality, but I think he is a very flawed one. That win in Helsinki was his big moment of triumph, and he exploited it for all it was worth. Fair enough. He made the most of one race, one win. He got more out of that race than many of us get out of a whole season. He went on to be a thorn in my side for some time afterwards.

A couple of months after Helsinki, Mike Whittingham secured me a deal with the car firm Mazda, and Du'Aine questioned the decision, suggesting that it should have gone to him as the European champion. There was also an implication that the fact that he was a black athlete and I was white had had something to do with it. Of course I'll never know what it's like to be black, but if there's one thing I take umbrage with, it's the suggestion that there is an edge between myself and black people.

Elsa got very upset about it: 'Sometimes you've got to stop being so understanding and you've got to put your foot down. He is out of order. Does he not realize what you have achieved? You can't turn round everything just because he beat you in one race.' In the end I was so angry too that I had to pick up the phone. Du'Aine maintained he had not meant his comments to be interpreted in that light, but it was an incident I could not forget.

One of the greatest compliments I ever had was when Linford Christie called me 'Roger the Nigger'. It was partly a joke, because my name was Black, but it was also a term of endearment. The colour of someone's skin has simply never been a factor for me in any relationship. If it was, I would have had to change my girlfriend and many of my friends. I resent the assumption which some people may have that I have become rich on the back of being a white athlete. When I have been offered extra money for being a white competitor – and it has happened – I have refused on principle.

People will say, 'Yeah, you're white. It makes a difference.' To me it doesn't. I'm an athlete, and to me it doesn't matter who I'm running against. But to some people in the outside world it's a far bigger issue. I recall stepping into a hotel lift in Monaco in 1997 and discovering I was sharing it with Primo Nebiolo, the president of the International Amateur Athletic Federation, who took the opportunity to tell me that he was my greatest admirer. 'I watch your career a long time. I really admire you.' Then he added with a little chuckle, 'You're the only white 400 metres runner in the final and your name is . . . Black.' Primo, no doubt, thought he'd cracked an original joke. I chuckled along with him out of politeness even though I'd heard the same thing numerous times before.

The fact that for a long while I have been a white man in an event dominated by black people is something of which I am often reminded. People have come up to me since 1996 and asked, 'Did you realize you were the only white guy to win a medal in any of the Olympic sprints, 100, 200 or 400?' It hadn't even occurred to me. Many people do see things that way, though. In 1991, at a joint press conference with Michael Johnson before we ran against each other in Bratislava, the whole discussion seemed to turn on the fact that I was white and he was black.

I don't like to think about it, but to a lot of people I'm the white hope. I was in Milan once when a woman came up to me and said, 'You're my favourite athlete. Because you run well. But you run well against all those *savages*.' When you come up against that kind of attitude, it is almost a waste of breath arguing, although I do.

It was a topic Des Lynam brought up in conversation with

myself and Linford Christie when we were off air while working with the BBC during the 1997 World Championships.

Des was asking us why there weren't any white sprinters. Linford said it was because white people just felt they weren't good enough; this idea that black people are physically faster was, in his opinion, rubbish, though it is automatically assumed as true by many people. And I agreed. I know that's one of the reasons why I've done so well – because I've never seen it as black and white. This physical excuse is a bit of a cop-out. For instance, the three fastest British 400 metres runners of all time are white: myself, Iwan and David Grindley. The 400 metres counts as a sprint.

When I was seventeen I ran in a race where I was the only white runner, and everyone was saying, 'Wow – the white guy is going to win!' I never thought of it like that. A lot of young kids, however, do assume that black people are better at sport. There's that wonderful moment in the film *Soul Man*, where the man takes these pills to become black. And when they pick the basketball team, he automatically becomes the No. 1 pick. It doesn't necessarily mean he can play, though. I was reminded of the expression 'never judge a book by it's cover' while training with Kriss Akabusi, Derek Redmond and Phil Brown one day in California in 1987. We were striding down the track together, preparing for a session. As usual Daley Thompson was close by and locked in conversation with a man-mountain called Cedric, a retired professional American footballer, full of testosterone and attitude.

'Hey,' he said to Daley, 'who are those guys?'

'That's the British 4x400 metres relay squad,' Daley replied.

'Yeah, I can see that, man. They look good. Real good.' Cedric then paused to enquire, 'But who's the white boy?'

And Daley replied with a grin, 'He's the fastest of them all!'

The year after the European Championships turned out to be full of frustration for me. I trained well in the winter, but as the 1995 season came on I began to get sharp pains in the back of my left knee, especially when I was sprinting. It didn't stop me racing, but I was getting a lot of treatment, and it was a case yet again of my mind being taken up by a physical problem when I raced. Somehow I managed to equal my personal best of 44.59sec that year in Lausanne. I don't know how I did it, I was in absolute agony after the race. My hip and left foot would have seized up but for the efforts of my sports therapist Mark Zambada.

That was the pattern for the whole year. And before I even ran a step at that year's World Championships I knew I had a problem. I got to the final but I was in real discomfort and came seventh. My focus was on the Olympics, which were a year away. But I knew I couldn't go to them with my knee in that state.

While I was struggling, however, 1995 turned out to be an astonishing year for another British athlete – Jonathan Edwards – who made a sudden rise to being the world's No. 1 triple jumper which was all the more astonishing given that only six months earlier he had been suffering from the same Epstein-Barr virus I had had in 1993. During his illness, Jonathan had given me a call to ask my advice about getting back to fitness. He was very distressed and concerned. There was a chill of recognition for me when I heard the tiredness and detachment in the voice, and became aware of his lack of confidence. You can always hear that doubt in an athlete. And I knew all about it . . .

I told him a few things about nutrition and acupuncture. I recall passing on something I was told once by one of my friends when I was despairing of getting back into action because of my broken foot. He had simply said, 'Well, it's not going to be broken for ever.' It may sound obvious, but there is an important truth in that. One day you'll be better, you just don't know when it'll be. I told Jonathan he had to have patience, which may be easier said than done. But I had done it myself, and he knew that, so I hope it was of some help to him. The incredible thing was that he went out the following year and took the triple jump into completely different territory. His view on that in retrospect was that maybe his body had needed the enforced rest. But there was no doubt that he was surprised by what he achieved in 1995 – world records, a world title – because it was the last thing he had been expecting in the circumstances. I don't think he ever really saw himself as a world record holder. Obviously I felt particularly pleased that he had come back from adversity to do all that.

It was hardly surprising that Jonathan should be voted Athlete of the Year for 1995. I was there to see him receive his award at the British Athletics writers' dinner, which came just before I was about to undergo the operation on the knee which had caused me to have such a disappointing season. I recalled the time in 1986 when I had stood where Jonathan was, and I simply couldn't imagine standing there again. But a year later, after the Olympics, I was.

Jonathan gave his speech, and in typical fashion he was play-ing his achievements down. He said he felt very proud to be standing there, but he just wanted to give a special message to other athletes in the room to persevere with their problems because their time would come and they deserved good luck as much as he did. And as he said that he appeared to glance towards me, and I thought to myself, 'Did he look over at me then or not?' Jonathan subsequently told me that he was think-ing of me, among others, at that point in his speech. I had tried to help him and now he was trying to help me. It really was a message of 'Hang in there.'

I have always got on well with Jonathan. He's got a wife and two children, is a devout Christian, and one of the nicest people you could meet. We have often roomed together at champ-ionships because we both love to play chess. He is in many ways an anomaly. He doesn't look like an athlete. There is this thin, almost puny figure who looks more like an academic than an athlete. Of course that is what he is, because he was a physics graduate from Durham University who worked in a genetics laboratory before taking up the sport full time.

You see him up against these huge, motivated hulks from Cuba and America – and he's the world record holder and world champion. But underneath that nice exterior there must be a man with a huge need. And I think since 1995 Jonathan has had a conflict in himself as to what that need is, and at the time of writing he is having to re-assess that. It is a problem that is especially acute for someone who achieves the dramatic success he did. Where do you go from there?

In 1996 he was expected to win at the Olympics and was beaten to the gold medal by Kenny Harrison, but I think he was almost relieved to win the silver medal, because psychologically he was all over the place in that year as he was still trying to come to terms with being world record holder and world champion. Remember, this had happened to a man who was devoted to his wife and family and to the Lord. And suddenly he found himself a hugely famous and wealthy world record holder. Many people would have loved it, would have relished it. For Jonathan I think it caused a lot of deep conflicts in his life. He could not find peace within himself.

You can sense when an athlete is at one with himself. Before the Barcelona Olympics of 1992, I was training in Monte Carlo along with a number of other British athletes, and at one point I was in a hotel room with a group including Linford Christie. I didn't know him particularly well at the time, and he was just sitting on a bed signing autographs. But there was something about him, about his manner, which made me think, 'He is going to be the Olympic champion.' He knew. You could feel it. You can tell when somebody is on a roll, when they are physically and mentally ready. People felt the same thing about me in 1996. But I did not feel that with Jonathan in that year.

It was a different story in 1997. I roomed with Jonathan at the Athens World Championships that year, where he was beaten by Yoelvis Quesada of Cuba. I was fully aware of how bitterly disappointed he was by that and I had to try to help him through it. There was no sense of relief that time in winning the silver medal. He was upset, because he had rediscovered his hunger for the event and had really felt he could win it. When we returned to the room following his defeat he was absolutely devastated. Completely disillusioned. He was just empty. I remember him looking at the medal in front of him and saying, 'It means nothing.' That's the pressure of being a world record holder. It's not a world I have been in.

The position any athlete wants to be in is a zone of absolute oneness with himself, both physically and mentally. To be the best in the world, physical and mental elements have to be side by side. If the physical side is 100 per cent and the mental is 50 per cent you can get away with it if you are very good. If the physical is not 90–100 per cent then you usually cannot get away with it, although there have been exceptional performances achieved by some athletes over the years despite the fact that their bodies have been in bad shape. The concept of 'mind over matter' is one that all athletes have to remind themselves of during both training and competition. My trainer Joe Picken would always remind me of this during long hard weight sessions on cold winter nights. 'Mind over matter, Roger,' he would shout, 'and remember I don't mind and you don't matter!'

I have no doubt that Jonathan Edwards will go on to win many things, because he is a truly great athlete. But all people tend to see is athletes going out there to perform – they don't see what's underneath the surface and what we are all having to deal with internally. I am not a devout Christian, but I wonder about the questions he asks of himself at such times of disappointment.

I think Jonathan needs athletics infinitely more than he allows himself to admit. Or is allowed to admit because of his Christian faith. The problem for someone like him is that deep down they know how much they need success, but they are not necessarily able to admit it to themselves. You can compete for many reasons – whether it is for yourself, for money, for fame or for the Lord. But the most important thing is that when you stand up there you know why you need to do it. And only you know the true answer to that question. And if you are not comfortable with why you need to do it, it will show in your persona off the track and your performance on the track. I think that Jonathan is a lot more driven than he admits.

He has maintained his business connection with Andy Norman following the latter's removal as promotions officer of the British Athletic Federation in the wake of a scandal in which a coroner's jury concluded Norman had been a 'contributory factor' in the suicide of the *Sunday Times* athletics correspondent Cliff Temple, whom he had accused of sexually harassing female athletes. But there has never been any question that Andy Norman is a man who can deliver as an agent and promoter. One may not agree with his methods, but his results speak for themselves.

One thing I realized after the 1995 World Championships was that my relationship with Mike Whittingham had changed. There had come a point during the season when I was doing things I didn't really want to be doing and we weren't communicating as well as we should have done. And after the World Championships in Gothenburg, with the Olympics less than twelve months away, I was sitting there with a sore knee, feeling that if I kept things as they were I couldn't be sure they were going to get any better. They were just going to be good. And I hadn't come this far just to be good.

The truth was, I felt the straight coach–athlete relationship between Mike and myself had run its course. I needed something else, but what was it? What could I do? Mike had always told me that a coach has done a great job when the athlete becomes empowered, and by that token, he had done a great job. It was a very, very hard decision because Mike is someone I value as a great friend and will do for the rest of my life, somebody whom I can trust implicitly and who has always had my well-being at heart. What made things even more difficult was the fact that I wanted Mike to remain as my business manager and still be involved, in some way, in my training preparation.

What had happened between Mike Smith and me back in 1989 had to happen. If it hadn't, I would probably not have continued running into my thirties. But I went through the same thing with Mike Whittingham to a lesser degree.

If you are going to run from 1985 to 1998 you are going to have to evolve as a person. I didn't see it clearly then, but the split with Mike Smith was the beginning of me taking control of my destiny, and the shift in the relationship between myself and Mike Whittingham was another element of that process. I hated upsetting Mike, but in athletics you've got to do what's right for you.

Now the opinion of most people is that the best 400 metres coach in the world is John Smith, who works out of California. He had been a world record holder for the 440 yards, and had trained a number of world-class athletes including the previous two Olympic champions at 400 metres, Steve Lewis and Quincy Watts, as well as Kevin Young, who won the 1992 Olympic 400 metres hurdles in a world record, and even John Regis, who had joined his group for work over 200 metres.

And I thought, 'Maybe I should just go and join John Smith.' John Regis had, to good effect. He must be doing something right. Many people were very suspicious of his methods, but that's just the same old thing of people jumping to conclusions. I felt that it would be a really significant step for me. I was saying 'I want to do this right. I want to train with the best coach in the world.'

I didn't have a group of athletes I could work with. I was feeling isolated really. I spoke to Mike about it, and he was obviously upset. But he understood that he had done his job, he had empowered me to make my decision, and he was not going to stand in my way – nor would it affect either our friendship or our business relationship.

So I made contact with John Smith and met him when he was next in London. I came away feeling confident that I would be under his guidance in Olympic year. From then onwards, I had to go through his lawyers, which I found a little bit strange.

It didn't feel quite right, to be honest. Then it transpired that John wanted to manage me as well as coach me. I said that was just not feasible, because I had absolutely no wish to drop Mike from that role. He had built up a business in the previous five years, and I was his major client. I pointed out that John didn't manage John Regis or Tony Jarrett when they joined his group. Nor does he manage another of his top athletes, Marie-Jose Perec, who was then world 400 metres champion. As Marie-Jose is a close friend of Elsa's, I had spoken to her about the move and she thought it would be a good idea.

I was given the impression that they understood my position and had come to terms with it. I was all set to go, and I had spoken to John Regis, telling him I was going out. Then I got a phone call from John Smith's lawyer saying 'Sorry, no go.' I don't really understand the reasons. Whether it was because I was a Reebok athlete and he was contracted with Nike – that was a reason they gave. Maybe he didn't really believe I was worth taking on. Whatever, it was a no.

So there I was in a situation where I couldn't go back to Mike because that would have meant the reasons for leaving him had been false. I sat on a sofa in my flat after taking the phone call – I was alone at the time – and thought, 'What the hell do you do now? You're really on your own now.' And then I asked myself, 'Who are the people apart from Mike that I speak to about my athletics?' There were obviously two – one was Kriss Akabusi and the other was David Jenkins.

I phoned Kriss. 'What do you think? Would you be interested in being involved?' I asked.

'Yeah, yeah, I could come and train with you. I could be there,' he said.

'Let's get real here. Would you have the time?' Kriss was so busy then with his television career, presenting *Record Breakers* and other programmes, or prancing around on stage in pantomime, that there was no way he could spare the necessary time. Kriss was just my friend, someone I could bounce ideas off. He was never going to be my coach.

Then I phoned Jenks in America and explained, 'I'm faced with this situation, Jenks. And I'm really turning to you now and saying, you've always been involved as far as being a voice on the end of the phone, but it's never been real involvement. It's been detached and opinionated. But what do you think? Would you be prepared to have a greater and more official involvement with me?'

He thought long and hard about that and his initial reaction was 'No.' Because he was so busy – he had built a flourishing business selling protein powder by then – and he felt that he couldn't be a coach as well. I wasn't asking him to be a coach, though. We talked for a long time, and again the following day. In the end, he asked, 'What are you after?'

'Well, I just want something different. I'm nearly there, but I just want a different approach. It's Olympic year, and I want to get it absolutely right.'

So he agreed he would help. Once I went to California for my warm weather training, he would do some research for me and put together some ideas. But he was very scared of me thinking that I wanted him to be there at training sessions because he knew he wouldn't be able to do that. He told mutual friends in America that he was really not sure whether I was asking him to do too much.

For all that, I was in control of my destiny at that point. Through his decision, John Smith had forced me to take full responsibility for myself. It was as if I grew up properly at that moment. As I looked around it was quite clear that if I wanted help there were people who could provide me with it. I could have the almost perfect set-up. Mike Whittingham, who is second to none at aerobic/anaerobic preparation, would ideally help me with my winter preparation, providing he was willing to have me back on that basis. I started work with a friend of mine, Tony Lester, who has a group of sprinters near my home in Guildford, and I asked him to look after my sprinting. I'd never really focused specifically on the technical aspect of sprinting – I was a floater, not necessarily a sprinter. But I realized that here was a new way in which I could improve my overall performance. And I was asking Jenks to oversee the whole Californian thing, particularly the mental side. I could tap into three people who were all hugely capable in their particular fields. I was compartmentalizing my requirements.

Mike was great about it. It was difficult for him to be told a few weeks earlier that I would be going off to train with someone else in America, because he had always believed that if I stayed healthy I was going to run well. But Mike being the person he is said he would still help me even though I had changed my plans once again. Tony did a very good job. And Jenks and I were on the phone two or three times a week. He was great, because he had no input into what I did during the winter, he just said, 'Mike knows what he's doing. Leave it to him, and when you get to California we'll take over the next phase.'

After the Tokyo World Championships of 1991, which had raised my profile and Kriss's enormously, it was quite clear that we needed the services of a manager. Mike had been doing bits and pieces for us, and made the decision to leave his job running a council leisure services department to go full-time with us. It was a bit of a risk for him, because you become dependent on the health of your athletes. If your athletes don't run, you don't earn. But one thing Mike has always striven to do is put athletics before commercial considerations. It's paid off, because I have come back and done well. He has been my manager ever since, but more importantly my friend. On the face of it, managing Roger Black sounds easy, but that does not take into account the times when I have been either ill or injured, and not making any money.

I think Mike's honesty is a threat to a lot of people, particularly in the cut-throat world of athletics, where often it is those who aren't quite so honest who are perceived to have got things done. Mike has always had an underlying caring for athletics and over the years has done a great deal of consultative work for the British Athletic Federation which has taken up much of his time and effort. He is multilingual, which has been very useful to him in getting to know almost everybody on the circuit. You'll always find Mike propping up the bar with some Russian coach or French sprinter. As a coach, what he has managed to do is what most people in that position cannot – he has taken an athlete and eventually 'let him go'. Most coaches hate to do that, because often the coach's identity comes from his athlete.

Most coaches like to be there when their athletes are warming up before a race, because they often think that the athletes need them to be there. In my case, I didn't really need someone to be there with me. But it was an interesting side of my character, that what I wanted most was not to upset anybody. I wasn't grown up enough to say, 'Mike, I appreciate your intentions, but I really don't want you here right now.' Not because he wasn't important to me, but because this was me, this was where I was on my own. You looked around, and Linford Christie's coach Ron Roddan would be with him, and Derek Redmond's coach Tony Hadley would be with him. Clearly within the circle of coaches, the feeling was that to be a great coach you had to be with your athlete until the very last minute.

In 1991 Mike felt, in retrospect, that I had not been as composed and together as I seemed before the World Championship final. I was confident enough beforehand that I could win, and the comment that I made to him saying that it wouldn't come to a dip finish eventually turned out to be wrong. The issue, however, is that I shouldn't have been having that conversation at that point anyway. I didn't need to have that conversation with anyone except myself.

At the 1996 Olympics I had got to the point where I would turn up to the warm-up track and I wouldn't be with the British. I would go over to find my own little corner, which more often than not would be near where the Jamaicans gathered – perhaps I wanted to pick up a bit of their relaxed approach. I would tell Richard Simmons, the national coach, whose job it was to accompany me to the warm-up area in

Atlanta, 'Look, please don't come and stand with me, I don't want to see you. Just tell me when it's time to go.' And to his credit, he was great about it, even though he might have wondered, 'What am I supposed to be doing here, then?' He was a great help to me precisely because he didn't distract me by getting involved. Often that's the secret – let someone be by themselves. Certainly the difference in my requirements in 1991 and 1996 showed how far I had come as a confident athlete.

There was never a total split with Mike, just a dilution of his input. I think many coaches would have said, 'Well, if that's the way you feel, forget it. It's me or nothing, buddy.' That was the situation I had found myself in with Mike Smith, who wasn't prepared to let me move on. But Mike Whittingham merely said, 'I guess I've done a good job, because you are now empowered. You wouldn't have made this decision otherwise. Unfortunately in my business, if you do a good job you actually put yourself out of a job.' I think that magnanimity is the mark of the man.

Now if I have a problem, I will talk to Mike Whittingham, I will talk to David Jenkins, I will talk to Tony Lester. But the fourth person, and the one who ultimately makes the decisions, is me. It took ten years to get to that point. The day I did, I was ready to win an Olympic silver medal.

All my new arrangements felt right, and I had a fresh lease of life. But I still had a problem with my left knee. I needed an opinion, and it had to be a good one. I went to see a specialist in London who felt that there wasn't a lot he could do. He didn't want to operate. But then I was very lucky, because Sally Gunnell told me about a Swiss doctor called Roland Biedert who had done a good job of mending her damaged Achilles tendon. Coincidentally, the doctor was in Britain with the Swiss football team as part of their preparations for the following year's Euro 96 competition. I went to see him in London, and he took one look at my knee and said, 'You need to have a cartilage operation.'

So I jumped on a plane and went to his clinic in Switzerland,

and he performed the operation on 18 December 1995. And one thing I do know – if things had worked out with John Smith's group, I probably would have gone straight to America without having my knee operated on. Or I would have gone over and my knee would have started playing up and I would have had to have the operation closer to the Olympics, which would almost certainly have ruined my chances.

Biedert removed some torn cartilage from my knee, but he did it under an epidural, which I found somewhat bizarre. He doesn't like putting athletes under anaesthetic, so I was awake during the whole operation and was talking to him and watching it on video. Having an epidural numbs you from the waist downwards, which led to one of the most unpleasant experiences of my life about six hours later. I was sitting in the hospital bed, and my bladder was painfully full, but I was unable to relieve myself. Couldn't pee. So I had to call the nurse – and the catheter had to go in . . . Putting a catheter in is not too painful. But taking it out again . . . A few hours later, when my senses were back to normal, I had pain I'll never forget. When I had to have my right knee done the following year, I made sure I was totally empty before I went to the operating table!

The rehabilitation time was about eight weeks. A lot of people think you go in and out on these operations, but Biedert is someone who says 'stay on crutches for three weeks, and don't start pushing it for seven to eight weeks.' Which is very wise. But it meant I was looking at being on crutches in January and being out of action in February. Not the best way to prepare for the Olympic Games which were to take place in July.

I'd done a lot of aerobic work with Mike up to that point in December, so I was phenomenally fit, and I was able to maintain that by running in water. I was also having intensive physiotherapy. I was able to start jogging at the beginning of February, and I carried on the process when I got to California. The operation was a total success. I have never had problems with that knee since.

So I was able to sit down with Jenks, and we talked for hours and hours about what I wanted to achieve and how I was going to do it. We agreed that the emphasis in training should be on my speed but my aerobic capacity must not be neglected. It wasn't a huge shift, but it did mean my load was not so hard as in the days with Mike Smith, and maybe not in the days of Mike Whittingham either.

Jenks and I would meet up every two weeks. He watched me run just once. He didn't need to see me run, it wasn't about that. Of course you could say, 'That's all very well but it was your knee operation which made you healthy. That was what made you run fast.' And there was some truth in that. For the first time since 1986, I came into a season with not an ache in my body. After my knee operation nothing hurt. Mark Zambada was working on my hip and foot, keeping things at bay, and I no longer felt any effects of the glandular fever.

An athlete without a single ache or pain is a powerful proposition. You turn up for training and it's a case of 'Great, let's run.' You're lining up for the race, and it's 'Great, let's run.' I hadn't had that feeling for ten years. And I squeezed it for everything I could. I appreciated it. I also believed deep inside me that there had been a reason for all my ups and downs. I felt I had been held back for this year. I could feel the momentum.

There was a wonderful bonus for me when Jon Ridgeon, who had fought a long battle to regain fitness, rejoined our training group. For him to have made it back to the Olympic Games – his subsequent passage through the Olympic trials was the formality everyone expected – was an incredible achievement. Sven Nylander was there too, preparing for the 400 metres hurdles. We were playing poker. The Californian life was as sweet as ever.

During that time I ran two races in America. One was in the Olympic stadium, when I recorded 44.81sec, and the other was in Eugene, where I did 44.77. Two fast races to open up a season – obviously I was in shape. But more importantly I knew exactly what I was doing during the races, I knew exactly where I was in the race. I was at one with the distance.

208

When I returned to England I was ready. The big talk was of the Olympic trials, because the policy had been changed and now the first two past the post would get automatic places, a policy which had been instituted in consultation with the athletes. There were three individual places at stake, which meant that two good people were going to miss out, because apart from myself, the others in contention were Iwan Thomas, Jamie Baulch, Mark Richardson and Du'Aine Ladejo – all capable of running 44.5 on the day. Ladejo had the air of a man who thought he had the race in the bag. I was quietly very confident.

It was a remarkable evening, because it was a packed house at the Alexander Stadium in Birmingham – the crowd were crazy. And there was so much expectation involved in that race, there was so much anticipation. Anyone could win it, and someone was going to miss out. And it really mattered because it was the Olympic trials.

I never once thought of any of the other runners. I didn't know what lanes they were in, I didn't think about how they were running, I didn't watch them in the semi-final. I was just programmed to focus on myself.

I felt totally in control, and I knew that whatever happened, they were going to have to react to me, I was not going to react to them. I was supremely confident and very calm. In earlier years I would have been very nervous, thinking, 'Oh gosh, here we go . . .' But not this time. I was going to do what I was going to do.

And as I crossed the line, in 44.39sec, the expression on my face wasn't utter joy, it was an expression of the real, raw determination that is deep inside me and only comes out now and again. I was back. I had broken the British record. I thought, 'Whatever happens after this day, remember it, because it is special.' I hadn't held the British record since 1986. Now, ten years later, I had broken it again in Britain in a high-pressure environment and I was going to the Olympic Games.

I remembered sitting in a jacuzzi in California three months earlier with Jon and Sven and the European 200 metres champion Geir Moen. I was in fabulous shape, I was training better than all of them, and they all knew it. And the funny thing was, all three of them said, 'We know we're going to the Olympics, but you don't.' Sven and Geir were pre-selected while Jon had no competition at 400 metres hurdles. The one person in the jacuzzi who couldn't guarantee a place at the Olympics was the person who was running better than anyone else. That played on my mind for much of the time. If I had made one mistake I would have missed out on a final Olympic opportunity in Atlanta. I couldn't have lived with that.

After doing a lap of honour I found out that Ladejo had come second and Iwan third, which meant that Mark Richardson and Jamie Baulch had missed out on individual places. Mark wasn't a close personal friend of mine at that point – he became one later and now trains with me. He had been No. 1 in Britain the previous year, but a week or so before the trials he got food poisoning.

It was important to me to speak to Mark, because I had been where he was. And he was devastated – you could see it written all over his face. But he showed his character two weeks later when he ran a personal best in Lausanne. And in my opinion he, along with Iwan, has all the attributes to take the 400 metres to another level when I retire. He subsequently said that what he saw me do that day and the way I was made him want to come and train with me. Because he realized then that there was a hell of a lot more to this business than just training.

After that race came the infamous press conference. We sat in a room full of press and television people because it was such a high-profile race. The first question to me was, 'Roger, congratulations, how do you feel?' I said that obviously the moment was very important to me, not just because I had got to the Olympics, but because I hadn't held the British record for ten years, and to regain it after all my ups and downs and struggles made me so happy, and so proud. Du'Aine was sitting next to me, with Iwan on his other side. After saying my bit, I congratulated Du'Aine for coming second because he had produced a fabulous run and a personal best of 44.66. Before the race, I didn't think he'd come in the top three. And I congratulated Iwan, who had almost certainly done enough to get the third place.

But when Du'Aine's turn came to say how he felt, I will never forget the tone of his voice. It was just a complete dismissal of what I'd done. 'Well, I hope Roger enjoys this moment because, like in 1994, I'm not ready yet, and he's not going to beat me again, and when it matters in the Olympics I'm going to be The Man, and I will hold the British record by the end of the year.'

I remember looking out of the window at that point as I sensed members of the press looking at me. I was really angry inside. I do believe fundamentally that you should be gracious in victory, and in defeat. It's an important part of sport. It's about respect for your fellow competitors. I don't mind people bad-mouthing me, I don't mind people not liking me. I don't crave respect from everybody. But I do expect it from my fellow competitors, especially my fellow British competitors who haven't been around for twelve years and been through what I have. I don't demand it, purposefully. But as I would give it to them when they perform well, so I expect it back. And in the twelve years I've been in the sport, I've had it from better athletes that Du'Aine Ladejo. Michael Johnson, for one.

I turned to him and said, 'Du'Aine. You are so predictable.'

'Why? Why?'

'You can't even be gracious. So you are going to break the British record by the end of the year are you? 44.39 – that's no good, right?'

'Yeah, I am. No problem.'

'Well put your money where your mouth is,' I challenged him.

Where that came from I do not know. He looked at me and said, 'Well, how much?'

'You tell me.'

'A grand.'

211

I just leaned over and shook his hand, then looked away.

Iwan Thomas could not believe it. He was staggered by the whole thing. I had given Du'Aine respect when he beat me in 1994, but he didn't give it back. Now Du'Aine will always say that it was just a bit of publicity and it was really good for us, because he comes from that world of 'got to get publicity'. Yes, get publicity, but don't do it by putting down another competitor. That was the mistake.

When Du'Aine arrived on the scene in 1994 I remember him giving me the impression that what he wanted was celebrity. But if all you want is celebrity, you don't choose to do athletics because it's too hard. I always thought that Du'Aine's PR and his self-publicity machine were second to none. You've got to hand it to him, a guy who won relatively little achieved a lot of celebrity, even down to his own TV show for a while.

The fact is that when he won the European Championship 400 metres in 1994, I was the only person he was up against, and I was coming back from glandular fever. Mark Richardson was injured, Iwan Thomas wasn't on the scene. And the truth, which he found out immediately the following year, was that he wasn't good enough to proclaim himself as the greatest 400 metres runner we've ever had. Du'Aine is actually a nice bloke, but his love of celebrity for its own sake made him miss the point.

And he has not made himself widely popular among black people by some of the things he has said and done in recent years. Soon after the Olympics, Frank Bruno came up to me and said, 'I was really pleased when you won that race.' And I said, 'Well. Actually Frank, I didn't win it, I came second.' And he said, 'No. No, no. Not that race. *That* race.' He was talking about the Olympic trials.

Du'Aine did the same thing before the Olympics when he talked about beating Michael Johnson. In the world of athletics, you can't hide. If you make statements like that, you've got to go out and do it. Talking about beating Michael Johnson and winning the gold medal – I'm sorry, but that was bordering on lunacy.

212

Nevertheless the episode at the press conference really upset me. It soured things for me. And Du'Aine did himself no favours with the other 400 metres runners. That could have caused a difficulty when we all had to run together in the relay team. He and other athletes went on to criticize me prior to the Olympics for saying I did not necessarily feel I could beat Michael Johnson. The man had run 43.5. I was running 44.39, or 44.37 as it was by then. He was in a different league, and all I was saying was, 'I'm not thinking about a gold medal or Michael Johnson, I'm thinking about executing my perfect race. And if I execute that and Michael Johnson messes up, I'll win the gold medal.'

I fundamentally believe that that was the right approach for me. Absolutely. It was not a defeatist approach – I think the result spoke for itself. I ran virtually to my personal best in the Olympic final. That mindset worked for me. And it doesn't mean I couldn't win the gold medal – everyone is beatable on the day. We've seen that with Michael Johnson subsequently. But if your focus is just, 'I'm going to win, I'm going to win,' and you are basically a second away from an opponent, where are you going to find ten metres in one race? I've never seen anyone do that. You have to show some form. I knew my limitations to a degree.

As things turned out, Du'Aine got knocked out in the second round of the 400 metres in Atlanta. And no matter what had gone before, I actually did feel sorry for him at the Olympics. Because he couldn't win. What could he do? He had set himself up to fall.

As we got ready to leave the athletes' village to warm up for the relay final, he was first reserve so he was obviously coming with us in case one of us got injured. We were standing by the bus when he walked up and asked, 'Are any of you guys injured?'

'No,' we replied.

'Would you mind if I didn't come down then?'

Iwan and Mark and Jamie were looking at me as if to say,

213

'Your decision, mate!' So I asked Du'Aine what was wrong, and he said, 'I'm just devastated by everything. I don't think I can go through with it.'

'If you really feel that way, don't come down.' I felt it would be wrong, it would have created a negative environment for the team. I remember seeing him walk away then as a broken man, and I felt for him. I hope he learned from that experience, because he has the ability and the talent to achieve.

As it turned out, I made a very, very bad decision there. I didn't realize that if one of us had got injured – and Iwan's hamstring was troubling him – we would have been disqualified if our replacement first reserve Mark Hylton had run instead. The rules state that if a relay runner is taken out of the team for any subsequent round he cannot be reinstated. Therefore, since Mark Hylton had run the first round heats but had been replaced by Iwan Thomas for the semi-finals he could not run in the final. Du'Aine Ladejo, however, could run in the final since he had run in the semi-final. Fortunately myself, Jamie, Mark and Iwan were able to run. If one of us had had to withdraw at the last minute (like Phil Brown at the 1986 European Championships) then an Olympic medal would have been thrown away. Perish the thought.

At the end of the season, I received a cheque in the post from Du'Aine's agent for £1,000. There was a suggestion that I should have a photo-call with Du'Aine for an official handing-over ceremony. No way. I mulled over in my mind how I would most like to enjoy the money, and eventually decided that I would invite a group of my best friends, including Kriss, Sven, Jon, my schoolfriends John and Kelvin, and blow it all in one night. We had very expensive wine and very good food. And champagne. And the toast at the end of every course was 'Du'Aine Ladejo'.

15

CAPTAIN ON THE SIDELINES

A year before I won my Olympic silver medal, I couldn't have imagined what lay in store for me. The same was true of the following year. I had got everything right, I was voted Athlete of the Year by the press, I was very complete as an athlete. I could have stopped then. But I was healthy, I was fine – and I felt I hadn't struggled that much to ignore the rewards of my Olympic success, so demands on my time were great. That feeling of completeness is a very dangerous thing to have as an athlete, because you should have a sense of desire. I couldn't pretend that there was much more that I desperately wanted to achieve, that I had to stay in the sport to do. I did, however, want to enjoy my achievement, to appreciate it, and just love life – which I did.

I was particularly aware of the preciousness of life at that time. One of the sad things about my Olympic success in 1996 was that one person who was special to me didn't live to see it. She was a Scottish woman called Maureen, somewhere in her late twenties, and incurably ill. Maureen wrote to me a lot, and she always used to get tickets to watch me run at British meetings. She was a big fan of mine, but she wasn't obsessive. I gave her my phone number and she would ring me from time to time but she never overdid it. One thing she did for several years was to videotape my races and present me with an annual compilation. That was something I really appreciated, and I have used some of the film she recorded in the motivational speeches I now give.

She died early in 1996, just before I was about to leave to train in California. Her brother rang me and told me, 'I just wanted you to know that she died a few hours ago.' I was on the list of people to phone. He said, 'I want to thank you for keeping in contact with her in the way that you did. It made a big difference to her.'

Adulation from excited screaming girlies is great – they are turning their attention to Jamie Baulch now because I'm getting a bit old for them – but it is the fans like Maureen who really make an impact on you.

I had tried to start 1997 in a normal way, getting back into winter training with the best intentions. Jon Ridgeon was running very well at the time, and Mark Richardson's arrival had added a lot to the group. But although I trained well in the winter, I didn't have that real focus and hunger which I had had the year before. In truth I didn't expect to have it. I've been around long enough to know the difficulty with continuous motivation. I would rather there hadn't been a World Championships in 1997. It's very difficult, both physically and mentally, for anyone to have Olympic success, and then just go back in and run in the World Championships. Even Michael Johnson found it a strain.

Soon another, more familiar strain became apparent.

When I started sprinting again in December, and my right knee started to hurt. I thought, 'Oh no, you are joking.' I had exactly the same symptoms as I'd had with the left one before. The difference was, as soon as it happened I knew the signs, whereas with the left one I had run the whole season on it before realizing that something had to be done.

I phoned up Dr Biedert again in Switzerland, had some scans, sent them over to him and he rang me and said, 'Get on the next plane.' I went to the same hospital, lay in the same hospital bed, and had the same cartilage operation on my other knee. The problem was that this was in January – six weeks later in the season than the first operation in 1995 had been – and that had a significant knock-on effect. It meant I had no time to have the operation, do some rehabilitation after the operation and some endurance work before going into the Californian phase. I was playing catch-up from that point onwards.

It was then that I really started thinking about my life after athletics. What was I going to do? I didn't feel I could, or needed to, top my Olympic success. What I wanted to do was make a smooth transition from being an athlete to having another purpose in life. So when I linked up again with Sven Nylander in California, the two of us took on the challenge to spend a lot of time reading, writing, researching, and attending motivational courses.

Sven had come fourth in the Olympics and had broken his personal best, so we had a joint celebration when we met up. But there was no hiding the fact that it was disappointing for him because he had desperately wanted a medal. I'd got a silver medal without running a personal best, and he'd run a personal best and come fourth. It shows you the power of that medal to the public. If you get a medal it matters, but if you come fourth it doesn't really have the same impact. That really hurt him, but he came to terms with that, and accepted that that is the way it is.

By the time I got to California, Mark Richardson was ready to run fast, while I had lost a lot of my aerobic base and I didn't have the focus. I felt, with all this catching up, that I wasn't in control of things as I had been the previous year. I got through the training, and I was moving reasonably well after the operation but it never felt the same. It wasn't firing.

When I got back to England, my performance in training dropped off dramatically. I won the 400 metres in the European Cup final, contributing to the overall victory of the British men's team, but those 400 metres felt like a long way and were a lot of hard work.

The week before I was due to run at an early season meeting at Sheffield I began sweating a lot, and I was very tired. It was exactly the same way I had felt in 1992. I said to myself, 'You've just got a bit of flu or something.' But really I knew then.

After I crossed the line – with Iwan Thomas a distant winner – I walked straight off the track thinking, 'I don't believe this. It's all happening again.' And then, fleetingly, 'I don't need this.' After the Olympics I had told myself that no matter what happened, I would be happy. That is true, basically, but moments like that really get you down.

Mike Whittingham came right over to me, we looked at each other and I told him, 'Mike, I've been here before. I need a blood test.' For once I didn't hang around to sign any autographs. I got in his car immediately and we drove straight home. The blood test was the next day, and the results later confirmed that I was suffering from a virus. I got in touch with a doctor in St George's Hospital in London who is an expert in that field and his advice was all too familiar. 'Look,' he said. 'You've got it. So you've got to rest.'

I had contracted cyto-mega virus, probably earlier that year while I attended two motivational seminars in California. I had been training hard up until that point and then proceeded to surround myself with two and a half thousand people for three days and one thousand people for four days. A lot of contact, not a lot of sleep and my immune system was obviously suppressed. I was exhausted at the end of it, the virus was around and I succumbed. I don't regret attending the courses, though, since they cleared my mind about what I want to do for the rest of my life and also better equipped me mentally to run even faster.

I had it badly, but I was tested every week and I knew it was gradually clearing from my body. Unlike when I had been ill with the Epstein-Barr virus in 1993, I felt there was some immediate hope, though I couldn't be sure of how soon I would recover. My diary entry from the time reads:

Yet again I have followed a good year with a bad year. Is this a pattern, and how do we address that? Maybe I'm just not strong enough.

I'm certainly sure it's the seminars which caused me to contract the virus, in which case I should have had the foresight not to do them.

But I was trying to balance what I wanted to achieve for that year and what I wanted to do with the rest of my life. So I had desperately wanted to do these seminars, to learn, to grow. I've decided not to attend any more of them until I retire. It's a foolish person who does the same thing again risking the same results.

Many people can get a virus and merely feel under the weather. When you are an athlete you are like a Ferrari, and being just 10 per cent out of tune means you underperform massively, whereas if a standard car is 10 per cent out of tune it still performs relatively well. Athletes are called upon to perform at 100 per cent. If you are only 80–90 per cent, it is the difference between running 44.5sec and 45.5sec.

One of the worst things about having a virus is not knowing when you are going to get better. You get sweats, and you are not sure whether that is because you are hot, or ill. At the World Championships in Athens my head was really tired and my eyes were so sore I had to put ointment in them throughout the fortnight – but I didn't know for sure if that was the virus, or the pollution. I didn't have a clue.

The virus had some alarming side effects. A week after I had run really badly in the pre-trials meeting at Sheffield I was with my old school friends John and Kelvin and feeling pretty low when I had a complete loss of memory. For about ten minutes it was absolutely bizarre. I felt a sense of total detachment from everything. I was saying things like, 'I've got an illness, haven't I? What is it?'

Elsa was away for her sister's wedding, and I was living on

my own. There was a strange sense of detachment, seeing myself in the national press and on TV, while I was feeling so ill at home alone. My family and friends kept saying, 'You need to get more people in. Can we come and help you?' But I just wanted to be alone. Elsa was supposed to come home for about ten days and then go back out for the actual wedding, and I told her not to.

I needed to be alone then. During times of trouble I am a very insular person, and I always get back on my own. When I'm at an athletics championship, I don't want my friends or my family around me. It's both a strength and a weakness. When I'm really up against it, I don't let people help me, I pride myself on the fact that I can dig deep into my personal reserves and get through. Also when you are alone you don't have to consider anyone else, so you can eat what you want, you can sleep when you want. If I hadn't been on my own at that time, I wouldn't have got to the World Championships.

A virus is probably the worst thing you can have, because it fills you with negativity. You doubt yourself. And even though you've sat down with the experts who have explained why you can't run fast, you still, as an athlete, have a glimmer of hope. I thought, 'The rest of my body's fine! My feet don't hurt. My hip doesn't hurt. My knees don't hurt. And I'm running fast enough, even coming off a virus, to make the British 4x400 team.'

There were times when I doubted whether I could even make the trip, though. I remember having one training session which was so bad I thought, 'Forget it.' I rang David Jenkins up and said I wasn't going, I wasn't going to risk doing myself damage and jeopardizing the following season. And Jenks, whose protein business was making him a stack of money, said, 'Rog, if I had a chance to get a medal in the World Championships in the relay and then salvage something from the rest of the season, I'd change places with you right now.'

And I thought, 'Yeah, OK, you're right. Sometimes we forget

how lucky we are.' But then he added, 'No, maybe I wouldn't. Because I'm making so much money out here!'

'Fine,' I said, 'I'll swap places with you right now, buddy!'

At the 1997 World Championships in Athens I found myself in a very strange situation: team captain for the first time, running in the 4x400 relay, but not picked for the individual event. The day after the British trials, which I had had to miss because of the virus infection, the selectors had given the third optional place to Jamie Baulch, who had finished behind Iwan Thomas and Mark Richardson. That decision by the selectors provoked a controversy which took me aback by its force. It also provided me with an unexpected opportunity to do some television work as part of the BBC commentary team. The issue, though, was not whether Jamie or I should have been selected, but whether I should have been given a week until the final entry deadline in order to prove my fitness.

In hindsight, I know I wouldn't have taken the place anyway, because the diagnosis made it clear that I wouldn't have been able to perform properly in four races over four days. So Jamie was the right man to do that. But at the time the decision was made the selectors didn't have that information. I believe they were wrong, and the way they handled it was symptomatic of the problems British athletics has had over the years.

I was upset about it. Not because I was insistent about running the individual, but because they didn't have the information, they didn't know what my diagnosis was. No one had asked me how I was feeling. I had done everything I could. I had written a letter to the chairman of selectors, David Cropper, I'd explained the situation, I'd told them who my doctor was, and Mike Whittingham had faxed many times to keep them up to date. I was progressing. But after the 400 metres final at the trials, Mike went to Britain's chief coach Malcolm Arnold and asked, 'Can you let us know what your thoughts are?' Malcolm replied, 'I think it's obvious – it's got to be based on today's performance. One, two, three.'

He had gone into the selection meeting with his mind made up and the selection panel were not strong enough to stand up against the national coach. But if that was how it happened, then why not call me before the meeting and say, 'Rog, I've made my mind up. You may not agree with it, but I thought you should know before anyone else?'

I've heard conflicting reports of what went on in the meeting. Ian Stewart, who was there as the head of the British Athletic Federation's promotions unit, told me he stood up and argued against choosing Jamie. He said, 'It's ridiculous, you are talking about leaving out the Olympic silver medallist for a runner who didn't break 45 seconds in the trials.'

Eventually they made their decision. Fine. I can live with that. What I find so hard is that not one person in that room thought, 'What are the implications of this from a press and PR point of view? What are the implications of this for Roger personally? Obviously, we should have the decency to let him know first, if for no other reason than to cover our backs before all hell breaks loose.' No one had that foresight. It was, 'Oh well. Who cares?' And I'm sorry, but in the professional era we are in, and with people like myself who are high profile and whose actions have implications for the sport, not to understand that was unacceptable. It would have been so easy to co-ordinate the correct action – but it didn't happen. And so I found out when a journalist left a message on my ansaphone. And later I confirmed it on teletext.

Mike was furious about the whole thing. His feelings were much stronger than mine at the time, because I was ill, and I tended to think, 'Well, maybe I wouldn't have made it anyway.'

Mike said to me, 'You have done so much for the sport in the last two years. You have gone out of your way – against my advice at times – driving around the country, seeing other athletes, helping to set up the British Athletes Association. You put yourself out for the sport, you are team captain and

Olympic silver medallist, and they can't even show you the decency of giving you a week? That is not on.' Mike also felt that he personally had given a lot to British athletics – he had been working on and off for more than a year on surveying the sport and putting together an athlete services programme. And he felt disillusioned by what happened. He said, 'What's the point in trying to be a good guy? Yet again the good guy gets shafted.'

I wasn't asking for special favours. I was asking for what other athletes had been given – time to show their fitness. I had never felt the sport owed me anything. But in this situation, maybe for the first time in my life, I felt, that yes, the sport did owe me something. What it owed me was that courtesy. And that's all.

Malcolm's big line was, 'What sort of message does it send out to Jamie Baulch if we don't select him?' I think Kriss Akabusi answered that very well when he heard it. 'Break 45 seconds. Run faster and guarantee your place in the team by coming in the top two.' And as one journalist pointed out to me, the message that was sent out to Jamie by selecting him was, 'Even if you become Olympic silver medallist, we're not going to treat you properly.' I hadn't considered that, but when you think of it, any young athlete could think, 'If it could happen to Roger Black it could happen to all of us.'

I don't want to do anything to bring the sport bad publicity, but the reasons I made my stand were twofold: firstly, I felt I had been badly treated, but secondly, I believe this kind of thing has to stop. I don't want it to happen to someone else. The athletes must come first. Anyone who works for the sport should be working for the athletes. And I think in the way we were told about the decision the athletes didn't come first.

What made it more pathetic was that the morning the story came out, Mike phoned the chairman of selectors in outrage and said, 'Why have you not phoned Roger?' And the reply was, 'Oh, I was going to phone him in two hours' time', which was an hour before the official press conference. When he phoned me, what seemed to concern him most was the fact that I had learned of the decision the day before. He resolved to set about finding out who had leaked the information.

I gave Jamie a ring before the news became official – it was not his fault, poor guy. We both agreed, 'That's just athletics. That's the way it is.' But he accepted why it was such an issue for me.

The next day I seemed to have the whole nation on my side. The Sports Minister issued a statement. BBC News came round to my house to film me, and a report went out on the main news bulletin. Journalists were writing in support without me even having to speak to them. John Rawling from BBC Radio was outraged by the decision. David Miller, of the *Daily Telegraph* left a message of support on my mobile within about two minutes – he was absolutely fuming. Seb Coe, who was so famously left out of the 1988 Olympic team, was saying, 'Nothing changes.' It was all very encouraging from a personal point of view. The problem was that while all this was going on, I was still dealing with the virus.

Athens was my first experience of being team captain, following Linford's retirement from international competition. You have a collection of very different individuals in the British team – different sexes, shapes, sizes. Some run, some jump, some throw. They come from different backgrounds. What tends to happen is people go into their own little cliques, and there isn't the same sense of community that there would be in a football or a rugby team. There never has been, and there never will be. But we are a team, and the role of the captain has always been an ambiguous one. Linford was made team captain when we needed someone to pick up the European Cup trophy at Gateshead in 1989. He stayed in that position, and he played the role well because he led from the front on the track. And to his eternal credit, Linford always stayed with the team. That was something he felt very strongly about. He was always around, even though the team management never defined a role for him. They didn't seem to think team captain was an important role at all.

That's why the role is strange. In athletics, as the sport is at the moment, it is not like being captain in other sports. You're just a spokesperson, an ambassador. You don't direct the play or tell people what to do. But the media like to use the role to hang stories around so they make it bigger. When I was made team captain, I knew that I was only going to be in the role for about fourteen months because it was always my intention to retire after the 1998 European Championships. So I see my task as captain as creating a clear role for whoever is my successor. I think the team captain should stand up and motivate the team separately from the team management.

There's a relationship between the athletes based on the fact that we are all in the same boat. When I joined the team, Frank Dick, who was then national coach, always gave this speech asking whether we were mountain people or valley people. You heard the same old speech every year, and you always knew it was coming. We all laughed about it, but the message got through. You ask people like Kriss or Daley. You got keyed up, you got yourself in the right frame of mind.

When Frank left and Malcolm Arnold took over, all that disappeared since Malcolm was not a natural motivator. And that I thought was sorely missing. In the team meeting I stood up and gave a small speech. I did what I could to fill the gap. Even though I wasn't running in the individual event, the Championships in 1997 were still important to me. I was in the relay, I was team captain, and my new training partner Mark Richardson, who had joined my training group soon after the 1996 Olympics, was running in the 400 metres individual event. Mark is young and has the ability. Just as importantly, he has the intelligence to learn from other people's mistakes, and he has the fire in his belly – so he has it all. He also had a point to prove because he had missed out on Olympic selection in the individual after food poisoning had undermined his performance in the trials. I want to hand over to him when I retire and help him to go on and achieve, hopefully, everything that I did and more. The advantage he has is that he doesn't have to go through some of things I've been through because we can see it before it happens. And biased as I may be, I think Mark is the person who is going to achieve the most from the new generation of 400 metres runners.

There are some curious parallels in our careers. Mark was the No. 1 400 metres runner as a junior, but then David Grindley, his rival, came through to achieve greater success, while Mark was also undermined by a series of frustrating injuries. Once again, it underlines the fact that talent on its own is not enough to succeed. David Grindley came along and then got injured. Mark Richardson got injured, and then said, at some point, 'No. The definition of insanity is to do the same thing time and time again and get the same results.' That's what Mark has done – he has made the step forward.

To be a great athlete you have to be prepared to do that. He approached me after the Olympics and said, 'I want to come and train with you. I want to learn from you. I think what you have done this year is incredible. I can see it, I can feel it, and I want to be a part of it.' That means stepping away from your first coach, from your familiar environment, making changes in your life. Even down to something like making the effort to drive an extra half an hour to go training. It means saying to yourself, 'What I'm doing now is good, but it isn't good enough. And I am prepared to take the step from being excellent to being outstanding. To do that, I have to take risks.' I have done that in my career, and it's difficult. Making the step is only part of it. You also have to use faith and intelligence, which Mark does.

All three British 400 metres runners reached the final in Athens, which was excellent for us. But none got a medal. Mark was the highest placed, finishing fourth in 44.47sec. – equal to the British record David Grindley had set at the 1992 Olympics.

Iwan Thomas was sixth after fading in the final straight with Jamie finishing seventh. Michael Johnson may not have been Superman on the day – despite the shirt he had on underneath his running vest – but he was still good enough to retain his title. Despite the way things turned out in Athens, Iwan Thomas was voted British Athlete of the Year. People forget Mark Richardson; but I believe they will not be able to do that for much longer.

I think Colin Jackson should have been Athlete of the Year for 1997 because of the way he raised his game to take the world silver behind Allen Johnson in the 110 metres hurdles. Although Iwan broke my British record, I feel medals are a fairer factor for deciding achievement – and Colin excelled to get his, while for Jonathan Edwards and Steve Backley, who also won silver at the World Championships, it was more a case of failing to get gold. Iwan did well because he was new, and young, and he broke the British record. But the fact is that in the world of athletics, what matters is the championships. They are the races that people really remember.

When it looked as if Michael Johnson was not going to take part in the World Championships, there was a sense of hope in Britain that Iwan could win the 400 metres title. After the final, Iwan tried to take some comfort in the fact that at least he had gone for gold even with Johnson running. But he could have won the gold anyway if he had played it differently, because Johnson was coming off an injury and was clearly not the force he had been at the Olympics. I think if Iwan had gone through 200 metres 0.2 to 0.3 seconds slower, he would have got a medal. How he hung on that long is incredible. I'm not really criticizing Iwan, because I did the same kind of thing for the first eight years of my career. What I'm saying is that you have to learn from other people's mistakes.

I was very pleased for Mark, though, because he ran it right. He may not have got a medal, but he couldn't have run any faster than he did. Mark had listened and learned, and when he got to the World Championships he executed his perfect race.

He was gutted at not getting a bronze medal. I sat with him that night and tried to tell him that, yes, it was a natural reaction to be disappointed, but that he must take personal satisfaction from running a personal best. And I asked him, 'Where did you make a mistake?' Truth was, he hadn't made a mistake.

I always thought the fact that I was a late maturer would give me a long career, which it has done. Iwan is a Grindley-like character who matured early. He is definitely a lot stronger than me physically. It seemed that Iwan could not run badly in 1997, he was so fit and strong. I know the signs, because that was me in 1986. But like all 400 metres runners at some stage, he's going to have to get hurt. And the test for Iwan will be the test of coming back like I did. But will Iwan Thomas still be running at the top level when he is thirty years old? That will come down to one person and one person only – Iwan Thomas.

Steve Backley's performance in the javelin at the World Championships was technically one of his worst. He had been on the brink of being seen as a failure and getting slated in the press, but with one throw, his last, he came from nowhere to take the silver medal. That changed his destiny – but it also did the same for his friend, Mick Hill, because Steve knocked Mick – whose overall performance had been far more consistent and free of error – out of the medals. In athletics, if you win, someone else must lose – and that someone could be your best friend. Steve is going to have to carry that, and it is quite a heavy load for him because as he said at the time, if Mick had got a medal he would have been able to give up his job and concentrate on throwing full time because of the bonuses he would get. But it didn't turn out that way. It just goes to prove the point that despite every effort, you cannot control the final outcome of this business – so much of what happens to you as an athlete can be governed by matters beyond your control.

In Athens, although I was on television and I was team captain and involved at least partially in the competition, the underlying thought I carried with me every minute of the day was of my illness. I had missed the whole of 1993 with glandular fever; in 1997 I was suffering from a cyto-mega virus, which is another glandular fever-type virus.

Although I trained quite hard in Athens, it was a struggle. I knew I was not 100 per cent, and before the relay I was very scared. The previous year in Atlanta I had been the rallying point of the team; this year I was the one who needed rallying. We did a time trial before the competition, and I was significantly faster than the other two reserves so I was obviously going to run to create the best team we could. But I knew I was not the man I had been in Atlanta. I also knew that in running I could do myself damage for the rest of the season.

We finished up taking silver in the 4x400 behind a US team which did not include Michael Johnson or Butch Reynolds – just as we had done the previous year at the Olympics. I regard both races as wasted opportunities.

Jamie's split time for the World Championship 4x400 was the same as mine, 44.20 sec. But I felt he laid himself open to criticism for his relay legs in both the Olympic and World Championship finals, because running the relay is not about what times you run, it's about doing a job. That's why we won in the Tokyo World Championships of 1991. There is no doubt that in Athens, job descriptions were not adhered to. Iwan was unable to hand over the baton to me with a first leg lead, which effectively meant our gameplan went belly up. He was tired, and he had been troubled by his hamstring. These things happen. The task for all of us had been to give Mark the baton either five metres in the lead, or up an American's backside. I did my best but I was not in outstanding shape and was unable to make any impact on the American lead. Jamie had a chance to do better than I had. He was not going to hand over a five metres lead to Mark, but he was in a position to leave him right on an American's shoulder. Unfortunately in the excitement of the moment he felt he could give us a five metres lead, which proved to be overambitious. As his energy flagged, he handed over five metres down. Mark, not surprisingly, was unable to close that gap.

These young British runners have got, I hope, many years ahead of them to get it right. But we had a chance that day to win a gold medal and it didn't happen. Anyone can make mistakes – but you have to learn from them. It was frustrating for me that I wasn't in great shape. It was even more frustrating for Mark, because if he had been in a position to win it would have meant a lot of welcome recognition for him.

1997 was a difficult year for me in terms of athletics, although not because of losing my British record to Iwan Thomas. That's not what I'm about, I'm a championship performer. Obviously when he did it I thought, 'Oh no, there goes my record,' but I'm pleased for Iwan who is a great talent and a good bloke. I hope he and Mark can sit down in seven or eight years' time and do what I'm doing now without the very mixed story that I have to tell.

I suspect that if they're still running, they will have had a rough ride, because that's in the nature of the 400 metres. It's an event that's so demanding physically that, historically, it has injury problems. But it's an event that's evolving, and the next great 400 metres runner will be like Michael Johnson, a natural 100/200 metres sprinter with the strength to take the event on. That person hasn't come along yet. The coaches in the country will be now looking for that sprinter who is not scared of the 400 metres. The event needs taking up one more level. Iwan and Mark could do that. Maybe Jamie could do it as well. But I'm sure there's somebody else out there who will come in and hopefully push them.

I got through the season, but it was no fun getting beaten. It was no fun running sub-standard performances. I established a new goal for myself – winning that third European 400 metres title which had eluded me in 1994. Whether I win again or not at the 1998 European Championships matters to me personally, but it's not going to make or break my life now. When I look back, I feel so lucky. People say to me, 'You've been so unlucky with all your illnesses and your injuries,' but I don't see it like that. Because I've been lucky – the European and Commonwealth titles, the Olympic and world medals, the relays – these moments more than make up for all the difficult times I have had. I don't dwell on the bad times, but it is definitely the bad times that have changed my character. I think of all the athletes who had as much talent, if not more – the Danny Harrises, the Derek Redmonds, the Jon Ridgeons, the David Grindleys – and I count myself fortunate to have sustained a career in the 400 metres.

That I have remained in athletics until 1998 was largely a reflection of my need to challenge for a third European title. If you get out too early you run the risk of ending up thinking, 'Damn. I could have kept going.' It gives me a feeling of satisfaction to have been around at the top level for a twelve-year span. I've always wanted to choose the day I retire from athletics; I've never wanted to be retired by the sport. I'll know the day I should choose to go, and when I choose it, that will be it, and it will be time to concentrate on other things in life which have had to wait. I want to start a family. I want to get more involved in a media career. I want to develop my speaking career. I want to run a marathon – some day! And I want to take a lot of pressure off my shoulders. Daley said to me the other day, 'You want to stay an athlete as long as you can. Because when it's over, you're a long time retired.' I said, 'I'm not scared of retirement. In fact, to be honest, I'm looking forward to it.'

There comes a time when the scales start to tip, and athletics prevents you doing a lot of things you want to do. I think age is irrelevant, it is merely a number – look at Linford Christie, look at Merlene Ottey – it is the desire that can wane before the body is too old. If your mind is saying, 'I'd rather be doing something else', then your days are numbered.

I went into 1998 really believing I could rekindle the fire one more time. It was a challenge; and I do love a challenge. I strongly believe that my misfortunes in 1997 occurred for a reason. I believe it was a wake-up call: 'Roger, if you are not 100 per cent focused on athletics, you're not good enough to make the British team.' The task for 1998 was to look after myself, be smart in training and do everything right. It was a measure of my renewed sense of commitment to the sport that I postponed my wedding to Elsa, which had been scheduled for autumn 1997, for a year, because I didn't want to go through visiting Martinique, organizing a wedding, taking a few weeks out and then coming back. If I was going to carry on for the European Championships, I had to do it right.

And I had a huge commitment to Mark Richardson as well, especially after what happened to him in Athens. Mark can win the Olympic gold medal in 2000. But both he and I know we have to do it right if we are to have a chance of achieving our goals. And we can help each other do that.

16

'TV TIMES'

If you had to choose a way to miss the World Championships, it was not too bad to have the whole nation behind you feeling you should have been there, and for the runners who did get there not to get a medal, and for you also to get to do a bit of television, which is what you want to do in the future anyway. My bad luck before the championships turned into good luck – I had three great days working with the BBC which I enjoyed and which were very useful given my choice of future career. It meant getting a grandstand view of the action alongside fellow commentator Linford Christie, who announced his retirement during the championships, after an international career which had started around the same time as mine.

When you are sitting with Des Lynam, David Moorcroft – another regular member of the BBC team in Athens – and Linford you simply chat away. What you don't think about – and shouldn't think about – is that there are seven or eight million people back home watching you. Someone once said to me, 'Just imagine you are talking to one person in the sitting room,' which was good advice. The secret of television is to forget the cameras are there. Sitting watching athletics and talking about it afterwards was an absolute pleasure.

I first did some presentation for BBC South in the early 1990s, and in October 1997 I started doing the same kind of job for the BBC's twenty-four-hour news service on cable, which involved anchoring a regular Saturday afternoon sports show. I was still considering the offer while in Athens, and I took the opportunity of speaking to Des about it. He said, 'Take it. It's a wonderful opportunity for you.'

But while I am looking towards a future presenting sport, you cannot do the job solely on the back of being an ex-athlete. That's why I wanted to go and learn my craft before coming into the mainstream. That's what Sue Barker did after she finished playing tennis. She worked for years on Sky television, and when she went to the BBC everyone said, 'Gosh, she's really good.' She had done her home work. I have learned from athletics that you can't make the Olympic final if you haven't put your training in; it will be the same for me in television. I realize it requires a lot of practice and concentration, not least because you are autocueing while the producer is talking in your ear.

Being a pundit is not particularly taxing. You are just talking about something you should know about. And it's a wonderful way to watch athletics as well, because you have monitors and you can see replays of everything and you get all the trackside interviews relayed back to the studio.

Des is wonderful because he is so laid back. If he was more laid back he would be asleep. But I always get the feeling he's not particularly into athletics. He's a football man, really. I remember one incident – it was such a shame it was off-air – when Britain had just qualified for the final of the 4x400 metres relay. And Des turned to me and asked, 'So who's going to come in for the final?' I replied, 'Well, Des, I think it could be me.' And he just collapsed in his chair. He creased up laughing and said, 'I don't believe I just said that.' Another thing which gave us all a chuckle did happen on air. Dave Moorcroft was describing Fermin Cacho's fast finish in the 1500 metres, and it came out as 'a late burst of speed from Fidel Castro'.

Watching Des in action it came home to me that it is easy being interviewed and it is hard to do the interviewing. Des had to talk to Maurice Greene, the quietly spoken, God-fearing American who had just won the world 100 metres title, and I was sitting next to him while he did it. Maurice was very shy and unassuming and was still trying to come to terms with becoming world champion. And it was one of those interviews where Maurice would say something and you would expect him to carry on ... but he would just stop. So Des, who only had a little factsheet in front of him, had to keep the conversation going. I was off-camera at the time, and I was looking at Des's face as he did it. And he was saying, 'Yeah? ...' and then throwing up another question. He did a fantastic job. That's when you realize just how good he is. As Maurice left the room, Des turned to me and said, 'Fast runner. Slow talker.'

My emotions while I watched the 400 metres final were mixed. All athletes are the same – you want people to do well – and you certainly don't wish any bad luck on anybody – but you don't want them to do too well! I wanted the British guys to do well in Athens – but it didn't do me any harm that none of them got a medal. That's the truth, and I think most athletes would understand that. You are always striving for that balance – I want to be a nice person, but there has to be the competitive edge. Linford told me exactly the same thing. He too always wanted the others to do well, but not too well. That's your ego talking, that's what makes you a great athlete. And we are all judged by each other.

Sometimes, though, that attitude can tip over into something unacceptable. Ever since I've been in athletics I've been surrounded by many people who just don't want others to do well in any circumstances. I was aware, particularly in my younger days, that certain people got great pleasure when you didn't do well. And I certainly had the same feeling immediately after the 400 metres at the 1997 World Championship trials, when Fatima Whitbread interviewed Jamie Baulch at the trackside for Channel 4 and appeared to gloat over the imminent prospect of him taking the last, optional 400 metres place at my expense. Fatima would deny that that was the case, I'm sure, but many who saw the interview felt there was a smug-ness there, a sense of 'Ha ha ha, Roger Black isn't going to make it' which was uncalled for.

The first person on the phone to me afterwards was Kriss, who has a history of crossing swords with Fatima and her husband, Andy Norman, the promotions officer who effectively ran the sport as he put on his meetings throughout the 80s and early 90s until he was dismissed from the British Athletic Federation in 1994. Kriss was furious. He said it was so obvi-ously a case of her taking the opportunity to settle old scores.

He was referring to a business deal which Fatima arranged in 1992 for Britain's 4x400 world champions in her role as an official with Chafford Hundred, the athletic club established to promote and market Britain's élite athletes. Fatima agreed to alter the terms of the deal, which involved a television commer-cial for Mars, after the runners concerned – Kriss, John Regis, Derek Redmond and myself – had discovered she was taking what we considered an unreasonably high percentage of the fee. She accepted that she had made a 'misjudgement'. An understatement to say the least. John Regis, in particular, was seeing red every time her name was mentioned.

I told Kriss that what had been said at the post-race inter-view didn't really bother me, because to a degree I expected that sort of thing. Athletics, by its essentially individual nature, has always tended to be a fragmentary sport. Athletes have their own coaches and all coaches like to compete with other coaches. Then you've got managers and agents doing the same thing. At the time of the 1997 World Championships, the management group Nuff Respect were looking after Linford, Colin Jackson and Jamie, Andy Norman had his athletes, such as Iwan and Jonathan Edwards and Kelly Holmes, and then you had Mike Whittingham, who looks after people like myself and the Frenchman Stephane Diagana, who won the world 400 metres hurdles title. Obviously if one athlete does better than another one it means more money and endorsements for them. That's the natural way of things, and we all accept and understand that. But when it becomes personal, and you don't want specific individuals to do well, then it becomes unacceptable.

I remember when I first came into the sport there was far less choice for athletes seeking to maximize their commercial potential. As soon as I began to achieve success on the track, Todd Bennett and Mike Smith both insisted, 'You've got to get in with Andy Norman.'

My first experience of the unconventional way Andy operated came immediately after I had won the European 400 metres title in 1986. On my return from Stuttgart, Andy offered me £10,000 to run at a meeting he was putting on at Crystal Palace. To me it was a staggering sum of money. Before the European Championships I was getting £500 per appearance. But the problem was that Andy insisted I should run the 400 metres, and he had brought over to race against me an American runner called Darrell Robinson, who was world number one that year.

I was knackered. My gut feeling was, 'I've been through all this', and I really didn't want to run another 400 metres. because I didn't think I could win. I didn't want to come straight back from the championships and lose in Britain. I wanted to run a 200 metres.

Kriss was acting as my manager then, and he met Andy, who was adamant that I run the 400 metres. In the end he turned round and said, 'Well, if you run half the distance, you get half the money.' And I said, 'Fine'. So there it was, £5,000 gone. To a kid for whom this was a lot of money. It was that day I realized that, when it came down to it, I would never be sucked in by money in the sport. I would always use my gut feeling and my valued judgement as an athlete. I've been consistent with that through my whole career and it has always paid off.

So I ran the 200 metres, and I ran really well, winning in 20.62secs. And four weeks later, when the cheque came through the post, Andy paid me £10,000. It's funny because Andy Norman and I have never been what you would call good friends. I've never been one of his athletes. Obviously, he's a controversial figure who a lot of people are against, but he didn't *have* to pay me that money. If he hadn't, it wouldn't have bothered me; I didn't expect it. That was his way of saying, 'You deserve it.' But I was as surprised as anyone when it came through.

The important thing is that I have always performed well enough not to have to ask for any real favours from Andy, but many other athletes have been broken by the fact that, in the early days, Andy was Mr Big in British athletics. He could make life very difficult for you, as an athlete. He did that to Kriss.

You would hear stories of Andy pulling athletes out of meetings and saying they were never going to run there again. He controlled what athletes did and didn't do. Linford said as much in his book, and put a lot of his success down to Andy. Many people felt that was the only way to do it, and he did create an awful lot of success in the sport, both for Britain and athletes individually. But there are many ways to climb a mountain, and, in the end, I think his results were outstanding but his methods were unacceptable. And Kriss and I on principle stood up to that; we couldn't be managed by a man who basically told you where to go, what to do.

I cannot work with somebody who simply tells me what to do. I'm not saying that because I always want to do what I want, but I need to have a good personal relationship with those I work with. And Andy Norman and I are very different people. I could not work with him and he couldn't work with me and I think he knew that. We have never had a bad word with each other directly, because I've always had another person to get involved for me. In the early days it was Kriss, and he and Andy had some real run-ins. Later Mike Whittingham had to deal with him.

But my God I had to keep running well. If you run fast, you are always going to be asked to meetings, and you are always going to get endorsements. But not all athletes were fast enough or had sufficient resolve.

The great thing I can say is: I don't owe Andy Norman

anything. There are no favours to call in. You make life very difficult for yourself adopting that position in relation to Andy. You lose out in the early days, but you maintain your independence, and in the end you maintain your integrity.

Paradoxically, the reason I couldn't work with Andy Norman – the enormous control he exerted over his athletes – is precisely what a lot of athletes need. Most athletes don't want to have to deal with anything taxing on the commercial front. Mike Whittingham does an enormous amount of work for me, but ultimately he knows he doesn't have to be sitting on my shoulder the whole time.

I had a long conversation with Linford once while we were waiting to go on air in Athens, about what makes him special and what makes me special but not quite to his level. What drives Linford Christie is totally different from what drives Roger Black, although we are both undoubtedly driven people. I think a lot of his drive is for respect, for recognition, a drive against the system, against the way he feels he has been treated. A lot of his anger comes from that. At times he appears dominated by this need to be respected by the world.

We are very different people, and he has done things on many occasions which have grated on me. I have sat round a table with him and others when he has spent the whole evening complaining and moaning about things in the sport. I feel he is too quick to criticize and blame, particularly when it comes to the press he gets – which, given the amount of generous things that have been written about him over the years, has always struck me as bizarre. My ultimate frustration with him is that I just want to say, 'Can you just please not think the whole world is against you? It just isn't the case.' He's won everything, he's done everything. He has respect from all points of view. But because of his confrontational nature, many are wary of him. I find that intensely frustrating.

During one of the broadcasts from Athens, Linford said, 'Second doesn't matter, nobody remembers who came second.'

Instinctively I exclaimed, 'Oh, cheers mate!' It was good television and I don't believe he was consciously winding me up. Linford was sitting there as a former world and Olympic champion, a man who single-mindedly goes for that gold medal, and he's achieved it. So he has a unique perspective, and for him second doesn't cut it. Linford has to be the best in order to satisfy his drive and motivation.

For me, second does cut it. If I know I've done the best I can, that's all I can ask of myself. Mine is an internal motivation. If I can walk away from any situation knowing that I gave it my all, then you can't tell me that the colour of the medal is going to change that. It's not.

When Linford gives his opinion about second not counting, he's not criticizing anyone who gets a silver medal. He's just giving his view from his point high up on the mountain: if you're not the best it's not worth doing. And I disagree with that, because I've struggled. He hasn't had the setbacks with injury and illness that I have. If I'd lived by Linford's rules, I wouldn't have won an Olympic medal. I would have been lost to the sport at twenty-four if my only drive had been to win a gold medal.

And – here's the rub – if he has that attitude for the rest of his life it will be frustrating at times. Someone who invests everything in winning during his athletic career is going to have to do something pretty spectacular after athletics to remain a satisfied man. The Linford Christies and the other great Olympic champions of our time carry that weight with them for the rest of their lives. And as Olympic silver medallist, I think it's going to be a bit easier for me. I'm not saying I'm right and they are wrong. It's simply a question of different motivations.

Daley Thompson would side with Linford on this one. He said to me recently, 'In the past, I would have killed to win.' I have never, ever come close to feeling that way, even though I discovered when I had glandular fever that I needed the sport a lot more than I admitted.

You could argue that to be a great performer, to go beyond

the usual and become extraordinary, you have to have that certain something, that certain drive, that I would say from my experience Linford Christie had, Daley Thompson had, Sebastian Coe had. I don't have it. Steve Cram didn't have it. Akabusi didn't have it. Most of us don't have it.

Only a few have that something whereby they don't *hope* to do the best they can, they *know* they are going to do their best – it is not even an issue. And combined with that is 'I want to beat these bastards. I need this.' When push has come to shove, winning has never mattered to me to the degree of 'Forget everything else.' What drives people is a fascinating question because everybody is driven by something different. You don't have to come from a broken home with no money to rise through to be a great athlete, although that can be a huge motivation. You can still be motivated if you come from a secure background and you've not faced prejudice, and you've not had massive pain in your life. You can still be a fierce competitor. The world of athletics is not a subjective one. If you cross the line first you are the winner, it doesn't matter who you are, what you look like or where you're from. For many people who face prejudice in their daily life, sporting success provides a welcome escape. Perhaps that is one of the reasons why many black people are good at sport.

That, obviously, can never be a motivation for me. But for whatever reason, there's a part of myself that says, 'Give it 100 per cent when you have to, or don't do it.' I couldn't have won what I've won if I didn't have that. I don't carry it with me obsessively, but it's in there. It's got to be in there. If it wasn't, I wouldn't still be doing this after so many operations.

My primary question in life is, 'Am I doing the best I can?' When you are an athlete you know if you are or not. That's what drives me. So it is not a matter of thinking to myself, 'I'm going to prove to these others, Iwan Thomas, Mark Richardson, Jamie Baulch or whoever, who's the No. 1.' Some athletes have to hate their opponents to perform to their full capacity. I don't hate my opponents. I never have. I do believe if you focus on other things you are not focusing on what you can control, which is yourself. I've never had that competitive need to prove anything to others. But then again, ten O-levels, three A-levels, relatively good looking, secure background, loved by a family that hasn't broken up. What big point would I need to prove?

I have, however, felt I had to prove things to myself. That's not when the gun goes, though. That's when you wake up and you don't want to go training, but you make yourself get up and train anyway because you couldn't face yourself if you didn't. That's why I've always come back from adversity, because I don't think you can do that if you're merely trying to prove something to somebody else.

I think a lot of my attitude comes from my father. Now I look back I can see that he wasn't particularly gifted academically, he struggled to get through medical school, and he worked very, very hard. I'm very proud of what he's achieved. So, somewhere along the line what was instilled in me was, 'Do the best you possibly can – or don't do it at all.'

Linford knows I always give my best. He has no problem with my silver medal. What frustrated Linford at the World Championships was all the young pretenders in the British team who he thinks shouldn't even be out there because they are not doing it properly. There are British athletes, some of whom were in Athens, who could do so much more and always find an excuse why they haven't. Linford would point to the young sprinters. They were good – but they weren't going to cut it. He doesn't agree with the way they all give interviews after the heats, and I am with him on that.

Mr Nice Guy and Mr Controversial. Isn't it funny that when they performed at major championships they behaved in exactly the same way when they crossed the line in the heats? They both walked straight down that tunnel. I'll tell you why. Because they were already thinking about the next round. They don't want to hang around to say things like, 'That felt really good, thanks Mum, how are you doing?'

Linford and I don't know each other very well, and there are a lot of things we don't agree on. But we have a common understanding that all athletes who have achieved share, and that is a strange and precious thing.

17

THE ROAD TO RUIN

On 14 October 1997 I was doing a TV show with the rest of the British 4x400 team when I got a call on my mobile phone from Jonathan Edwards. 'There's going to be a press announcement this afternoon,' he said. 'BAF has gone bankrupt.' Now I knew things weren't great with the British Athletic Federation, but I didn't realize it had come to that. Anyway, I had to do the show – and when I got back to my mobile I had six messages on it, all about the same thing. It seemed Jonathan was right.

The first task was to call an emergency meeting between the athletes and the administrators who had taken over the Federation's affairs – and there the whole sad story was laid bare. BAF's financial collapse was precipitated by the terrible mess it had got itself into two years earlier and never had a chance to fully resolve. The reality was a direct conflict between athletes and the British Athletic Federation over money and also over the way they had been treated. At the heart of the dispute was a terrible communication problem between the sport's leading competitors and the man at the head of the sport, Professor Peter Radford, who resigned as executive chairman of the BAF between Christmas and New Year 1997.

From a personal point of view, I was not deeply involved in any acrimony. The parties who felt most aggrieved were athletes such as Linford Christie, Colin Jackson and John Regis, who were unhappy about adjustments that were made to the levels of their appearance money. But it was then that I realized

I had become a senior statesman in the sport, and with that position comes a degree of responsibility, and you can't just stand back and watch all the strife going on. I felt I was in a position to do something about the conflict. I didn't know Peter Radford, to be honest. Perhaps that highlights part of the problem.

I was getting a lot of information from Jon Ridgeon, who was working at the time for the sport's main marketing firm, owned by Alan Pascoe. It was clear that the acrimony in 1995 caused the sport enormous damage to relationships with sponsors – both individual meetings' sponsors and ITV, who were coming towards the end of their contract with British athletics and eventually did not renew it. It was disastrous in terms of PR. Neither side – neither Linford and Colin and co, nor Peter – were giving one second's thought to the way it was all affecting the sponsors. In sport you have got to keep sponsors happy, and the position was especially acute for athletics, given that it had been set up in such a way that it was almost entirely dependent on that revenue.

For the good of the sport the dispute should have been sorted out in private. But there were stories all over the press. And the situation became farcical when, supposedly after an agreement had been reached, some of the sport's top names such as Christie and Jackson turned up at the London grand prix at Crystal Palace solely for the purposes of signing autographs and giving television interviews. The fans must have thought, 'This is ridiculous. We don't want to see these athletes signing autographs, we want to see them running.' Fans don't care what you are getting paid, they just want to see you performing. The bottom line was that British athletes were failing to perform in Britain.

I think that was wrong. Rumour has it they were paid to do that. I couldn't say if that was true, but if it was, it must be viewed as bad financial management and a slap in the face to those who actually competed that night. But athletes such as Linford and Colin were wealthy enough to pick and choose events for their own needs, financial or otherwise. Some would argue that this had the effect of holding the sport to ransom. Perhaps they were, though they also had genuine grievances.

I've spoken to Linford about it subsequently, and for him and Colin the issue was the way they had been treated by Peter Radford. Colin had objected to being called in to Peter's office to account for himself after pulling out with an injury halfway through the AAA championships and running abroad the following day.

Linford was told that athletes' fees were too high and they were going to have to accept a cut in their appearance fees because of diminishing income. If the BAF had stuck to the set fee the row could have been avoided. If the BAF had been more consistent and applied the cut across the board there would have been fewer problems. If everyone had had to take a percentage cut it would have been fair. If the sport couldn't pay that much, then fine, 'I'm getting cut by that percentage, he's getting cut by the same.' But when Colin was offered a bigger fee than Linford, after both had been told there was no more money, Linford perceived that they had been played one against the other. It was mismanagement. It was a mess.

Peter misjudged the situation. These guys were not bigger than the sport, but they were pretty damn big. They had financial muscle. You couldn't say to them, 'Sit down, or you are not going to get your money, boys.' Because they didn't really need the money, they needed to feel they were being treated correctly. It was certainly true that the sport did not have the money it had had in previous years, but Peter's communication skills fell below an acceptable level.

There was a real, widespread feeling of discontent among the athletes then which was like nothing I had ever felt before. Everyone was blaming each other and moaning about everything. It was not a pleasant environment to be in. Athletics is the worst sport in the world for people moaning and complaining without doing anything. Perhaps it is because an athlete's basic instinct has to be to safeguard their resources in what is an unpredictable and often short-lived career.

I had a conversation at an airport with Mick Hill, the javelin thrower, during which he said to me, 'You know who you should speak to about all this? Geoff Parsons.' Mick pointed out that Geoff, who had briefly been British high jump record holder before the arrival of Dalton Grant on the scene in the late 1980s, had been concerned for a long time about the way the Federation was being run. He was the kind of person who would do something about it, writing letters, even canvassing for support within the media. He also knew a lot about the Federation's workings because he had attended many council meetings and AGMs.

Although my initial perception of Geoff was as an abrasive, person, I thought, 'I will, because something has to be done.' So I spoke to him and we set up a series of meetings with athletes all over the country to discuss how relations within the sport could be improved.

This was the pre-Olympic year, remember, and I recall Mike Whittingham was always on to me about the amount of time I spent on this project (even though he had been the key instigator in setting up better communications between athletes and the sport). He used to say, 'Why are you spending all these hours driving around?'

Both Geoff and I felt that what was missing was any kind of representative voice for the athletes. There was simply no line of communication with the Federation – hence no communication at all. We set out to create one. We spoke to Peter Radford. He had always claimed that the athletes were the most important thing in the sport – he would talk about it being an 'athlete-centred sport' – but saying things and doing something are not the same. The initiative to set up a line of communication came from the athletes' side, not the Federation's, although Peter encouraged and welcomed it, which is something he should be credited for.

We held a meeting in a London hotel and got sixteen of the

top British athletes – including Linford, Jonathan Edwards, John Regis, Sally Gunnell, Kelly Holmes, Jon Ridgeon, Steve Backley and Mick Hill – sitting round a table for the first time ever. Usually when athletes get together they just moan. So that was a significant moment of solidarity with a very positive aim.

Things snowballed, and the result was the formation of the British Athletes' Association early in 1996, and, though cynics would say that Peter just teamed up with the athletes because he knew he wasn't going to be around for much longer, he certainly put his money where his mouth was, because BAF did fund the BAA.

It was not easy. We didn't want to have a set up exactly like the old International Athletes Club, because it lost its sense of why it was there, and besides, many of its functions are now being carried out through National Lottery funding. What we decided upon was something that we felt was valid and open to everybody, and we did some important work sitting in on meetings with actual or potential sponsors to assure them of the goodwill of the athletes, and calm their fears about any repeat of the 1995 fiasco.

What happened at Crystal Palace then was a perfect example of the sport not working as a team. The reality is that the athletes, the federation and the sponsors are one big package and we all have to work with each other. If we don't the athletes won't be paid, as we discovered in 1997 when many of us were left being owed large sums of money. If we don't keep the sponsors happy, they will walk away. They can sponsor anything. TV channels can cover whatever they want, and there are plenty of other sports striving for the position athletics has occupied.

And that was where the BAA came in, to offer guarantees of good will to the sponsors and assure them that there was a new sense of commitment among athletes. We were not just soft soaping – there genuinely was a positive attitude among the majority of British athletes, and let's face it, bad publicity would only have the eventual effect of damaging everyone in the sport anyway.

Soon after its formation, however, the BAA hit a succession of problems beyond its control. First Peter Radford announced his intention to resign as BAF's executive chairman, then the BAF financial director resigned, and then BAF itself went bankrupt. That undermined the very existence of the BAA, as it was financially supported by BAF. Geoff, who had been appointed as a full-time employee on the BAA's behalf, spent most of his time doing extra work to cover for the BAF because they were simply running out of bodies. Suddenly the chief executive was gone, and Geoff had to help to prop the sport up as far as sponsors were concerned, which was not the role which had been envisaged for him.

The timing of Peter's resignation announcement shocked many people, as he had given an upbeat press briefing only a couple of days beforehand. It shocked me too, because he had been down at my house the day before for a meeting with the BAF chairman Ken Rickhuss, myself and Geoff. There was no doubt during that meeting that he was a man under enormous pressure. He wasn't answering the questions we were asking him, even though one of the successes of that year had been the fact that we had always been very open and honest with each other. There was quite clearly a problem, although I didn't know what it was. The following day I found out.

Peter has been accused of leaving a sinking ship. He will claim that he was being prevented from doing the job he was brought in to do, because the system in place did not allow him to make the decisions he needed to. Others would say he wasn't strong enough to sail the ship. You can see both sides. I think his vision and belief in the way athletics should be run and the way it should go forward will stand. I think he had his hands tied – but I don't think he was a strong enough communicator to lead British athletics.

There have been critics of the BAA who have accused it of being élitist. It wasn't set up as an élitist organisation; the intention was to serve every athlete. It certainly hasn't benefited any of the founders financially – indeed people like myself have lost money because of it when one considers the time we put into its formation. I still think it absolutely right to have an association within the sport with a separate voice for athletes. But they have got to use it, and athletes can be very lazy. Many people still expect everything to be given to them.

I think the BAA totally justified itself in the months following the BAF bankruptcy announcement. It gave the athletes a focus where they could sit round a table and discuss the ramifications of what had happened rather than all go off to fight their own little corner and try to get their share of the money. We are now properly informed about what is going on through Geoff Parsons. Before we never were.

In my position as a founder of the BAA I have had to placate television and sponsors on many occasions. Most of my talking with television people took place after ITV had decided to pull out of athletics. I was meeting representatives from the prospective new sponsors, Channel 4, who eventually signed a four-year deal in 1996. Channel 4 wanted to know why they should get involved in the sport when the top athletes weren't necessarily going to turn up because they kept falling out with the federation, and I had to say, 'We are doing our utmost to improve the situation. I can't give you a cast-iron guarantee, but in my opinion it won't happen again.' And it hasn't. Even Colin Jackson, who had said he would never run in Britain again, has done so, because there is a new sense of belonging.

The other thing the BAA tightened up on was athletes making personal appearances outside meetings. In 1996, a lot of promised appearances were not honoured. In 1997 they were all delivered. If the sport is to move forward, you have to deliver value for money both on and off the track.

If I could fast forward to the future, I would like the future British administration of the sport to be funded primarily by the Sports Council and the National Lottery. The whole thing should be overseen by David Moorcroft, who received widespread support when he was chosen as BAF's chief executive a matter of days before the collapse.

The reality is that if the sport is to survive into the twenty-first century, it can no longer be dependent on television and sponsorship money. And it is going to have to be run professionally by professional people. There should be someone to make sure the finances are ticking over, and a commercial director, someone who can liaise with the sponsors and television to make sure they are getting value for money and that the sport gets paid what it should. There should be a performance director whose sole job is the development of the sport, the coaching structure and the welfare of athletes. This could all be funded by the Lottery – that's what Lottery money is for.

The athletic meetings in this country should be owned by BAF, or a new body, and they should be leased out to a separate organization which would have responsibility for putting them on. BAF tried to do it all. And you can't do it all.

Before he was sacked as promotions officer in 1994, Andy Norman managed it. But, although he certainly got things done, he did it in a way that upset a lot of people. You can argue though, that if you had the amount of money he had to play with, anybody could have got things done. After all, ITV had come in with a £10 million contract in the 1980s.

I think Andy probably could have got things done even without that amount of money. No one else has been able to replace him. The promotions unit has never since been able to match his sheer output of work. If you wanted somebody to get athletes together and put a meeting on, it would be Andy Norman because he is just consumed by the business.

You need to keep the commercial side away from BAF. Let someone else do it whose livelihood depends on it. And then put on a good meeting. BAF owns the rights, so they get paid. The athletes get paid by a separate company, so they are fine. And then BAF can do what it is there for, namely developing the sport without being dependent on these big meetings to finance the whole operation.

Of course the crisis with BAF affected athletes in the most direct way possible. I was among many top performers who were owed large sums of money. The BAA held a crisis meeting attended by the administrators, and when we asked them about which creditors would get paid first, obviously the question on all the athletes' minds was, 'When will we get our money?'

They said it would depend upon the result of the legal case being pursued by Diane Modahl, who is currently suing the Federation for half a million pounds following her successful appeal against a drugs ban. If she won, she would be the primary creditor, along with the office staff, and after that the athletes would get a percentage. So it seemed we were pretty low down the list.

Then Jon Ridgeon asked, 'What about your own fees? You're primary creditors too, aren't you?' And they said, 'No. No we're not.' Now that came as a total surprise. Everyone was saying, 'Really? Is that right? So you boys are down with us then?'

To which they then replied: 'No. We're pre-primary!'

The best place to be, without a doubt.

Whatever happens, talented athletes will always be out there. I didn't need Lottery money to help me win medals – I just did it. It's true that looking back it has been very tough at times, and it shouldn't have to be that bad. It is still not going to be easy for youngsters coming through – and it shouldn't be.

The crisis won't affect the strength of the British athletics team. What it will affect is whether people can actually make a good living or not. Of course, the argument is that if people are going to do it professionally they have to be able to make a decent living out of it. I would certainly agree with that. If I couldn't have made a living out of it, I don't know that I would have lasted this long. The future for athletes could be in serious jeopardy if the sport does not take this opportunity to look at itself and make radical changes.

There are good people out there. Moorcroft is a popular man who has the support of most people in the sport. That's easy to say because he hasn't any baggage. As long as he has the freedom to make the right decisions and to do the right things, then the sport can move forward. But if his hands are tied like Peter Radford's with power struggles and clashing egos, then people will spend all their time fighting and what they are fighting for will disappear. Then there's nothing left to fight over – and that's what happened.

What professional athletics is about is giving young people the opportunity to compete, to compete for their country, and to be part of the product that is televisual, attractive to sponsors, and therefore money-making for both the individual and the sport.

The blame for the crisis has to lie with bad planning, with thinking that sponsorship from television would always be there, and always be lucrative. There was too much bureaucracy. There were management boards, the council, all this unwieldy structure – a system which did not allow anyone to make the big decisions quickly – which is essential in the business world. Any successful business must be organized so that there are people who can make important decisions without having to go and ask somebody else. This cumbersome set-up has now been swept away – and it could be for good, we'll have to wait and see.

Questions have been raised, following the demise of BAF, about athletes being overpaid. There are probably many in athletics who feel that. But I would say what I have always said that there is not one athlete, and there is not one athletic environment. The world I live in is very different from that of the club athletes, although their reasons for doing it are the same as mine – to fulfil their true potential, to train as hard as they can, to run as fast as they can, or jump as high as they can, or throw as far as they can.

When you get to a certain level – and very few athletes get there – and perform on the world stage going from meeting to meeting, you become a commodity. You are a commodity for television, for sponsors for interviewers after a good story. It is a highly competitive world where you have to give twenty-four-hour, full commitment to get anywhere. You can try doing it part-time, but very few people get away with that in today's athletic world, when so many athletes from so many countries are competing that a great degree of professionalism is required to succeed.

The word professionalism, which many regard as a dirty word, is not just about making money from the sport, it's about how you conduct yourself. When I have been reported in the press as saying that British athletics is being run by amateurs, I don't mean that they're useless people. I don't mean that they're people who don't care and who don't want to do well. I mean that many of them are part-timers. You cannot run the business side of the sport in that way.

At the beginning of every year I sit down with my manager, Mike Whittingham, and we decide on race fees for Europe and Britain. I get paid more in Britain. We are in a commercial marketplace. When Linford Christie and Colin Jackson were getting paid as much, or more, to run in Europe as in Britain, obviously they were going to make their decisions on where to run accordingly. Most of us get paid three times more in Britain than we do in Europe. Sometimes more, proportionally, because the British TV audience ensures we are worth more here. It's market forces. The finger was pointed at athletes for being too greedy – and I can understand people thinking that when you look at the sums of money involved – but fees have always been agreed by promoters, so you assume the sport can pay. If someone was being too greedy, the promoters would simply say, 'We can't pay you that much.'

In 1997 I was paid more for my races than ever before – as Olympic silver medallist. I assumed the money would be there, but now, like many others, I am waiting. In his defence, I think Ian Stewart, the BAF promotions officer, thought it would be there as well.

I don't know of anyone who is really struggling as a result, but people have been hit. I think many people are realizing that the money side is totally out of our control now. It's a salutary lesson for the athletes of the future. It teaches them that if running is their business, there is the possibility that one of their paymasters may go bankrupt. Therefore athletes should always be prudent and realize two things: one, they could be injured tomorrow, and two, until they have seen the money in their bank account they shouldn't assume it's there. I'm not sure I would like to be a young athlete now.

18

THE JENKINS FACTOR

In the course of the past twelve years I have become increasingly fascinated by the difference between those who fulfil their potential, and those who underachieve. Why do some people who have enormous talent never fulfil it? Why do those with less natural ability manage to achieve more? What is it that makes the difference? In the world of athletics, with the intense focus that is required on oneself, it is important to address these questions, although they are equally valid for the world outside sport.

The philosophy in sport that mental strength is of the utmost importance – that success is 90 per cent mental and only 10 per cent physical – is clearly absurd. If you are physically unable to perform, it doesn't matter how mentally strong you are, you are simply not going to win. The primary element in an athlete's performance is physical ability. But the mental aspect of the performance, particularly at the highest level when you have to assume that everyone else is also an excellent athlete, is the difference between being excellent and being outstanding. It's a small step, but it is fundamental to success.

As a young athlete I had a naive approach. I worked on my physical performance, and it was a wonderfully simple routine, but now in my thirties the mental aspect of maintaining peak performance has become vitally important. It becomes increasingly important as you get older. The problem with sports psychology is that most athletes know they should do it, but they don't take it upon themselves to find out about it. They expect other people to do it for them.

I started reading books on psychology in 1993 when I got glandular fever and was obliged to ask serious questions of myself about my own motivation. I realized that there was an area of mental preparation which was crucial, and I do believe that the vast majority of athletes do not tap in to their mental abilities. I think the reason for that is in the nature of athletics because you do it young, you achieve young, and then you become scared of accepting that there is anything more to it, that there is another side. Athletes still think that if you just go out and train hard you are going to get the results. Well, yes, you have to train hard to get any results. But there are a lot of other things you can do mentally which I know have worked for me and for people like Sven Nylander: the power of visualization, the power behind the questioning approach. Asking the right questions of yourself, and getting the right answers.

I have found the answers to these questions in a lot of self-development books. America is the home of self-improvement. It is the natural habitat for psychoanalysis, and therapy – and in California it is like an epidemic. I am fully aware that too much analysis can be self-defeating, but I do believe you have to be open to new things, you have to evolve.

Over the past few years I have read a lot, and with Sven have researched and attended seminars in America. Now this interest has taken on a new turn. There is a market among companies to have sports celebrities as motivational speakers. The only thing that gives me the same buzz as performing on an athletics track is delivering a positive motivational speech, a speech that could contribute to an individual's development, a speech that could make a difference.

When I started speaking to business people, I quickly realized that it was not just my sporting achievements which interested the audience, but the development, the self-knowledge and the evolution that underpinned those achievements.

The concept of achieving the perfect performance is as relevant to any individual as it has been to me. The environment and the arena for those peak performances may be different – they may not be running around a 400 metres track – but once someone has identified what they want to achieve I can supply the tools to help them reach their goal.

I have achieved my professional goal. What I focus on in my talks now are the questions I have had to ask myself to get there:

1. Do I have the desire to reach my full potential?
2. Am I driven by a need to achieve, or by the fear of failure?
3. Do I just want to win, or do I need to win?

We do things for two reasons, to avoid pain (fear of failure) or to gain pleasure (need for achievement). Fear of failure is a motivator, but it is not the ultimate motivator. I had experienced these things before I ever picked up a book on the subject. And when I read about it it made sense, because I had been developing this philosophy myself. I had already mastered the process of goal-setting, a necessity for any athlete with serious aspirations.

The process of implementing a proper training programme, and surrounding yourself with training partners – I had Kriss Akabusi, Sven Nylander, Jon Ridgeon and Mark Richardson – was also something I had done in practice before reflecting on in theory. I also mention teamwork, and what could be a better example of that than the 1991 World Championships quartet, who won the gold medal by changing the running order, putting egos to one side, and recognizing that the greater good of the team is more important than any individual. That is the essence of teamwork.

And I have personal experience of the principle of synergy – the principle that one plus one can equal more than two. It is an accurate reflection of my relationship with Kriss Akabusi.

Talking about those fundamentals is the basis of my motivational speaking. It is my main aim to get that across to people – but I always end on the frustrations of success and on my defining moment of Olympic achievement.

People often come up to me afterwards to discuss different elements which have interested them. For some, it is the business of goal-setting. Often, it's about the fear of failure. When I admit my fear of failing, and how I have worked to turn it round, it seems to strike a chord with many people.

While I am developing a career in television at the moment, the main thrust of my future will be to develop my motivational speaking to a point where it can really influence change in people. I know how to get through the bad times. I know, and hopefully I can convey that to others, how to reach a point of self-development where you can stand behind your own metaphorical line, ready to run your perfect race. It has happened to me, and I would like to draw on my experiences to help others.

Success is a balancing act. I do not believe anybody should strive to achieve their personal goals at the cost of everything else in their lives, but I do believe they should *try* to fulfil their potential. To change oneself is hard work, though, and you have to continue to work on that development. And to do that you have to be open to other influences.

There was somebody I had to phone after winning my Olympic silver medal. He was at home in California at the time, and when I said, 'Hi Jenks. It's Roger . . .' there was a silence on the other end of the line. Then David Jenkins started chuckling, and I started chuckling, until he said to me very quietly, 'Thank you.'

'What do you mean?' I asked.

'Thank you for allowing me to complete my athletic career,' he said.

Jenks had failed as an athlete. He had had the talent, but that was not enough, because, as he never tired of telling me, talent is something that has to be applied. And he had made mistakes in life, big mistakes. He admitted having taken drugs for some years while he was running because he didn't have confidence in himself, even though they didn't actually help improve his performance.

We have always talked together as one British 400 metres runner to another. And he felt he had been able to set right the mistakes he had made in his career through helping me to realize my potential. He needed to exorcise his demons through me.

Before the Olympics, Jenks had been talking about getting me a mobile phone so I didn't need to worry about not being able to contact him at any time. But in the end he didn't go ahead with that plan, which showed how well he knew my character, because at that stage I felt utterly ready for what lay ahead, and my natural inclination at such times is to retreat into myself. He realized that he would have been seeking regular advice in my situation, but that that did not mean it would be the right thing for me.

Our communication throughout the Games was all one-way as Jenks sent me a succession of telegrams via the British Olympic Association office. The tone of his messages was very consistent, reminding me of the fundamental points we had been through earlier in the year. It was as if I was programmed to do what I was about to do. This fax he sent to me before the Olympic trials gives the flavour:

Man, I would love to be in your shoes this weekend. You can stamp it down and show them. You can enjoy it for all it's worth . . . relishing every step, every moment. All the preparation . . . all that preparation. You are in your zenith. A fabulous time to be alive. And we only go around once. So . . . Enjoy it . . . Enjoy it . . . Enjoy it!

No matter the weather. No matter the wind. No matter the lanes. No matter who. No matter how. I wouldn't want to race against you this weekend. You know what to do. You know how. You know it all in every fibre of your body. YOU ARE READY.

It's been a pleasure and a privilege. Sincerely, Jenks.

Messages reached me in Atlanta after every round of the Olympics. The last one before the final read: 'You are in control. This is your destiny. All you have to do now is execute it.' Afterwards, I realized a curious detail. Such was the delay on the telegrams that every one had had to be sent before the result of the previous race was known. That is what you call confidence.

The key to my performance in 1996 lay in one conversation I had with Jenks once he had agreed to oversee my Olympic preparations. He started by asking me what my goals were for that year.

'Well, I'd like to win an Olympic medal and I'd like to break the British record.' I said. 'Right. You can forget that right now.'

'Well, OK, so . . . ?'

'From this day onwards you will have one goal, a simple one you will carry with you every day, and that is the goal of running your perfect race,' Jenks said.

Then he asked me what my perfect race was. We talked it through and tried to analyse what it was for me. It certainly wasn't to go off too quickly and die. It wasn't to go off slowly and let it come home. We broke down the whole race. But the idea of the perfect race didn't just apply to a race. It meant trying to make every training session perfect. Everything I could control had to be done right – look at my nutrition, do my yoga and stretching. And there was to be no worrying about the opposition, not even thinking about them or the Olympics. Just taking every day, every session as it came. Not thinking ahead too far – just one week at a time.

That one shift of emphasis crystallized everything for me. I really started to run with enjoyment. I made myself enjoy what I was doing. It all fitted into place. I missed the Seoul Olympics,

I was injured in Barcelona, so only one thing could happen in Atlanta. I started to believe things like that. I wasn't thinking about gold, silver or bronze medals, because all that had gone. I was thinking, 'If I run my perfect race on the day I'm asked to do it, then I'm going to be a hard man to beat.'

Jenks always said other people shape their own destiny and you can't alter that. So if someone else were to come along and run their perfect race and beat me, then so be it. I think what he was telling me was, 'Rog, I spent my whole career worrying about other people. I spent my whole career choking when it really mattered. I spent my whole career needing it so badly and being so insecure about it all that I resorted to drugs. I spent my whole career analysing things to the point of analising it. Whereas in the end it is very simple. If you focus on what you can control and you don't put yourself under the pressure of worrying about what everybody else does. Another man may beat you in a race, but he cannot take away from you your own personal sense of achievement. You can control that.'

That was very liberating for me. Some people have questioned my approach to the Olympic Games. The conventional wisdom is that you have got to think you are going to win it, that you are going to get the gold medal. I'd been around for ten or twelve years, and I believed in the concept of running your perfect race. I absolutely believe I did the right thing. I absolutely know that I if I had reacted to Michael Johnson I would not have done so well. This was neither the time nor the place to experiment. I did see myself getting the silver medal. I saw the whole race exactly how it panned out. Now there's an issue. Is that negative? Seeing yourself with the silver medal?

Some psychologists might say 'You came second because you didn't see yourself coming first.' But I think anyone who understands the situation, who understands who you are up against, who understands the folly of trying to run somebody else's race, who is significantly faster than you on paper, will know that the Olympic final is not the time to try and run

43.5sec when the best you've ever run is 44.37. If I had tried to do that I would have finished fifth or sixth.

I was thinking of running the perfect race and I knew that if I ran my perfect race, at best, what would it be – 44.10sec, 44.20? That wouldn't beat Michael Johnson – unless Michael Johnson had an injury. I just kept seeing the silver medal. I kept seeing myself coming second.

Many people feel 'I've got to win, I've got to win, I've got to win. If I don't win it's not worth doing.' But only one person is going to win. If winning is everything to you, then ultimately you are going to be disappointed. But you can always win by saying, 'I ran my perfect race.' Because the rules for your success are not dependent on a gold medal. Or a silver.

In March 1996 I was looking round an art gallery during one of my training visits to California. It had been at the back of my mind to see if I could chance upon any inspiration in what was an Olympic year, when I was drawn to a magnificent sculpture of a gymnast hanging on a point of sublime balance over a pommel horse. As I read the notes on this sculpture I was thrilled to discover that it was a small scale copy of the official Atlanta Olympic sculpture which stood outside the city's Georgia Dome. The artist had been inspired by an Olympic motto I had never heard of until then:

'The essence lies not in the victory, but in the struggle.'

The more I thought about it, the better it got. This phrase summed up my entire career. To me, the message is that there is no point in achieving any goal if you have not learned from, or enjoyed the journey. I bought the sculpture.

Four months later in Atlanta, an Olympic silver medallist, I made my way to the Georgia Dome to see the original. And as I stood in front of it, admiring it once again, I felt that a long and testing journey had been completed.

19

END OF THE ROAD

My goal in 1998 was a very clear one – to end my career where it all began by winning the European 400m title for the third time. I had my Olympic medal – I'd even run my perfect race and, in athletic terms fulfilled my potential – yet I still had this goal of finishing where it had all begun: on top with another European title. In Stuttgart in 1986 I was twenty years old and naïve – maybe all that was different in 1998 was that I was thirty-two years old. I was still naïve.

I had always wanted to choose the day I finally hung up my spikes but even I could not have foreseen the controversy and chain of events that eventually resulted in my final lap of honour.

I began my winter training in October 1997 following a similar programme to previous years: a usual week comprised of two weights sessions, two track sessions and plenty of aerobic running and circuit training. The key sessions, such as 8 x 200m or 6 x 300m with short recovery times, would always leave my legs heavy and full of lactic acid. As I walked off the track in pain after each session, I took comfort in the knowledge that I would never have to put myself through this ordeal day in, day out again. Each session was ticked off as the last of its kind and this gave me all the motivation I needed to give 100 per cent. Mark Richardson, Mark Hylton and the young sprinter Marlon Devonish provided the company and quality of training partner for most sessions, although now and again I would choose to train alone, running up a steep hill six to eight times fighting gravity just for old time's sake. This was a part of my training that I'd enjoyed during my early days in Southampton in 1985/6 and I wanted to recapture some of those days in my final winter's training.

For Mark Richardson and I, those winter months gave us the opportunity to train consistently together and by March we were eager to fly to California, ready to move up a gear and get down to the hard 400m training in the sun. Our relationship both on and off the track had matured and even though time was never going to allow us to experience synergy to the level that Kriss Akabusi and I had enjoyed, we both felt fortunate to have each other around – even though we were both pursuing the same goal. From the outside looking in it may have appeared that he had by far the better part of the deal as it seemed that I provided the experience, stability and strength that he required and he could just follow me in training and step up a gear now and again. Many people were concerned that I was sacrificing myself for him in training but if he had not been around I know I would not have been able to motivate myself to train to such a high level day in day out. He was my bench mark, and if I was to become European champion I had to beat Mark Richardson to do so. In hindsight, the reason we could never synergize perfectly was that my strength was his weakness and vice-versa – I would dominate any speed endurance session and Mark would dominate every speed session. There was never any middle ground; we could improve each other's individual weaknesses but could never experience moving forward together – we were two individuals on the same track whereas Kriss and I had at times become one.

If an athlete is to receive help and advice the person giving assistance must do so unconditionally for it to be of real value. By the beginning of May I knew that I was not doing so with Mark – I wanted him to improve, to run fast, to become one with the 400m but on one condition – that he didn't beat me. As he began to run spectacular times in training my confidence began to lower and I was beginning to believe that I couldn't compete with him. He had simply moved on to a higher level and no matter how much I tried to pretend it didn't affect me, his performances in training were becoming the focus of my attention. I was becoming a reactive athlete but I had been around long enough to know that I had to become proactive if I was to have any chance of becoming European champion. Mark and I spoke at length about the situation and agreed that it would be best if we trained separately from that point on. All the hard work had been done, we were both mean enough and ugly enough (in his case anyway) to take on the rest of the world individually and it was time to see each other as competitors, not partners. A huge weight was lifted off both our shoulders and from that moment on he knew I meant business and respected me for it, although his confidence was so high I'm sure he didn't see me as a serious threat.

When an athlete is fit, healthy and running fast times in training then lack of confidence is never a problem. Throughout my career the stopwatch would always tell me what sort of shape I was in as I began to run my first races of the season. I was not an athlete who left his running on the training track – I would always perform well under race conditions, especially if my training had been going well. As I flew back home from California towards the end of May, I knew I was fit, healthy and focused but my training times were not quite at the usual level – I felt I needed to find another gear and would do so by racing.

It was a conversation with Kriss Akabusi that allowed me to face up to the reality of my situation and the challenge that lay ahead. Kriss said to me, 'Roger – let's look at the facts – you're thirty-two years old, you had a virus in 1997, you've ultimately fulfilled your potential and the 400m is a young man's event. I know you can become European champion, but it won't be as easy as it was in 1996.' He then produced a pearl of wisdom that seemed to sum up my situation: 'During my last couple of seasons I used to tell myself the following: I may not be as good as I once was but I can be as good once as I ever was!'

That was it, that one phrase summed up exactly how I felt. I was unable to perform consistently in training at the level I had prior to the Olympics but I had to respect my body and mind enough to know that it was going to be hard to run consistently around 44.5 seconds. However, when it mattered, when I would be called upon to dig deep and find once more the form that had won me so many medals over the years, then I could be as good as I ever was. In effect, that meant that only two races mattered – the AAA Championships (the European Trials) and the European Championships. Every other race was just a stepping stone towards competing at those events.

My first race of the season was supposed to be in Seville on 30 May, but a strike by Spanish Air Traffic Control put a stop to that. As a result I found myself lining up in Bratislava the following week against both Iwan Thomas and Jamie Baulch for my first 400m of the year. I won the race in 45.36 seconds – a despondent Iwan Thomas coming third in 45.70 seconds. As we waited to be presented with our medals a very anxious and worried Iwan Thomas was clearly struggling with nausea and fatigue.

'Great race Rog,' he said. 'Christ knows what happened to me – I feel terrible.' 'Iwan, you'll be fine,' I replied. 'You've been injured. Go back, get healthy, get focused and come back when you're ready.'

In hindsight, of course, I should have kept my mouth shut and just let him wallow in his misery. I believe that race was the turning point for Iwan, not just in his season, but possibly his career, since he found out just how hard a career at 400m is and that you cannot afford to be unprepared. The test for the champion is to come through the bad times a stronger athlete and Iwan went on to win European and Commonwealth 400m titles in 1998 and prove himself to be not just a great athlete but, more importantly, a true champion.

Athletics has always been and always will be an individual

sport, yet once a year a British team competes for the European Cup. The British men's team went to St Petersburg in Russia towards the end of June as Cup holders, and I had the privilege of being team captain. On paper we were expected to come third behind the Russians and the Germans but, due to some outstanding performances from the new breed of young talent, we found ourselves still in with a chance of retaining the Cup with just one event remaining. Fortunately for Britain the last event was the 4x400m relay and with the team comprising of myself, Jamie Baulch, Iwan Thomas and Mark Richardson it was a safe bet that we would win the race, keep hold of the Cup and, more importantly, silence the Russian crowd. As expected we dominated the race, winning by a clear thirty metres. Receiving the European Cup as British team captain was a memorable occasion, particularly as it turned out to be my last appearance for my country. That victory proved, once again, that Britain has an athletics team it should be proud of – a team that can dominate in Europe despite the administrative and financial problems of its federation.

That evening the 400m squad celebrated victory with the rest of the team, knowing full well that the following day we would have to put our friendships to one side, go our separate ways and prepare individually in search of the European 400m title.

As the AAA Championships approached, Iwan Thomas, Mark Richardson and myself were the clear favourites to take the first three places with the outsiders being Mark Hylton, Jamie Baulch and the unpredictable Solomon Wariso. (I say unpredictable but if there was one thing about Solomon that was predictable it was his unpredictability.) Solomon is fundamentally a 200m runner who has, over the years, flirted with the 400m. He is a wonderfully fluid athlete whose natural ability is clear for all to see. Before 1998 he was best known as the athlete who was banned for three months from the sport in 1994 for taking a supplement called, somewhat bizarrely, 'Up Your Gas', which contains excessive amounts of a stimulant on the banned list. Solomon is somebody I like very much and over the years our paths had crossed, not so much on but off the track – he's a fast-talking hyperactive person who at times can make statements so perplexing that even the most level headed of athletics journalists have been heard to proclaim: 'The man's raving mad!'

I shared a room with him in Rieti, Italy, in 1994/5, at a time when he was considering retiring from the sport. We talked for hours about opinions, beliefs and goals and I kept remind-ing him that our days in athletics are precious ones that we must appreciate and keep struggling through in order to fulfil our potential. Solomon was subsequently to recite this conversation to many a journalist in the coming weeks, claim-ing that I had helped keep him in the sport instead of quitting. Once again, with hindsight, I should have kept my mouth shut and got a good night's sleep and let him join the many talented athletes who give up far too early when the going gets tough.

The selection policy for the European Championships was a clear and accepted one – the first two athletes in the AAA Championships would gain automatic selection (so long as the required qualification standard was achieved) and the third place would be left to the discretion of the selectors who had up to two weeks to make that final selection.

As usual the men's 400m was the main focus of the public's attention. All the main contenders made it to the final, includ-ing Solomon Wariso whose personal dramas began to take place the morning of the race. His goal for 1998 was simply to be in the 4x400m relay team at the European Championships – a team that should come home with a gold medal, some-thing that he rightly wanted to possess. Individually, however, he felt he had a better chance of success at the European Championships in the 200m, the heats and finals of which took place the same day as the 400m final. Solomon felt that if he made the 400m final, but only ran the 200m final, he would have done enough to merit a place in the 4x400m squad at the Championships. He claims he discussed this with the national coach who categorically said that if he wished to be considered for the 4x400m team, he had to run the 400m final. So in effect, what was left was an athlete who would have to sacrifice individual success in the 200m for a relay medal – it was Catch 22 for him and in the end, at thirty-two years old, he wanted an almost certain European gold medal in the 4x400m relay. For a national coach to give an athlete such an ultimatum is both unfair and unwarranted – the precedent for 4x400m selection had been set many times before, most notably in 1990 and 1991 when John Regis, a 200m runner, ran in both the European and World Championship-winning 4x400m relay teams.

I had cruised through the heats and semi-finals and felt confident that I would run fast in the final – I had got my timing right and Kriss Akabusi's words were proving to be apt. Ultimately in athletics you can only try and do your very best – that had become my rule for success and I knew that I had the ability to run between 44.4 and 44.7 seconds at that moment in time. On paper only Mark Richardson and Iwan Thomas were capable of running that fast and so, in theory, I would at worst come third in the final. The beauty of sport, however, is that the unexpected can always happen and on Sunday 26 July at 7.50pm it came in the form of Solomon Wariso. With 100 metres to go Mark Richardson, Iwan Thomas and myself were about neck and neck with the rest of the field apparently beaten – I was relaxed and closer to Mark than I had been over the preceding weeks. As we searched for the line, Mark and I began to tire and Iwan came through to win in 44.50, Mark was second in 44.62 and I dipped for the line so close to them both I believed I must have got the third place. As I stumbled and fell over the line I noticed a shadow to the far right of the track . 'Who the hell was that?' I thought and before I had time to answer my own question the body of Solomon Wariso was spread-eagled on the floor. 'Surely not?' I thought. 'This could be very inconvenient.' The scoreboard flashed up the result:

1st	Iwan Thomas	44.50
2nd	Mark Richardson	44.62
3rd	Solomon Wariso	44.68
4th	Roger Black	44.71

Three hundredths of a second – not even the width of a vest – three hundredths of a second over 400m – the difference between third and fourth. I congratulated Iwan, Mark and Solomon and walked off the track stunned. I picked up my tracksuit and headed straight for the warm-down area. I had two thoughts as I walked from the stadium. Firstly I was proud that I'd run 44.71 seconds – I knew I'd done the best I could and felt it deep inside – it's an inner knowledge that all competitors can feel and I had no complaints regarding my personal performance. I had performed when it mattered and had certainly given Iwan and Mark something to think about. My second thought was that I now had two weeks in which to build on this performance – I had to find some races to run consistently around 44.5 seconds, which I knew I would have to do if I were to gain the third place in the team ahead of Solomon. Yes, he had beaten me on the day but it was only by three hundredths of a second and surely that could not be enough for the selectors to instantly give him the discretionary place.

As I jogged around the perimeter of the warm-down area I began to focus on the task that lay ahead – to forget today's race and to prepare to claim my place on the team – I would have to perform superbly to do so, I accepted that, but it was a challenge I believed I was up to facing and I had to begin to focus on it immediately if I was to succeed.

I tried to look ahead, to be positive, but underneath it all I was becoming choked with emotion and disappointment that I'd given it all I had on the day but it just hadn't been enough. From a distance I could see my old friend Jon Ridgeon walking towards me. As he reached me it just set me off – I sat down with tears in my eyes and said, 'Jon, I gave it everything, everything I had.' 'You did yourself proud,' he said. 'Everyone who

271

understands this sport knows how well you ran tonight.' Alan Pascoe joined him and reiterated his words and they both just assumed that we would have to wait two weeks to find out who would get the third place in the team.

All I wanted to do was get in my car and drive down the M40 to home but to add insult to injury first I had to go through the inconvenience of a drug test which, I can assure you, is the last thing you feel like doing after an emotional race. Afterwards, as I made my way to my car Mike Whittingham told me that many people felt I'd actually done enough to be selected ahead of Solomon. I found this somewhat hard to believe but was later to discover that in the post-race press conference Solomon himself said that I should be selected and that he only ever wanted to run the 200m and the 4x400m. A quite bizarre situation had arisen, yet all I wanted to do was get home, get some sleep and wake up the next morning ready to focus on possibly the most challenging two weeks of my career.

As I drove home I began to look at the options facing the selectors that evening; at the same time I understood that it was their job to select the best possible team for the championship. To compare myself and Solomon as 400m runners would be unfair to him. The only thing we had in common was our age. I was a tried and tested championship performer with fourteen major medals to my name; he was an athlete who had always been disappointed at major championships. To judge us on just one race would be equally unfair to me, especially since the margin of victory was so minuscule. The more I looked at the situation the more apparent it became that the selectors did not have enough evidence on which to make an immediate decision and fortunately for them they did not have to make a final decision for two weeks. It was a situation that clearly showed the sense of having a selection policy that is not simply first three past the post.

I was sure the only sensible and logical option the selectors had was to give us two weeks to improve our cases for selection and make their job easier. The pressure would be on me and I would have to run very fast – a couple of 44.3s to 44.5s would suffice – a very tough task, but at least I would have a chance.

Due to my championship record, experience and quite simply because I'd earned the right, many felt I could have been selected immediately even though I'd come fourth. At the time I thought that would be as unfair to Solomon as it would be to me if they selected him immediately. The more I looked at the situation, the more it became clear that the only logical option was to wait for two weeks and see if I could prove beyond any doubt that I was the right man for the job.

I had been at home for no more than half an hour when the phone rang.

'Roger, this is Graham Knight (the National Sprint Coach) speaking. I'm phoning to let you know that we've had the selection meeting and have decided to take the first three from today's race.'

For a moment I was speechless. 'But Graham, you didn't have to make that decision now. One race Graham, three hundredths of a second. Your job's to select the best man for the job. How can you make that decision on one race?'

'It wasn't an easy decision Roger, but in the end all the selectors were unanimous.'

Now that was a statement I found particularly hard to believe. 'Why can't you give me a chance to prove myself? I expect no favours but at least give me a chance.'

'There's nothing you could do in the next two weeks.'

'Yes there is,' I replied, 'I could break the British record in Brussels or Sheffield.'

I tried to make my case but in the end it was futile trying to carry on the conversation. The decision had been made and it was final. At least this time the selectors had had the decency to let me know my fate personally before notifying the press.

'Thank you for your call, Graham.' I added, 'You've just made a very big mistake.'

I put the phone down and just sat there feeling numb, trying to come to terms with the fact that the one goal I'd had left in my athletic career had suddenly vanished and more to the point I felt that it had been taken away from me. Before it had had time to sink in the phone rang.

'Roger, hi, it's Jenks – how did you get on?' It was David Jenkins phoning from America to get the results – his sense of timing was so ironic.

'Jenks, I...' I couldn't speak I was so choked with emotion.

'What happened?'

Eventually I began to talk. 'I ran 44.71, I came fourth to Wariso who ran 44.68...and they've just selected him.'

'Arseholes' was all Jenks could say. 'Don't they understand anything about this business – it's not first three past the post – can't they see your timing is right and you will be ready for the Europeans? So Wariso got lucky, so what? You're a champion, can't they see that?'

Unfortunately none of the selectors had such vision. Their decision surprised the vast majority of the athletics world – athletes, fans, journalists and even Solomon Wariso himself. 'I feel like I've shot JFK,' he was later to proclaim. We talked a couple of days later and he clearly felt bad about the whole situation. I assured him that it wasn't his fault and that he should try and prove the selectors right, although we both knew that to do so he'd have to at least win a bronze medal at the Europeans – something he should do easily on paper, but with his championship record you wouldn't bet on it.

As it turned out, Solomon struggled at the European Championships and was disqualified in the final after coming seventh. Some of the very same people who had put so much faith in him weeks before, decided to drop him from the relay team, which meant that he was unable to challenge for his main goal of the season...something else we now had in common.

Contrary to public opinion Solomon never at any point offered me his place in the team. As a fellow athlete I never expected him to do so but would I have taken up the offer? Damn right I would!

I just couldn't understand how the selectors could be so

short sighted and inept. Were they simply looking at one race and one time? If the same situation had arisen with, say, someone with Linford Christie's character, would they have come to such a quick decision and risk facing his wrath? Was it something personal regarding me? I didn't think so as I knew most of them and we bore no grudges. In the end I put it down to committee mentality and how the necessity to make a decision collectively can often cause rational, sensible individuals not to stand up and be counted. I say this in the knowledge that at least three people in the room that night have subsequently voiced deep regret that they allowed a decision that they knew was both wrong and unnecessary in the circumstances to be made that evening.

The press had a field day and made all the salient points in my defence without me having to speak to any of them. Sebastian Coe – a greater champion than I – who suffered a similar fate in 1984 simply said, 'Oh well, nothing changes there then!' Public debate on TV, radio and in the written press showed that 90 per cent of people felt I had been badly treated. Many fans wrote scathing letters to the selectors – some demanding resignations – but in the end a decision had been taken and would stand.

So that was it, I wasn't going to end my career battling it out for the European 400m title. What I had to do now was decide how I would end my career. It's a decision that an athlete shouldn't take either lightly or on the spur of the moment, so I decided to give myself two days to think things through before choosing how, when and where.

I spoke at length with the people who had played such important roles throughout my athletic career – Mike Whittingham, David Jenkins, Tony Lester, Joe Picken, Kriss Akabusi and Jon Ridgeon. I knew I had many options, from trying to become Commonwealth champion to just racing anywhere on the European circuit to make some money. They all knew what they would do in similar circumstances, but they understood that what might be the right decision for them might be the wrong one for me. In the end it was Sven Nylander who helped me see that there was only one decision I could make if I was to be consistent and true to myself. I had had only one goal in 1998, to try and win the European 400m title but that goal was no longer a possibility. Historically I was an athlete who performed when it mattered, I was motivated by clearly defined personal goals and had learnt that to survive in the competitive world of athletics you had to keep setting new goals, especially during periods of disappointment.

I now had to set new goals but they had to be away from the athletics track. There was no goal left athletically that could motivate me to focus to the level I expected of myself. Quite simply, there was nothing left that mattered enough and to hang around the track, training half-heartedly just to be part of a relay team that would win the European Championships with or without me was not the way I had wanted to end my career. I had had a long, fulfilling career, I had experienced what all athletes search for, I'd stood on the Olympic rostrum – my potential fulfilled – and had given it my best shot in 1998. I wasn't going to let this present situation tarnish all the great memories I'd had over the years.

I sat for two hours on a hill overlooking the countryside near my home and reflected on those thirteen years – the people, the places, the races, the victories, the defeats, the injuries, the oper-ations and, of course, the medals. I'd been lucky to have the talent in the first place, to have messed up that maths exam that set me on my way to an athletic career that reached its peak in Atlanta in 1996. From that perspective the events of the previ-ous few days seemed insignificant and as I stood up and turned my back on the view I felt comfortable with the decision I had taken: to run one more race, on my favourite British track in Sheffield a week later.

I'm sure the selectors would have wanted me to keep running until the end of the season and exit quietly from the sport but I had other plans and recognized the opportunity to announce my retirement in a blaze of publicity. I wanted to make an impact and, with the help of Jon Ridgeon and Mike Whittingham, a carefully orchestrated press conference was called for Thursday 30 July in central London. Together we prepared a written statement explaining the reasons for my decision. I wanted people to appreciate the anger I felt towards the selectors without looking like a whiner who couldn't take rejection.

I'd given many press conferences in my time, but none of them like this. As I entered the room it was full of press, TV and radio, the familiar faces of the athletics writers lost in the crowd. I sat down and paused, knowing that what I was about to say was being covered live on both TV and radio. During such moments, when everything revolves around you, it is often tempting to say or do something outrageous but I resisted the urge to drop my trousers in front of the nation and began to read my statement. I'd never needed to prepare or read my words at a press conference before and it all felt unnatural and rehearsed, which of course it was. As a result, I was pleased to finish and take questions from the floor. This allowed me to express myself properly. I don't think my decision to retire took anyone in the room by surprise, but most of the press seemed genuinely disillusioned by the way I had been treated by the sport. Once I'd given everybody a one-to-one interview as well I was ready to get out of the room and on with my life. It had been a hectic and emotional few days. As I sat down to lunch afterwards with Jon and Mike we were pleased with the impact the press conference had made and I began to look forward to running my final race on Sunday 2 August.

It's a very strange experience to know that you're about to do something that has been your main focus in life for the very last time. I knew that after that it wouldn't matter if my body hurt, or that I hadn't had enough sleep. I wouldn't have to train again, warm up again or watch carefully what I ate. I would never put on a pair of running spikes again or experience the nervous tension and adrenalin rush that top level competition produces. But I would never again experience the thrill of competing in front of thousands for both myself and my country.

I knew it would be an emotional occasion, as it would be for anyone under similar circumstances – it certainly wasn't just another race. I warmed up in the same way I had always done, listening to music, stretching each muscle in the usual order – a habitual sequence of exercises that told my body to prepare itself for one last 400m. My mind however was elsewhere and had no intention of focusing on the race ahead – I wanted to savour the whole experience and try not to get too emotional. As I walked into the stadium the reception from the crowd was unlike any other I'd received and something I will never forget. As I was called to my blocks for the very last time I instantly focused on trying to win the race – the competitor in me still came through even though the result on this occasion was irrelevant. With 100 metres to go I thought I had the race won, but both Mark Richardson and Iwan Thomas were too strong for me and I finished third. As I crossed the line I was relieved that it was finally all over and felt it appropriate that I should be accompanied on my final lap of honour by the two athletes who have both the talent and ability to go one step higher than me on the Olympic rostrum.

20

A NEW CHALLENGE

For fifteen years my identity had been clear: I was an international athlete. Everything I did revolved around that fact, it was my main focus in life – I had a clear purpose and each day I woke up I rarely had to question what I was about. Now all that had to change as I began my new life as an 'ex-athlete'.

To be officially retired when you're only thirty-two years old is a somewhat strange situation to be in but all sports people have to find a way to fill the time that was once taken up with training and competition. To succeed in the highly competitive world of top-class athletics you cannot afford to compromise – the sport demands your time and attention and any plans for future employment have to be put on hold if you want to make it to the top. I had signalled my commitment to athletics the day I decided to leave medical school and had maintained that level of commitment up until my most fulfilling day at the Atlanta Olympics. Looking back now, the moment I stepped down from the Olympic rostrum was the beginning of the end, since from that point on I was willing to compromise my athletic performance in order to prepare myself for a successful transition from athlete to 'ex-athlete'. Athletics was still my main focus but I spent a lot of time and energy growing my speaking business, appearing on television and, in 1998, promoting the hardback edition of this book!

The first few weeks of retirement were fun-packed as I was now able to do all the things I couldn't do whilst I was running because of the risk of injury. I had to improve my tennis quickly in order to beat Daley Thompson and Kriss Akabusi again – they had both been in retirement for over five years and had secretly been preparing for my re-appearance on court! I ordered some football boots, golf shoes, golf clubs and finally got to use the pair of roller blades I'd bought months earlier. I went ice skating many times and enjoyed the freedom of knowing that it didn't matter if I fell and twisted my ankle. It was liberating to be able to do all these sports just for fun and for no other reason. I didn't have to be any good, I just wanted to take part. It made me appreciate the motto 'It's the taking part that matters' which is true if the level of your performances isn't that important but certainly wasn't the case when I was an athlete. I never just 'took part' in athletics – it was far more important than that.

When your body has been your 'tool', or even your 'temple', for fifteen years, it deserves a well-earned rest – running or going to the gym were quickly replaced by fine wines, rich sauces and junk food. I no longer had to take my time searching for the healthy option on the restaurant menu and I would regularly stop off at the local bakery or fish and chip shop on my way home – bargain buckets of Kentucky Fried Chicken were no longer a rare treat and during any visit to France every meal began with plenty of fois gras!

I knew my lack of physical exercise since retirement would come in handy when the BBC asked me four months later to present a fitness video aimed at people who knew they should exercise but couldn't find the time to do so. I was chosen more as an example of supposed perfect fitness than for my presentation skills, but deep down I felt I could relate to both the participants and the viewers since I too knew I had to make exercise more of a priority in my life. Ultimately, vanity is not a strong enough motivation for me to exercise more since I could get away with little or no exercise for a few years before it really starts to show so. But being a goal-orientated person, and as a result of a very drunken night with two equally drunken friends, I have committed myself to running the London Marathon in the year 2000 – a goal that is both challenging and immovable since they both foolishly agreed to accompany me on the twenty-six or so miles around town.

My early retirement also resulted in me being asked once again by the BBC to work as a pundit alongside Desmond Lynam and Linford Christie at the European Championships in Budapest in August. I'd always planned to be in Budapest at this time anyway, but had intended to be running out on the track. Once that was no longer a possibility I was happy to get paid to watch the championships from the best seat in the house. I'd performed the same role a year earlier at the World Championships in Athens but was then still an active member of the British team. This time it was different – I was part of the BBC team, staying in the BBC hotel, travelling in BBC cars, on BBC expenses, eating with David Coleman, Stuart Storey, Brendan Foster and Des Lynam. I felt like a young junior athlete on his first senior international trip amongst such all-time greats. When I was a competing athlete at a championship my mind was continually focused on the races ahead – each hour of every day was a nervous countdown to the 400m final. I never took much interest in any other event and rarely experienced the atmosphere of a major championship outside of the athletes' village or the stadium – I often envied people who just went to watch and enjoy the whole occasion without the pressure to perform. But I went to Budapest as a pundit and a spectator knowing that, even though I wasn't competing my body clock was still on countdown towards the final 400m final. It wasn't a physical awareness, I didn't get a sudden urge to warm up before each race, it was more of a psychological build-up. I could imagine what the athletes would be feeling, killing time throughout the days, preparing for each race, building in confidence, going through the same routines again and again with the pressure on them mounting as the final got closer. Whether I was walking around town, playing tennis or sitting in the studio, I could always imagine how Mark Richardson or

Iwan Thomas would be feeling. A part of me envied them, yet I was happy to be free from the pressure. I was aware that until the moment when they went to their blocks for that race I wouldn't be 100 per cent sure how I really felt about the events of the previous few weeks. I'd convinced myself that I wouldn't feel anger, bitterness or jealousy but knew that my true feelings would only come out as that moment approached. I remembered watching the French footballer, David Ginola, being interviewed just after France had won the World Cup saying that nobody could be happier than he was to see his former teammates victorious – the right words to say on TV but I thought that deep down he must have felt bitter at being left out of the squad and perhaps all he could really feel was alone.

I realized that people were eager to hear my thoughts and impressions on how the events of the 400m would unfold, especially since any comments regarding Solomon Wariso would obviously have extra meaning. True to form, Solomon's unpredictability nearly resulted in him not progressing past the first round as he misjudged his finish and underestimated the opposition to come fourth in his heat. Since only the first three athletes in each heat qualified by right it meant he had an anxious wait of about half an hour to see if he would qualify for the second round as one of the four fastest losers. I couldn't help but have a wry smile to myself, knowing that those thirty minutes would be nervous ones for Solomon but absolute hell for the selectors, who must have been dreading the headlines that the press were waiting to write. For me it would have been a highly amusing end to a ridiculous affair. Although I criticized Solomon's lack of judgement in the race, I knew he'd run fast enough to progress to the next round.

Later that morning I bumped into one of the selectors and couldn't resist saying, 'Worried that you might have made the wrong decision now?' Sheepishly, he replied, 'No, not at all.' He then made his get away before I could carry on the conversation.

All the British athletes made it to the 400m final with Iwan and Mark the joint favourites for the gold medal. On paper there was only one hundredth of a second between them and they had both looked impressive in qualifying for the final. Opinions were raised as to who would become European champion. I felt that a lot depended on the lane draw for the final with Iwan, who was drawn inside, having a slight advantage over Mark since he would have him in sight for the first 300 metres at least. My allegiance was obviously with Mark since he had been my training partner but there was something about Iwan's manner that made me sense that he needed to win this race more than everybody else. Throughout the rounds he had looked so focused and determined - his body language portrayed a man on a mission. He had a job to do and believed that nobody was going to get in his way, he was neither over-confident nor too relaxed, he looked eager to get on with the job at hand and appeared to be in the right physical and mental state to do so. Linford had decided early on to tip Iwan to win so, for television purposes and out of loyalty, I went for Mark instead.

As I sat in the studio waiting for the athletes to enter the stadium I began to feel nervous but couldn't tell whether it was for Iwan, Mark or myself. The BBC studio was located high up above the crown of the first bend, so sitting in my chair I had a choice of how to watch the race. I could look from a distance over the crowd and on to the track or I could turn away from the action and watch the many television sets in the studio with close-ups and camera angles taking the viewer right into the heart of the action. No matter how skilled the cameraman or commentator, television can never fully capture the unique atmosphere created by a packed stadium prior to and during a major championship final. I wanted to savour that atmosphere so I looked out over the stadium. Since we could still hear David Coleman's commentary in the studio, it seemed like the best of both worlds. As they entered the stadium I could relate to the intense focus on their faces but I still didn't feel as if I wanted to be out on the track with them. As they prepared to go to their blocks Linford said, 'You should be down there.' I just nodded, then Des asked me, 'Would you rather be out there?'

'Of course,' I replied, knowing it was the expected answer. But deep down I knew that I was lying – I had experienced the loneliness of the last few minutes before the start of a championship final many times before but this time I was content to experience it away from the track. The truth was I couldn't imagine myself down on that track and begun to wonder how I'd ever managed to go through such an ordeal so many times before. I was happy just to be a spectator and that was the moment when I knew, without any doubt, that I was free to get on with a life away from athletics.

As the athletes went down to their blocks my heart was pounding. I knew how important this race was to both Iwan and Mark, since in forty-four seconds there would be only one European champion. As the gun went off my focus was on Mark out in lane six, willing him to run his perfect race. I expected to see him quickly find his usual relaxed rhythm and was immediately concerned to see him attack the first 120 metres so hard that he lost his natural rhythm and by the time he reached the halfway point I knew the race was over. Iwan maintained his form superbly throughout the race to become European champion in 44.52 with Mark trailing in third in 45.14. He had chosen the wrong time to forget his pace judgement and run the worst race of his life.

Once my post-race comments had been made I left the studio to look for Mark, who I knew would be in a state of both shock and disappointment. I found him outside the stadium with a blank expression on his face – people were trying to comfort him but he was in no mood to listen.

As I looked at him he said, 'Roger, I don't know what happened.' 'Yes you do,' I replied. 'What?' 'You just ran the worst race of your life. It was crap – total crap.'

This was not a time for comforting – this was athlete to athlete, 400m runner to 400m runner. He knew the truth and so did I. 'I cannot relate to what you just did,' I added. 'I ran bad races now and again but never as bad as that in a major final.' He began to smile. 'But guess what?' I added. 'You'll never do it again, that's for sure. If you remember how you feel right now, you'll never let it happen again.'

The test of the true champion is how you get through the bad times and that moment was a defining one for Mark Richardson. For the week following the European Championships he was about as depressed as an athlete can get and lost all confidence and self-belief – it's incredible how one bad race can change the way an athlete views himself. He knew deep down that he had choked under pressure because he didn't have the confidence to just run his perfect race. He'd reacted not to Iwan Thomas but to the whole occasion – he went off too quickly and paid the price over the last 100 metres of the race. After much analysis, including an evening with Daley Thompson - which is enough to make any athlete feel like an Olympic champion - Mark went on to win the Grand Prix final two weeks after that defeat. I was in the studio with Brendan Foster who questioned Mark's presence in the race so soon after the European Championships. I defended Mark's decision to run by saying, 'If you fall off a horse, the best thing to do is to get back on it as soon as possible.' Brendan responded, 'No it's not – you should actually get on a different horse!' I still don't really understand the meaning of that statement but it sounds like a wise one.

A few weeks later Mark went to the Commonwealth Games in Kuala Lumpur and once again was beaten by Iwan – this time, however, he could be proud of his performance, not just because he ran 44.60, but because he proved to himself that he has the heart of a champion by winning the personal race that I believe most athletes would have been scared to run.

I think that the next two years will bring out the best in both Iwan and Mark – theirs is a friendly rivalry built out of a mutual respect. I look forward to seeing them take on the likes of Michael Johnson and Tyree Washington at the 1999 World Championships and the 2000 Olympic Games.

My professional challenge during that time will be to make the move from being a pundit to a presenter. With the BBC securing exclusive rights to televise British athletics for the next six years there will be many opportunities to serve my apprenticeship and learn my trade – i.e. plenty of chances to cock up live on air!

British athletics has gone through a difficult two years politically and financially in 1997 and 1998 and a period of stability is required – the BBC contract should provide the sport with the opportunity to move forward and reach a larger audience than ever before.

The two men at the helm of the sport are David Moorcroft as Chief Executive and David Hemery as President. Both are highly respected by most of the people in athletics and both are capable of creating a shared vision. It won't be easy since the issue of drugs in the sport will always make the headlines and the recent scandal regarding the acceptance of bribes by members of the International Olympic Committee will probably result in much change in the way our Olympic sports are governed. Some would argue that the Olympic ideals are outdated and impossible to live up to in today's society – that bribery, corruption and drug taking are part of life and the Olympics should be a reflection of that. I believe the Olympics are everything to the honest athlete and those chosen to sit on the International Olympic Committee have a responsibility, above all, to those athletes.

Following the successes at the European Championships, Britain has high hopes of medals at the World Championships in Seville in 1999 and the Sydney Olympics in 2000. I believe we will see the Union Jack raised a few times in Sydney since we have athletes who have realistic chances of winning medals – Jonathon Edwards, Denise Lewis, Colin Jackson, Steve Backley, Ashia Hansen, Iwan Thomas and Mark Richardson are all capable, on their day, of beating everybody in the world. To do so in the Olympic final will be their greatest challenge. Britain needs Olympic champions and with the support of National Lottery money a lot is now expected from our athletes.

For me the pressure is off – for the first time in my career I can be certain that I will be going to the Olympic Games – the selectors at the BBC have already guaranteed me my place on the team! I look forward to going to Sydney knowing that, from the comfort of the studio, it really is the taking part that matters.

CAREER RECORD AT 400 METRES

Date	Event	Position	Time
1984			
4 July	Portsmouth	1st	47.70
15 July	Portsmouth	1st	48.20
5 August	High Wycombe	1st	49.40
1985			
12 January	The Cosford Games (indoor)	1st	48.06
26 January	Cosford AAA Indoor	3rd	47.86
	(1st s2 25 Jan 47.77)		
16 February	Genoa GB v. Italy GB Debut		47.24
	(1st r2)		
2 March	Athens European Indoor		49.67
	(3rd h3 2 Mar 47.36, 4th s2 2 Mar 49.67)		
9 March	Cosford England v USA	3rd	47.92
16 March	Cosford AAA Under 20 Championships	1st	48.19
15 May	Crystal Palace	2nd	46.90
18 May	Portsmouth Hampshire Championships	1st	47.50
26 May	Antrim UK Championships	4th	46.05
15 June	Crystal Palace Southern Championships	1st	45.91
6 July	Kamen GB v Germany	1st	46.78
14 July	Crystal Palace AAA Championships	6th	46.34
	(2nd h5 13 July 46.14)		
19 July	Crystal Palace Grand Prix		46.42
	(3rd r2 46.42)		
20 July	Swansea Welsh Games	DQ	47.20
3 August	Birmingham AAA Under 20 Championships	1st	47.33
24 August	Cottbus European Junior Championships	1st	45.36
	(1st s1 23 Aug 46.98)		
31 August	Hendon GRE Cup Final	1st	46.10
8 September	Beijing Under 23 Tour	2nd	46.30
11 September	Nanjing Under 23 Tour	2nd	46.02

Date	Event	Position	Time
1986			
25 January	Cosford AAA Indoors	1st	47.22
	(1st h1 24 Jan 49.13, 1st s1 24 Jan 48.36)		
8 March	Cosford England v USA	2nd	46.82
26 May	Cwmbran UK Championships	3rd	45.48
	(1st h2 25 May 46.60)		
4 June	Madrid	1st	45.46
21 June	Crystal Palace AAA Championships	2nd	45.16
11 July	Crystal Palace Grand Prix	3rd	45.18
27 July	Edinburgh Commonwealth Games	1st	45.57
	(1st h1 26 July 46.66, 3rd s2 Jul 47.27)		
13 August	Zurich Grand Prix		45.00
	(7th r3)		
29 August	Stuttgart European Championships	1st	44.59
	(1st h1 27 Aug 45.50, 1st s1 28 Aug 45.33)		(UK record)
1987			
28 May	Seville	1st	45.46
20 June	Portsmouth England v Cze, Ita	1st	45.55
27 June	Prague European Cup	2nd	44.99
17 July	Birmingham England v USA	1st	45.58
22 July	Rome Grand Prix	5th	46.13
2 Aug	Crystal Palace AAA Championships	4th	45.92
	(1st h4 1 Aug 46.22)		
1988			
No racing			
1989			
16 September	Jersey	1st	46.20
1990			
23 January	North Shore (NZL)	1st	45.56
22 April	Walnut (USA)	2nd	45.90
26 May	Granada	3rd	45.25
30 May	Seville	5th	45.36
3 June	Cardiff UK Championships	1st	45.63
	(1st h1 2 Jun 47.30)		
22 June	Portsmouth GB v USA, Kenya	2nd	45.97
29 June	Gateshead GB v GDR, Canada	1st	45.61
6 July	Edinburgh Grand Prix	2nd	45.20
20 July	La Coruna	1st	45.48
7 August	Malmo	2nd	45.41
10 August	Brussels Grand Prix	4th	44.91
15 August	Zurich Grand Prix	5th	45.05

289

Date	Event	Position	Time
17 August	Gateshead England v Commonwealth Int Sel	2nd	45.13
30 August	Split European Championships	1st	45.08
	(1st h1 28 Aug 45.53, 1st s1 29 Aug 45.46)		
16 September	Sheffield	1st	45.47
1991			
25 May	Granada	1st	44.79
20 May	Seville	4th	44.96
19 June	Crystal Palace GB v Germany	1st	44.91
29 June	Frankfurt European Cup	1st	44.91
12 July	Crystal Palace Grand Prix	2nd	45.14
15 July	Nice Grand Prix	2nd	45.03
3 August	Monaco Grand Prix	3rd	44.87
5 August	Malmo	1st	44.71
9 August	Gateshead	1st	45.19
29 August	Tokyo World Championships	2nd	44.62
	(3rd h5 25 Aug 46.02, 3rd q3 26 Aug 45.39		
	1st s2 27 Aug 44.64)		
10 September	Berlin Grand Prix	2nd	44.85
13 September	Brussels Grand Prix	1st	45.04
15 September	Sheffield	1st	44.98
20 September	Barcelona Grand Prix Final	1st	44.97
1992			
1 June	Bratislava	2nd	45.08
7 June	Sheffield UK Championships	1st	44.84
	(1st h1 6 Jun 45.79)		
19 June	Edinburgh GB v Kenya	1st	45.12
2 July	Stockholm Grand Prix	3rd	45.53
6 July	Lille Grand Prix	2nd	45.63
10 July	Crystal Palace Grand Prix	4th	45.19
15 July	Nice Grand Prix	1st	45.15
3 August	Barcelona Olympic Games		44.72
	(2nd h9 1 Aug 45.94, 3rd q1 2 Aug 45.28)		
11 August	Monaco Grand Prix	4th	45.33
1993			
22 May	New York Grand Prix	6th	45.86
11 June	St Denis Grand Prix	3rd	46.55
1994			
12 June	Sheffield UK Championships	1st	44.94
	(1st h1 11 Jun 46.75, 1st s2 11 Jun 45.83)		
25 June	Birmingham European Cup	1st	45.08
1 July	Gateshead	2nd	45.30

Date	Event	Position	Time
15 July	London Grand Prix	3rd	45.10
2 August	Monaco Grand Prix	4th	45.08
11 August	Helsinki European Championships	2nd	45.20
	(1st h1 8 Aug 45.88, 1st 2 9 Aug 45.79)		
17 August	Zurich Grand Prix	4th	45.17
28 August	Rieti	1st	44.78
30 August	Berlin Grand Prix	3rd	45.09
3 September	Paris Grand Prix Final	4th	45.39

1995

Date	Event	Position	Time
27 May	Granada	1st	45.15
20 June	Madrid	1st	45.07
5 July	Lausanne Grand Prix	3rd	44.59 (PB)
7 July	London Grand Prix	2nd	45.16
23 July	Sheffield	2nd	45.54
9 August	Gothenburg World Championships	7th	45.54
	(1st h1 5 Aug 45.81, 3rd q1 6 Aug 45.01, 4th s1 7 Aug 45.32)		
21 August	Gateshead GB v USA	4th	45.20
27 August	London	2nd	45.18
1 September	Berlin	4th	45.23
5 September	Rieti	2nd	45.42

1996

Date	Event	Position	Time
18 May	Atlanta	3rd	44.81
26 May	Eugene	2nd	44.77
16 June	Birmingham AAA Champs/OG Trials	1st	44.39 (UK Record)
	(1st h1 14 Jun 46.05, 1st s1 15 Jun 45.02)		
3 July	Lausanne Grand Prix	2nd	44.37 (UK Record)
12 July	London Grand Prix	2nd	44.88
29 July	Atlanta Olympic Games	2nd	44.41
	(1st h1 26 Jul 45.28, 1st q2 27 Jul 44.72 1st s1 28 Jul 44.69)		
14 August	Zurich Grand Prix	4th	44.83
19 August	Gateshead GB v USA	1st	44.64
25 August	Sheffield	1st	45.05
7 September	Milan Grand Prix Final	5th	45.42
16 September	Tokyo	1st	45.33

1997

Date	Event	Position	Time
31 May	Long Beach	1st	45.79
21 June	Munich European Cup	1st	45.63
29 June	Sheffield Grand Prix	7th	45.70

291

Date	Event		Position	Time
13 August	Zurich Grand Prix		4th	45.07
17 August	London GB v International select		4th	45.30
24 August	La Chaux de Fonds		1st	45.22
26 August	Berlin Grand Prix		3rd	45.58
7 September	Gateshead		4th	46.59

1998

26 July	Birmingham AAA Champs/EC Trials		4th	44.71

Fastest 400m Relay Legs

3 August 1996	Atlanta	43.87
31 August 1986	Stuttgart	43.95
1 September 1990	Split	43.96
14 August 1994	Helsinki	43.96
28 June 1997	Prague	44.16
10 August 1997	Athens	44.20
26 April 1987	Walnut	44.30
9 August 1997	Athens	44.33
19 August 1996	Gateshead	44.35
26 June 1994	Birmingham	44.60

Fastest Times over 200m

6 July 1996	Enfield	20.50
4 May 1996	Irvine	20.56 wind assisted
1 May 1997	Fort de France	20.57
4 August 1990	Birmingham	20.60
13 April 1991	USA	20.60
12 September 1986	Crystal Palace	20.63
28 June 1992	Birmingham	20.65
7 September 1986	Stoke	20.68
28 June 1992	Birmingham	20.75
28 June 1992	Birmingham	20.75
25 May 1987	Derby	20.80
30 August 1997	Bedford	20.82
21 September 1996	Reduit	20.90

Fastest times over 300m

8 August 1986	Crystal Palace	32.08
11 August 1996	Crystal Palace	32.26
4 September 1994	Sheffield	32.45
21 June 1991	Belfast	32.58
9 August 1987	Coventry	32.90

Other Best Times

4 May 1996	Irvine	10.48 **100m**
31 May 1987	Southampton	10.40 **100m**
3 February 1991	Reading	76.20 **600m**
17 March 1990	USA	1.52.10 **800m**

INDEX

293

The author and publishers have made every reasonable effort to contact all copyright holders. Any errors or omissions are inadvertant and anyone who for any reason has not been contacted is invited to write to the publisher so that a full acknowledgement may be made in subsequent editions of this work.